Sets

The Idea

A set is a group of things which belong together.

How to Use the Idea

Here are some of the symbols used to talk about sets.

W = {0, 1, 2, 3, 4,...} W is the endless set of whole numbers.

C = {1, 2, 3, 4, 5,...} C is the endless set of counting numbers.

C ⊆ W Set C is a subset of set W. 0 ∈ W Zero is a member of set W.

0 ∉ C Zero is not a member of set C.

Read each set description. Refer to the symbols above. Read each statement; then write out what it says and answer the question.

① J = {Jim, Jack, Janet, Jill} B = {Jim, Jack, Mike, Ben}

J ⊆ B *Set J is a subset of Set B.* Is this true? *no*

Jim ∈ J *Jim is a member of Set J.* Is this true? *yes*

Mike ∉ B *Mike is not a member of Set B.* Is this true? *no*

② W = {0, 1, 2, 3, 4, 5,...} E = {2, 4, 6, 8, 10,...}

E ⊆ W *Set E is a subset of Set W.* Is this true? *yes*

1 ∈ W *One is a member of Set W.* Is this true? *yes*

3 ∈ E *Three is a member of Set E.* Is this true? *no*

③ P = {red, yellow, blue} S = {red, orange, yellow, green, blue, purple}

S ⊆ P *Set S is a subset of Set P.* Is this true? *no*

orange ∈ P *Orange is a member of Set P.* Is this true? *no*

green ∈ S *Green is a member of Set S.* Is this true? *yes*

④ W = {0, 1, 2, 3, 4,...} F = {5, 10, 15, 20, 25,...}

F ⊆ W *Set F is a subset of Set W.* Is this true? *yes*

5 ∈ W *Five is a member of Set W.* Is this true? *yes*

3 ∉ F *Three is not a member of Set F.* Is this true? *yes*

⑤ C = {1, 2, 3, 4, 5,...} O = {1, 3, 5, 7, 9,...}

C ⊆ O *Set C is a subset of Set O.* Is this true? *no*

O ⊆ C *Set O is a subset of Set C.* Is this true? *yes*

9 ∈ C *Nine is a member of Set C.* Is this true? *yes*

A *set* is a group of things which belong together.

Back Page Exercises **Think of your classmates as a set. Divide this set into six subsets.**

Sets

The Idea

A set is a group of things which belong together.

How to Use the Idea

Here are some of the symbols used to talk about sets.

W = {0, 1, 2, 3, 4,...} **W is the endless set of whole numbers.**

C = {1, 2, 3, 4, 5,...} **C is the endless set of counting numbers.**

$C \subseteq W$ **Set C is a subset of set W.** **$0 \in W$** **Zero is a member of set W.**

$0 \notin C$ **Zero is not a member of set C.**

✱ **Read each set description. Refer to the symbols above. Read each statement; then write out what it says and answer the question.**

① J = {Jim, Jack, Janet, Jill} B = {Jim, Jack, Mike, Ben}

$J \subseteq B$ ______________________ Is this true? ________

Jim $\in$ J ______________________ Is this true? ________

Mike $\notin$ B ______________________ Is this true? ________

② W = {0, 1, 2, 3, 4, 5,...} E = {2, 4, 6, 8, 10,...}

$E \subseteq W$ ______________________ Is this true? ________

$1 \in W$ ______________________ Is this true? ________

$3 \in E$ ______________________ Is this true? ________

③ P = {red, yellow, blue} S = {red, orange, yellow, green, blue, purple}

$S \subseteq P$ ______________________ Is this true? ________

orange $\in$ P ______________________ Is this true? ________

green $\in$ S ______________________ Is this true? ________

④ W = {0, 1, 2, 3, 4,...} F = {5, 10, 15, 20, 25,...}

$F \subseteq W$ ______________________ Is this true? ________

$5 \in W$ ______________________ Is this true? ________

$3 \notin F$ ______________________ Is this true? ________

⑤ C = {1, 2, 3, 4, 5,...} O = {1, 3, 5, 7, 9,...}

$C \subseteq O$ ______________________ Is this true? ________

$O \subseteq C$ ______________________ Is this true? ________

$9 \in C$ ______________________ Is this true? ________

A ______________ is a group of things which belong together.

Back Page Exercises **Think of your classmates as a set. Divide this set into six subsets.**

Subsets

The Idea

A subset is a group that consists of certain members of a larger set.

How to Use the Idea

P = {1, 2, 3, 4, 5} N = {1, 2, 3} W = {0, 1, 2, 3, 4,...} E = {2, 4, 6, 8,...}

Set N is a subset of Set P.

Set W is the infinite, or endless, set of whole numbers. It is not possible to name all the members of such a set. Many infinite sets are subsets of W. For example, one is the infinite set of even whole numbers. Is it possible to name all the members of this set? No, because whatever even number you name, you can add two and get another even number. Since every even number is also a member of W, we can say $E \subseteq W$, Set E is a subset of Set W.

Look at each pair of sets. Tell if one is a subset of the other. If not, tell why not.

① X = {4, 5, 6, 7, 8}
Y = {5, 6, 7}
$Y \subseteq X$

② O = {1, 3, 5, 7, 9,...}
W = {0, 1, 2, 3, 4,...}
$O \subseteq W$

③ E = {2, 4, 6, 8, 10,...}
T = {3, 6, 9, 12, 15,...}
no - each set has members not in the other

④ M = {7, 9, 11, 13, 15}
N = {9, 11, 13, 15, 17}
no - each set has one member not in the other

⑤ C = {1, 2, 3, 4, 5,...}
F = {5, 10, 15, 20, 25,...}
$F \subseteq C$

⑥ J = {Jim, John, Jan, Jennie, Joe}
B = {Jim, John, Joe}
$B \subseteq J$

⑦ F = {milk, eggs, bread, meat, coffee}
L = {milk, coffee}
$L \subseteq F$

⑧ P = {red, blue, yellow}
C = {red, orange, yellow, green, blue}
$P \subseteq C$

⑨ O = {1, 3, 5, 7, 9,...}
T = {3, 6, 9, 12, 15,...}
no - each set has members not in the other

⑩ S = {6, 12, 18, 24, 30,...}
T = {3, 6, 9, 12, 15,...}
$S \subseteq T$

A ___*subset*___ is a group that consists of certain members of a larger set.

Back Page Exercises Think of a large set. Break it into ten subsets.

Subsets

The Idea

A subset is a group that consists of certain members of a larger set.

How to Use the Idea

P = {1, 2, 3, 4, 5} N = {1, 2, 3} W = {0, 1, 2, 3, 4,...} E = {2, 4, 6, 8,...}

Set N is a subset of Set P.

Set W is the infinite, or endless, set of whole numbers. It is not possible to name all the members of such a set. Many infinite sets are subsets of W. For example, one is the infinite set of even whole numbers. Is it possible to name all the members of this set? No, because whatever even number you name, you can add two and get another even number. Since every even number is also a member of W, we can say E $\subseteq$ W, Set E is a subset of Set W.

Look at each pair of sets. Tell if one is a subset of the other. If not, tell why not.

① X = {4, 5, 6, 7, 8}
Y = {5, 6, 7}
Y $\subseteq$ X

② O = {1, 3, 5, 7, 9,...}
W = {0, 1, 2, 3, 4,...}

③ E = {2, 4, 6, 8, 10,...}
T = {3, 6, 9, 12, 15,...}

④ M = {7, 9, 11, 13, 15}
N = {9, 11, 13, 15, 17}

⑤ C = {1, 2, 3, 4, 5,...}
F = {5, 10, 15, 20, 25,...}

⑥ J = {Jim, John, Jan, Jennie, Joe}
B = {Jim, John, Joe}

⑦ F = {milk, eggs, bread, meat, coffee}
L = {milk, coffee}

⑧ P = {red, blue, yellow}
C = {red, orange, yellow, green, blue}

⑨ O = {1, 3, 5, 7, 9,...}
T = {3, 6, 9, 12, 15,...}

⑩ S = {6, 12, 18, 24, 30,...}
T = {3, 6, 9, 12, 15,...}

A ____________ is a group that consists of certain members of a larger set.

Back Page Exercises **Think of a large set. Break it into ten subsets.**

Intersection and Union

The Idea

The intersection of two sets is the set or list of members which belong to both sets. We write this A ∩ B, A intersection B, for Sets A and B. The union of two sets is the set or list of members which belong to either set. We write this A ∪ B, A union B, for Sets A and B. We use pictures called Venn Diagrams to show these relationships between sets.

How to Use the Idea

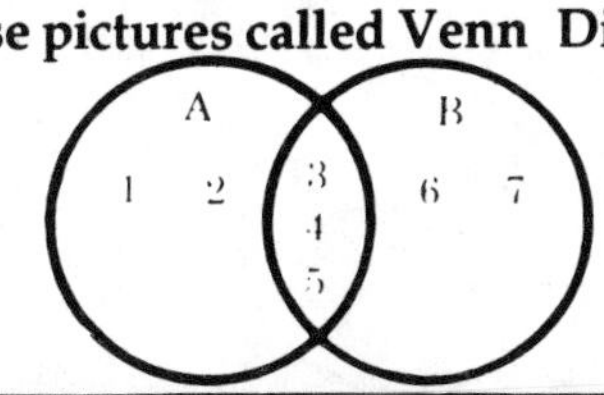

A = {1, 2, 3, 4, 5}
B = {3, 4, 5, 6, 7}

A ∩ B = {3, 4, 5}
A ∪ B = {1, 2, 3, 4, 5, 6, 7}

A For these exercises, you are given the sets and the Venn Diagrams. Give the intersection and the union for each pair of sets.

① C = {2, 4, 6, 8, 10, 12}
D = {4, 8, 12, 16, 20}
C ∩ D = *{4, 8, 12}*
C ∪ D = *{2, 4, 6, 8, 10, 12, 16, 20}*

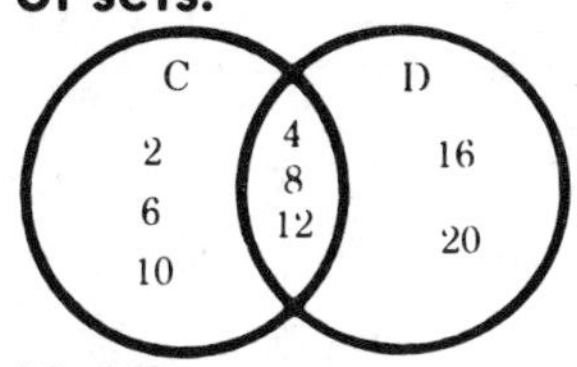

③ S = {1, 2, 3, 4, 5, 6}
T = {3, 4, 5, 6, 7, 8}
S ∩ T = *{3, 4, 5, 6}*
S ∪ T = *{1, 2, 3, 4, 5, 6, 7, 8}*

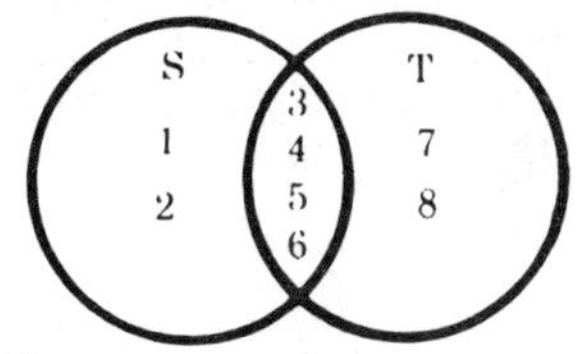

② X = {1, 3, 5, 7, 9, 11}
Y = {3, 5, 13, 15, 23, 25}
X ∩ Y = *{3, 5}*
X ∪ Y = *{1, 3, 5, 7, 9, 11, 13, 15, 23, 25}*

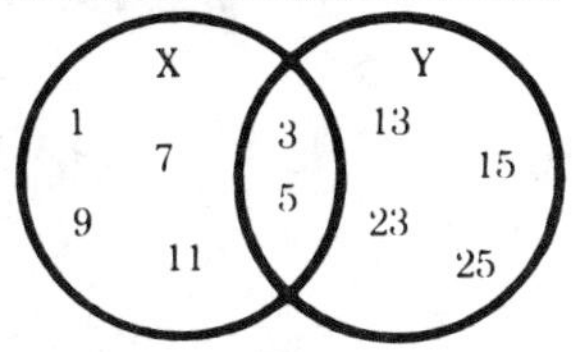

④ V = {1, 3, 5, 7, 9, 11, 13, 15}
W = {5, 10, 15, 20, 25}
V ∩ W = *{5, 15}*
V ∪ W = *{1, 3, 5, 7, 9, 10, 11, 13, 15, 20, 25}*

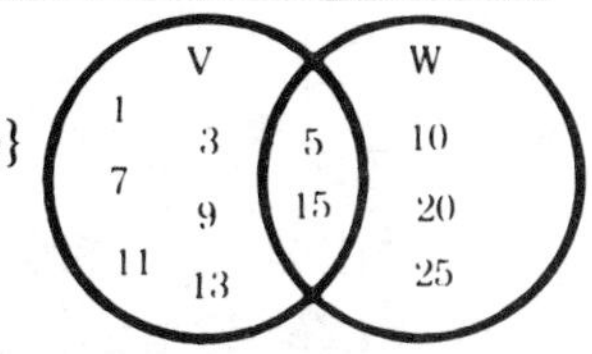

B For these exercises, you are given the Venn Diagrams. Give each set, then give the intersection and union of each pair of sets. Remember that each whole circle contains a set.

①

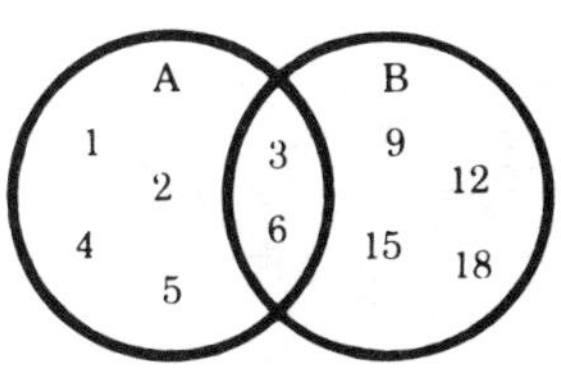

A = {1, 2, 3, 4, 5, 6}
B = {3, 6, 9, 12, 15, 18}
A ∩ B = {3, 6}
A ∪ B = {1, 2, 3, 4, 5, 6,
9, 12, 15, 18}

③

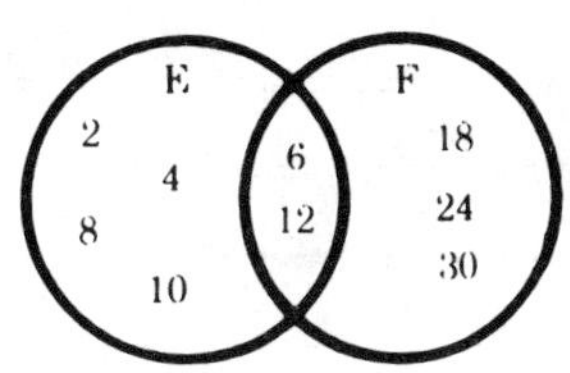

E = {2, 4, 6, 8, 10, 12}
F = {6, 12, 18, 24, 30}
E ∩ F = {6, 12}
E ∪ F = {2, 4, 6, 8, 10, 12,}
18, 24, 30}

②

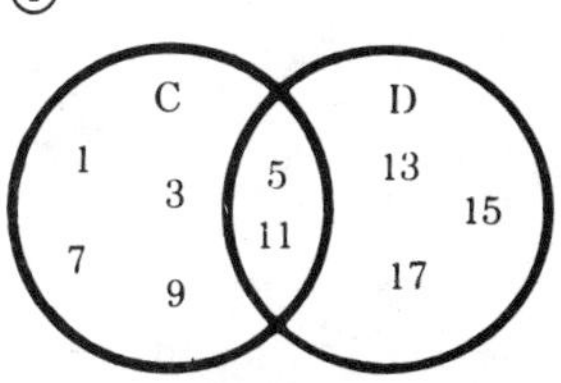

C = {1, 3, 5, 7, 9, 11}
D = {5, 11, 13, 15, 17}
C ∩ D = {5, 11}
C ∪ D = {1, 3, 5, 7, 9, 11,
13, 15, 17}

④

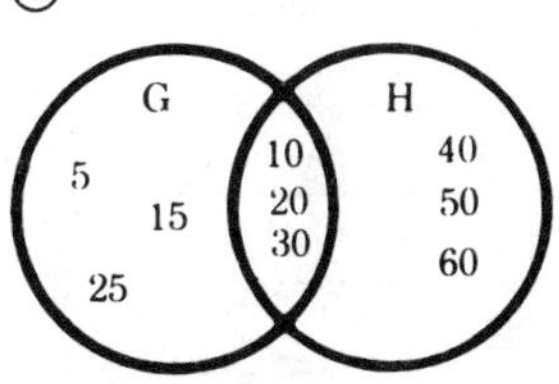

G = {5, 10, 15, 20, 25, 30}
H = {10, 20, 30, 40, 50, 60}
G ∩ H = {10, 20, 30}
G ∪ H = {5, 10, 15, 20, 25, 30,}
40, 50, 60}

An *intersection* of two sets is the set of members which belong to both sets. The *union* of two sets is the set of members which belong to either set.

Back Page Exercises Make a Venn Diagram of breakfast and dinner foods. Find the intersection and union of these sets.

Intersection and Union

The Idea

The intersection of two sets is the set or list of members which belong to both sets. We write this A ∩ B, A intersection B, for Sets A and B. The union of two sets is the set or list of members which belong to either set. We write this A ∪ B, A union B, for Sets A and B. We use pictures called Venn Diagrams to show these relationships between sets.

How to Use the Idea

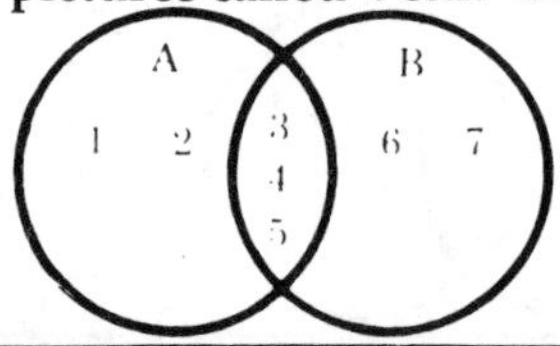

A = {1, 2, 3, 4, 5}
B = {3, 4, 5, 6, 7}

A ∩ B = {3, 4, 5}
A ∪ B = {1, 2, 3, 4, 5, 6, 7}

A

For these exercises, you are given the sets and the Venn Diagrams. Give the intersection and the union for each pair of sets.

① C = {2, 4, 6, 8, 10, 12}
D = {4, 8, 12, 16, 20}
C ∩ D = ____________
C ∪ D = ______________________________

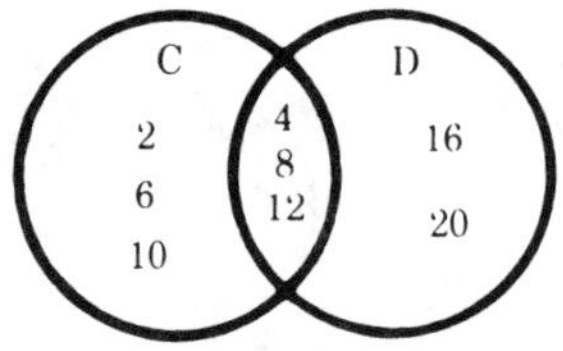

③ S = {1, 2, 3, 4, 5, 6}
T = {3, 4, 5, 6, 7, 8}
S ∩ T = ____________
S ∪ T = ______________________________

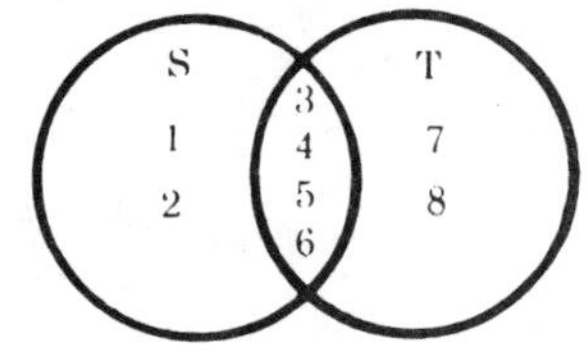

② X = {1, 3, 5, 7, 9, 11}
Y = {3, 5, 13, 15, 23, 25}
X ∩ Y = ____________
X ∪ Y = ______________________________

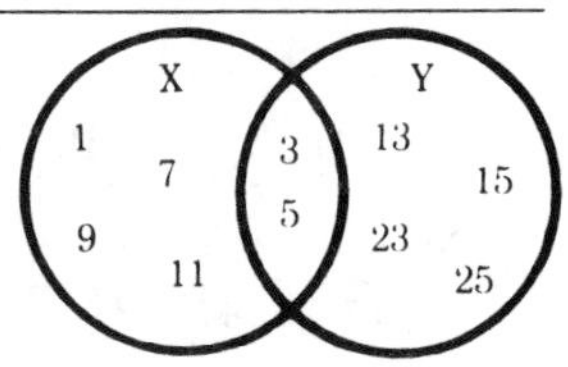

④ V = {1, 3, 5, 7, 9, 11, 13, 15}
W = {5, 10, 15, 20, 25}
V ∩ W = ____________
V ∪ W = ______________________________

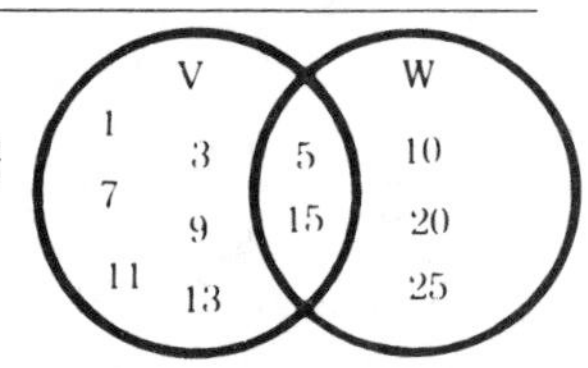

B

For these exercises, you are given the Venn Diagrams. Give each set, then give the intersection and union of each pair of sets. Remember that each whole circle contains a set.

① ______________________________
____
____
____
____

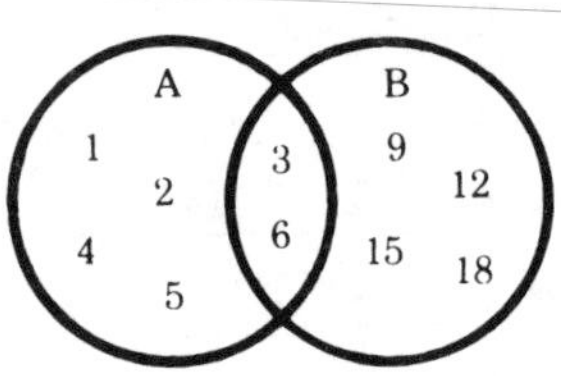

③ ______________________________
____
____
____
____

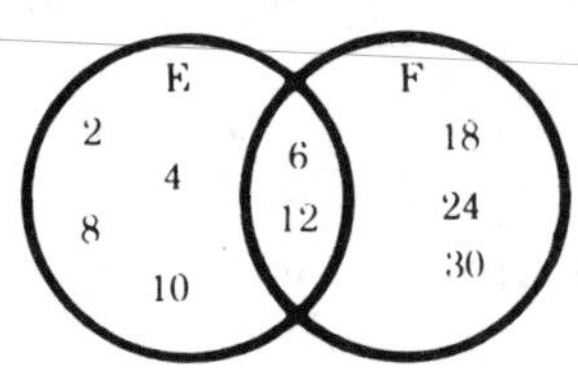

② ______________________________
____
____
____
____

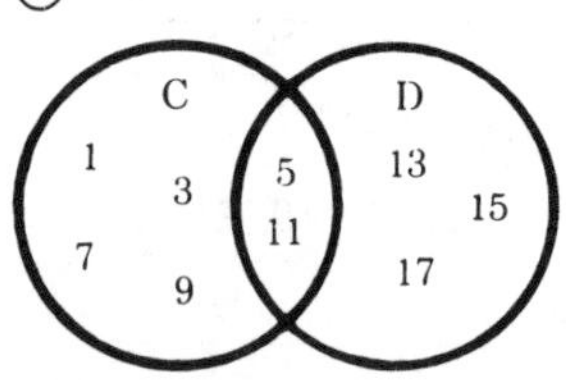

④ ______________________________
____
____
____
____

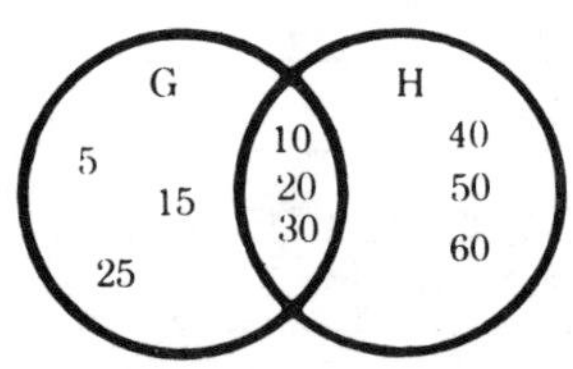

An ____________________ of two sets is the set of members which belong to both sets. The ____________________ of two sets is the set of members which belong to either set.

Back Page Exercises — **Make a Venn Diagram of breakfast and dinner foods. Find the intersection and union of these sets.**

Set Notation

The Idea

The symbols we use to tell facts about sets are called set notation.

How to Use the Idea

Study the table of symbols and examples.

$a \in A$	a is a member of A; a belongs to A.	$A = \{a, b, c\}$
$B \subseteq A$	B is a subset of A.	$B = \{a, b\}$
$A \cap B$	A intersection B; $a \in A$ and $a \in B$	$A \cap B = \{a, b\}$
$A \cup B$	A union B; $x \in A$ or $x \in B$	$A \cup B = \{a, b, c\}$
$d \notin A$	d is not a member of A.	

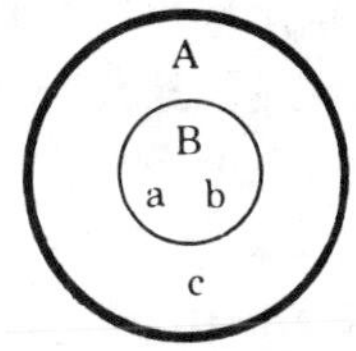

$W = \{0, 1, 2, 3, 4, \ldots\}$	W is the endless set of whole numbers.
$C = \{1, 2, 3, 4, 5, \ldots\}$	C is the endless set of counting numbers.
n(w) = endless	The number of members of W is endless or infinite.
	If $A = \{1, 2, 3, 4, 5\}$, n(a) = 5.

Answer the questions about the sets.

① $D = \{2, 3, 4, 5, 6, 7\}$
$E = \{5, 6, 7, 8\}$

Is it true that $E \subseteq D$? *no*
Is it true that $E \cap D = \{5, 6, 7\}$? *yes*
List the members of $E \cup D$. *{2, 3, 4, 5, 6, 7, 8}*
What is n(d)? *6*

② $F = \{1, 2, 3, 4, 5, 6\}$
$G = \{2, 4, 6, 8\}$

Is it true that $F \subseteq G$? *no*
Is it true that $F \cup G = \{1, 2, 3, 4, 5, 6, 8\}$? *yes*
List the members of $F \cap G$. *{2, 4, 6}*
What is n(g)? *4*

③ H = {bat, cat, hat, mat, rat, vat}
I = {hat, mat, vat}

List the members of $H \cap I$. *{hat, mat, vat}*
What is n(i)? *3*
Is it true that $I \subseteq H$? *yes*
Is it true that cat $\in$ I? *no*

④ $J = \{a, b, c, d, e, f\}$
$K = \{d, e, f, g, h\}$

List the members of $J \cup K$. *{a, b, c, d, e, f, g, h}*
What is n(j)? *6* n(k)? *5*
Is it true that $K \subseteq J$? *no*
Is it true that $d \in J$? *yes* That $d \in K$? *yes*

⑤ $L = \{3, 5, 7, 11, 13\}$
$M = \{1, 3, 5, 7, 9, 11, 13, 15\}$

Is it true that $L \subseteq M$? *yes*
Is it true that $9 \in L$? *no*
What is n(l)? *5* n(m)? *8*
List the members of $L \cap M$. *{3, 5, 7, 11, 13}*

The symbols we use to tell facts about sets are called *set notation*.

Back Page Exercises Using each symbol from above, write several set notations about problem 5.

Set Notation

The Idea

The symbols we use to tell facts about sets are called set notation.

How to Use the Idea

Study the table of symbols and examples.

$a \in A$	a is a member of A; a belongs to A.
$B \subseteq A$	B is a subset of A.
$A \cap B$	A intersection B; $a \in A$ and $a \in B$
$A \cup B$	A union B; $x \in A$ or $x \in B$
$d \notin A$	d is not a member of A.

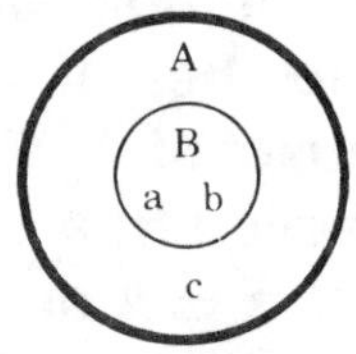

$A = \{a, b, c\}$
$B = \{a, b\}$
$A \cap B = \{a, b\}$
$A \cup B = \{a, b, c\}$

$W = \{0, 1, 2, 3, 4, \ldots\}$	W is the endless set of whole numbers.
$C = \{1, 2, 3, 4, 5, \ldots\}$	C is the endless set of counting numbers.
n(w) = endless	The number of members of W is endless or infinite.
	If $A = \{1, 2, 3, 4, 5\}$, n(a) = 5.

Answer the questions about the sets.

① $D = \{2, 3, 4, 5, 6, 7\}$
$E = \{5, 6, 7, 8\}$

Is it true that $E \subseteq D$? ________
Is it true that $E \cap D = \{5, 6, 7\}$? ________
List the members of $E \cup D$. ________
What is n(d)? ________

② $F = \{1, 2, 3, 4, 5, 6\}$
$G = \{2, 4, 6, 8\}$

Is it true that $F \subseteq G$? ________
Is it true that $F \cup G = \{1, 2, 3, 4, 5, 6, 8\}$? ________
List the members of $F \cap G$. ________
What is n(g)? ________

③ H = {bat, cat, hat, mat, rat, vat}
I = {hat, mat, vat}

List the members of $H \cap I$. ________
What is n(i)? ________
Is it true that $I \subseteq H$? ________
Is it true that cat $\in I$? ________

④ $J = \{a, b, c, d, e, f\}$
$K = \{d, e, f, g, h\}$

List the members of $J \cup K$. ________
What is n(j)? ________ n(k)? ________
Is it true that $K \subseteq J$? ________
Is it true that $d \in J$? ________ That $d \in K$? ________

⑤ $L = \{3, 5, 7, 11, 13\}$
$M = \{1, 3, 5, 7, 9, 11, 13, 15\}$

Is it true that $L \subseteq M$? ________
Is it true that $9 \in L$? ________
What is n(l)? ________ n(m)? ________
List the members of $L \cap M$. ________

The symbols we use to tell facts about sets are called __________.

Back Page Exercises — **Using each symbol from above, write several set notations about problem 5.**

Three-Digit Addition

The Idea

A three-digit number has digits in the ones' place, the tens' place, and the hundreds' place.

How to Use the Idea

When we add three-digit numbers, we sometimes carry to the hundreds' column.

1 1	1	1 1
347	283	586
+ 264	+ 134	+ 244
611	417	830

Find the sums.

① 352 + 549 = *901*	② 198 + 343 = *541*	③ 723 + 199 = *922*	④ 652 + 229 = *881*	⑤ 671 + 243 = *914*	⑥ 235 + 465 = *700*
⑦ 834 + 99 = *933*	⑧ 591 + 389 = *980*	⑨ 484 + 78 = *562*	⑩ 396 + 421 = *817*	⑪ 511 + 283 = *794*	⑫ 193 + 265 = *458*
⑬ 106 + 294 = *400*	⑭ 228 + 903 = *1,131*	⑮ 719 + 87 = *806*	⑯ 451 + 382 = *833*	⑰ 327 + 481 = *808*	⑱ 871 + 86 = *957*
⑲ 99 + 103 = *202*	⑳ 761 + 249 = *1,010*	(21) 87 + 223 = *310*	(22) 603 + 289 = *892*	(23) 507 + 98 = *605*	(24) 63 + 487 = *550*
(25) 876 + 55 = *931*	(26) 434 + 89 = *523*	(27) 578 + 78 = *656*	(28) 43 + 867 = *910*	(29) 62 + 199 = *261*	(30) 101 + 199 = *300*
(31) 169 + 903 = *1,072*	(32) 17 + 293 = *310*	(33) 297 + 54 = *351*	(34) 493 + 68 = *561*	(35) 555 + 66 = *621*	(36) 641 + 279 = *920*

A three-digit number has digits in the ___*ones'*___ place, the ___*tens'*___ place, and the ___*hundreds'*___ place.

Back Page Exercises Add the sums of problems 1 and 2, 3 and 4, 5 and 6, etc. You should have eighteen problems.

Three-Digit Addition

The Idea

A three-digit number has digits in the ones' place, the tens' place, and the hundreds' place.

How to Use the Idea

When we add three-digit numbers, we sometimes carry to the hundreds' column.

$$\begin{array}{r} {\scriptstyle 1\,1} \\ 347 \\ +\,264 \\ \hline 611 \end{array} \qquad \begin{array}{r} {\scriptstyle 1} \\ 283 \\ +\,134 \\ \hline 417 \end{array} \qquad \begin{array}{r} {\scriptstyle 1\,1} \\ 586 \\ +\,244 \\ \hline 830 \end{array}$$

Find the sums.

① 352 + 549 = *901*	② 198 + 343	③ 723 + 199	④ 652 + 229	⑤ 671 + 243	⑥ 235 + 465
⑦ 834 + 99	⑧ 591 + 389	⑨ 484 + 78	⑩ 396 + 421	⑪ 511 + 283	⑫ 193 + 265
⑬ 106 + 294	⑭ 228 + 903	⑮ 719 + 87	⑯ 451 + 382	⑰ 327 + 481	⑱ 871 + 86
⑲ 99 + 103	⑳ 761 + 249	㉑ 87 + 223	㉒ 603 + 289	㉓ 507 + 98	㉔ 63 + 487
㉕ 876 + 55	㉖ 434 + 89	㉗ 578 + 78	㉘ 43 + 867	㉙ 62 + 199	㉚ 101 + 199
㉛ 169 + 903	㉜ 17 + 293	㉝ 297 + 54	㉞ 493 + 68	㉟ 555 + 66	㊱ 641 + 279

A three-digit number has digits in the ________________ place, the ________________ place, and the ________________ place.

Back Page Exercises Add the sums of problems 1 and 2, 3 and 4, 5 and 6, etc. You should have eighteen problems.

Four-Digit Addition 6

The Idea

A four-digit number has digits in the ones' place, the tens' place, the hundreds' place, and the thousands' place.

How to Use the Idea

When we add four-digit numbers, we sometimes carry to the ten thousands' column.

$$\begin{array}{r} {\scriptstyle 1\,1\,1\,1} \\ 3{,}288 \\ 4{,}110 \\ +9{,}822 \\ \hline 17{,}220 \end{array}$$

Find the sums.

1	7,612	+ 2,309	*9,921*
2	6,843	+ 2,366	*9,209*
3	4,333	+ 2,487	*6,820*
4	3,416	+ 5,985	*9,401*
5	2,119	+ 4,864	*6,983*
6	1,099	+ 3,911	*5,010*
7	5,555	+ 6,743	*12,298*
8	4,861	+ 3,207	*8,068*
9	7,809	+ 899	*8,708*
10	1,588	+ 3,922	*5,510*
11	3,844	+ 2,207	*6,051*
12	8,999	+ 985	*9,984*
13	1,111	+ 9,999	*11,110*
14	3,482	+ 2,793	*6,275*
15	5,802	+ 3,944	*9,746*
16	1,006	+ 7,904	*8,910*
17	8,803	+ 1,197	*10,000*
18	9,734	+ 808	*10,542*
19	2,121	+ 9,888	*12,009*
20	6,464	+ 3,536	*10,000*
21	1,001	+ 8,999	*10,000*
22	888	+ 3,031	*3,919*
23	7,026	+ 937	*7,963*
24	6,304	+ 707	*7,011*
25	983	+ 9,083	*10,066*
26	3,214	+ 798	*4,012*
27	5,016	+ 395	*5,411*
28	4,333	+ 767	*5,100*
29	9,123	+ 838	*9,961*
30	3,576	+ 544	*4,120*
31	4,602	+ 733	*5,335*
32	9,763	+ 137	*9,900*
33	1,999	+ 2,101	*4,100*
34	4,326	+ 674	*5,000*
35	6,743	+ 975	*7,718*
36	975	+ 1,925	*2,900*

A ____*four-digit*____ number has digits in the ones' place, the tens' place, the hundreds' place, and the thousands' place.

Back Page Exercises — **Add the sums of problems 2 and 4, 1 and 3, 6 and 8, 5 and 7, etc. You should have eighteen problems.**

Four-Digit Addition

The Idea

A four-digit number has digits in the ones' place, the tens' place, the hundreds' place, and the thousands' place.

How to Use the Idea

When we add four-digit numbers, we sometimes carry to the ten thousands' column.

```
  1 1 1 1
   3,288
   4,110
  +9,822
  ------
  17,220
```

Find the sums.

① 7,612 + 2,309 = *9,921*	② 6,843 + 2,366	③ 4,333 + 2,487	④ 3,416 + 5,985	⑤ 2,119 + 4,864	⑥ 1,099 + 3,911
⑦ 5,555 + 6,743	⑧ 4,861 + 3,207	⑨ 7,809 + 899	⑩ 1,588 + 3,922	⑪ 3,844 + 2,207	⑫ 8,999 + 985
⑬ 1,111 + 9,999	⑭ 3,482 + 2,793	⑮ 5,802 + 3,944	⑯ 1,006 + 7,904	⑰ 8,803 + 1,197	⑱ 9,734 + 808
⑲ 2,121 + 9,888	⑳ 6,464 + 3,536	(21) 1,001 + 8,999	(22) 888 + 3,031	(23) 7,026 + 937	(24) 6,304 + 707
(25) 983 + 9,083	(26) 3,214 + 798	(27) 5,016 + 395	(28) 4,333 + 767	(29) 9,123 + 838	(30) 3,576 + 544
(31) 4,602 + 733	(32) 9,763 + 137	(33) 1,999 + 2,101	(34) 4,326 + 674	(35) 6,743 + 975	(36) 975 + 1,925

A ______________ number has digits in the ones' place, the tens' place, the hundreds' place, and the thousands' place.

Back Page Exercises Add the sums of problems 2 and 4, 1 and 3, 6 and 8, 5 and 7, etc. You should have eighteen problems.

Five-Digit Addition

The Idea

A five-digit number has digits in the ones' place, the tens' place, the hundreds' place, the thousands' place, and the ten thousands' place.

How to Use the Idea

When we add five-digit numbers, we sometimes carry to the hundred thousands' column.

```
 1 1 1 1 1
   63,522
   44,265
 + 43,534
  151,321
```

Find the sums.

① 56,429 + 34,073 = ***90,502***	② 44,327 + 46,849 = ***91,176***	③ 19,568 + 28,667 = ***48,235***	④ 70,765 + 19,446 = ***90,211***	⑤ 64,003 + 24,998 = ***89,001***
⑥ 39,202 + 52,799 = ***92,001***	⑦ 20,299 + 79,833 = ***100,132***	⑧ 49,777 + 48,483 = ***98,260***	⑨ 64,875 + 25,375 = ***90,250***	⑩ 11,999 + 79,322 = ***91,321***
⑪ 38,765 + 49,865 = ***88,630***	⑫ 22,830 + 69,109 = ***91,939***	⑬ 48,900 + 49,899 = ***98,799***	⑭ 37,037 + 52,983 = ***90,020***	⑮ 60,738 + 29,682 = ***90,420***
⑯ 39,801 + 53,809 = ***93,610***	⑰ 78,305 + 19,795 = ***98,100***	⑱ 29,009 + 43,113 = ***72,122***	⑲ 56,333 + 34,555 = ***90,888***	⑳ 34,766 + 22,466 = ***57,232***
㉑ 11,888 + 34,922 = ***46,810***	㉒ 61,223 + 29,887 = ***91,110***	㉓ 58,991 + 46,118 = ***105,109***	㉔ 20,663 + 49,664 = ***70,327***	㉕ 91,735 + 19,645 = ***111,380***

A five-digit number has digits in the ***ones'*** place, the tens' place, the ***hundreds'*** place, the thousands' place, and the ***ten thousands'*** place.

Back Page Exercises Add the sums of problems 1 and 6, 11 and 16, 21 and 2, etc. You should have twelve problems.

Five-Digit Addition

The Idea

A five-digit number has digits in the ones' place, the tens' place, the hundreds' place, the thousands' place, and the ten thousands' place.

How to Use the Idea

When we add five-digit numbers, we sometimes carry to the hundred thousands' column.

```
 1 1 1 1 1
   63,522
   44,265
 + 43,534
 --------
  151,321
```

Find the sums.

① 56,429 + 34,073 = ***90,502***	② 44,327 + 46,849	③ 19,568 + 28,667	④ 70,765 + 19,446	⑤ 64,003 + 24,998
⑥ 39,202 + 52,799	⑦ 20,299 + 79,833	⑧ 49,777 + 48,483	⑨ 64,875 + 25,375	⑩ 11,999 + 79,322
⑪ 38,765 + 49,865	⑫ 22,830 + 69,109	⑬ 48,900 + 49,899	⑭ 37,037 + 52,983	⑮ 60,738 + 29,682
⑯ 39,801 + 53,809	⑰ 78,305 + 19,795	⑱ 29,009 + 43,113	⑲ 56,333 + 34,555	⑳ 34,766 + 22,466
㉑ 11,888 + 34,922	㉒ 61,223 + 29,887	㉓ 58,991 + 46,118	㉔ 20,663 + 49,664	㉕ 91,735 + 19,645

A five-digit number has digits in the ________________ place, the tens' place, the ________________ place, the thousands' place, and the ________________ place.

Back Page Exercises — **Add the sums of problems 1 and 6, 11 and 16, 21 and 2, etc. You should have twelve problems.**

Six-Digit Addition

The Idea

A six-digit number has digits in the ones' place, the tens' place, the hundreds' place, the thousands' place, the ten thousands' place, and the hundred thousands' place.

How to Use the Idea

When we add six-digit numbers, we sometimes carry to the millions' column.

```
 1 111 11
  568,594
+ 456,867
---------
1,025,461
```

Find the sums.

① 114,683 + 238,729 = ***353,412***	② 680,972 + 289,338 = ***970,310***	③ 793,119 + 135,991 = ***929,110***	④ 449,391 + 453,729 = ***903,120***
⑤ 594,337 + 392,773 = ***987,110***	⑥ 843,677 + 117,333 = ***961,010***	⑦ 907,768 + 91,636 = ***999,404***	⑧ 711,806 + 283,441 = ***995,247***
⑨ 667,442 + 264,558 = ***932,000***	⑩ 199,784 + 715,556 = ***915,340***	⑪ 827,009 + 163,991 = ***991,000***	⑫ 559,662 + 233,745 = ***793,407***
⑬ 149,983 + 846,758 = ***996,741***	⑭ 385,763 + 192,784 = ***578,547***	⑮ 674,119 + 291,336 = ***965,455***	⑯ 732,147 + 249,386 = ***981,533***
⑰ 549,763 + 371,337 = ***921,100***	⑱ 229,123 + 487,377 = ***716,500***	⑲ 326,494 + 534,586 = ***861,080***	⑳ 791,679 + 129,423 = ***921,102***
㉑ 812,543 + 186,576 = ***999,119***	㉒ 100,999 + 901,001 = ***1,002,000***	㉓ 469,731 + 842,659 = ***1,312,390***	㉔ 735,112 + 375,888 = ***1,111,000***

A ___*six-digit*___ number has digits in the ones' place, the tens' place, the hundreds' place, the thousands' place, the ten thousands' place, and the hundred thousands' place.

Back Page Exercises — **Add the sums of problems 1 and 2, 3 and 4, 5 and 6, etc. You should have twelve problems.**

Six-Digit Addition

The Idea

A six-digit number has digits in the ones' place, the tens' place, the hundreds' place, the thousands' place, the ten thousands' place, and the hundred thousands' place.

How to Use the Idea

When we add six-digit numbers, we sometimes carry to the millions' column.

$$\begin{array}{r} {\scriptstyle 1\,111\,11} \\ 568{,}594 \\ +\ 456{,}867 \\ \hline 1{,}025{,}461 \end{array}$$

Find the sums.

1. 114,683 + 238,729 = *353,412*
2. 680,972 + 289,338
3. 793,119 + 135,991
4. 449,391 + 453,729
5. 594,337 + 392,773
6. 843,677 + 117,333
7. 907,768 + 91,636
8. 711,806 + 283,441
9. 667,442 + 264,558
10. 199,784 + 715,556
11. 827,009 + 163,991
12. 559,662 + 233,745
13. 149,983 + 846,758
14. 385,763 + 192,784
15. 674,119 + 291,336
16. 732,147 + 249,386
17. 549,763 + 371,337
18. 229,123 + 487,377
19. 326,494 + 534,586
20. 791,679 + 129,423
21. 812,543 + 186,576
22. 100,999 + 901,001
23. 469,731 + 842,659
24. 735,112 + 375,888

A ________________ number has digits in the ones' place, the tens' place, the hundreds' place, the thousands' place, the ten thousands' place, and the hundred thousands' place.

Back Page Exercises Add the sums of problems 1 and 2, 3 and 4, 5 and 6, etc. You should have twelve problems.

More Than Six-Digit Addition

The Idea

When we add numbers with more than six digits, we are using numbers starting with one million and getting bigger. Because our number system uses place value, we do not have to deal with all the digits in a big number at once. We deal with each column as it comes; moving from right to left. In the sum, the place of each digit tells us its value. We mark off the digits in groups of three, beginning on the right, to help us read them.

How to Use the Idea

When we add more than six-digit numbers, we sometimes carry to the millions' column.

```
  1 111 11
 2,637,894
+3,498,797
 6,136,691
```

A Find the sums.

① 7,193,202 + 1,926,435 = ***9,119,637***	② 86,247,126 + 13,555,248 = ***99,802,374***	③ 101,763,347 + 98,247,163 = ***200,010,510***	④ 379,642,101 + 502,159,880 = ***881,801,981***
⑤ 1,466,783 + 4,008,951 = ***5,475,734***	⑥ 21,765,344 + 19,235,856 = ***41,001,200***	⑦ 247,846,112 + 53,992,898 = ***301,839,010***	⑧ 461,505,239 + 49,619,333 = ***511,124,572***
⑨ 53,806,414 + 17,915,237 = ***71,721,651***	⑩ 673,928,110 + 338,172,983 = ***1,012,101,093***	⑪ 564,769,143 + 447,921,732 = ***1,012,690,875***	⑫ 276,560,488 + 439,733,122 = ***716,293,610***

B Work the problems.

① Write the number nine million, seven hundred three thousand, nine hundred ninety-one. Write under it the number eighteen million, six hundred twenty-three thousand, five hundred eight. Now, write the sum.

```
  9,703,991
+18,623,508
 28,327,499
```

② Write down and add the numbers one hundred thirty-two million, seven hundred thirteen thousand, twenty; and fifty-seven million, four hundred thousand, nine hundred fifty.

```
 132,713,020
+ 57,400,950
 190,113,970
```

The ___*place*___ of each digit in an addition problem tells us its value. We mark off digits in groups of ___*three*___ beginning with the ___*right*___, to help us read them.

Back Page Exercises Write out the answers to exercise A.

More Than Six-Digit Addition

The Idea

When we add numbers with more than six digits, we are using numbers starting with one million and getting bigger. Because our number system uses place value, we do not have to deal with all the digits in a big number at once. We deal with each column as it comes; moving from right to left. In the sum, the place of each digit tells us its value. We mark off the digits in groups of three, beginning on the right, to help us read them.

How to Use the Idea

When we add more than six-digit numbers, we sometimes carry to the millions' column.

```
   1 111 11
  2,637,894
+ 3,498,797
-----------
  6,136,691
```

A Find the sums.

① 7,193,202 + 1,926,435 = *9,119,637*

② 86,247,126 + 13,555,248

③ 101,763,347 + 98,247,163

④ 379,642,101 + 502,159,880

⑤ 1,466,783 + 4,008,951

⑥ 21,765,344 + 19,235,856

⑦ 247,846,112 + 53,992,898

⑧ 461,505,239 + 49,619,333

⑨ 53,806,414 + 17,915,237

⑩ 673,928,110 + 338,172,983

⑪ 564,769,143 + 447,921,732

⑫ 276,560,488 + 439,733,122

B Work the problems.

① Write the number nine million, seven hundred three thousand, nine hundred ninety-one. Write under it the number eighteen million, six hundred twenty-three thousand, five hundred eight. Now, write the sum.

② Write down and add the numbers one hundred thirty-two million, seven hundred thirteen thousand, twenty; and fifty-seven million, four hundred thousand, nine hundred fifty.

The ______________ of each digit in an addition problem tells us its value. We mark off digits in groups of ______________ beginning with the ______________, to help us read them.

Back Page Exercises Write out the answers to exercise A.

The Associative Property

The Idea

The associative property of addition holds that the sum will be the same regardless of the way in which a series of numbers is combined.

How to Use the Idea

We can call the associative property the grouping property. Suppose we want to add 7 + 8 + 4. We can add (7 + 8) + 4 = 15 + 4 = 19 or we can add 7 + (8 + 4) = 7 + 12 = 19. Changing the grouping does not change the sum.

Group each problem and work it two different ways.

① 10 + 9 + 8 = 27

(10 + 9) + 8 = 19 + 8 = 27

10 + (9 + 8) = 10 + 17 = 27

② 37 + 12 + 18 = 67

(37 + 12) + 18 = 49 + 18 = 67

37 + (12 + 18) = 37 + 30 = 67

③ 50 + 33 + 17 = 100

(50 + 33) + 17 = 83 + 17 = 100

50 + (33 + 17) = 50 + 50 = 100

④ 64 + 16 + 32 = 112

(64 + 16) + 32 = 80 + 32 = 112

64 + (16 + 32) = 64 + 48 = 112

⑤ 18 + 15 + 20 = 53

(18 + 15) + 20 = 33 + 20 = 53

18 + (15 + 20) = 18 + 35 = 53

⑥ 23 + 37 + 33 = 93

(23 + 37) + 33 = 60 + 33 = 93

23 + (37 + 33) = 23 + 70 = 93

⑦ 59 + 11 + 39 = 109

(59 + 11) + 39 = 70 + 39 = 109

59 + (11 + 39) = 59 + 50 = 109

⑧ 113 + 17 + 24 = 154

(113 + 17) + 24 = 130 + 24 = 154

113 + (17 + 24) = 113 + 41 = 154

⑨ 349 + 111 + 48 = 508

(349 + 111) + 48 = 460 + 48 = 508

349 + (111 + 48) = 349 + 159 = 508

⑩ 793 + 217 + 106 = 1,116

(793 + 217) + 106 = 1,010 + 106 = 1,116

793 + (217 + 106) = 793 + 323 = 1,116

⑪ 532 + 11 + 84 = 627

(532 + 11) + 84 = 543 + 84 = 627

532 + (11 + 84) = 532 + 95 = 627

⑫ 733 + 41 + 19 = 793

(733 + 41) + 19 = 774 + 19 = 793

733 + (41 + 19) = 733 + 60 = 793

The *associative* property of addition holds that the *sum* will be the same regardless of the way in which a *series* of numbers is combined.

Back Page Exercises Write a story for each of the first four problems.

The Associative Property

The Idea

The associative property of addition holds that the sum will be the same regardless of the way in which a series of numbers is combined.

How to Use the Idea

We can call the associative property the grouping property. Suppose we want to add 7 + 8 + 4. We can add (7 + 8) + 4 = 15 + 4 = 19 or we can add 7 + (8 + 4) = 7 + 12 = 19. Changing the grouping does not change the sum.

Group each problem and work it two different ways.

① 10 + 9 + 8 = 27

(10 + 9) + 8 = 19 + 8 = 27

10 + (9 + 8) = 10 + 17 = 27

② 37 + 12 + 18 = 67

③ 50 + 33 + 17 = 100

④ 64 + 16 + 32 = 112

⑤ 18 + 15 + 20 = 53

⑥ 23 + 37 + 33 = 93

⑦ 59 + 11 + 39 = 109

⑧ 113 + 17 + 24 = 154

⑨ 349 + 111 + 48 = 508

⑩ 793 + 217 + 106 = 1,116

⑪ 532 + 11 + 84 = 627

⑫ 733 + 41 + 19 = 793

The ________________ property of addition holds that the ________________ will be the same regardless of the way in which a ________________ of numbers is combined.

Back Page Exercises Write a story for each of the first four problems.

Using the Associative Property

The Idea

In addition, the associative property means that for any three numbers a, b, and c, $(a + b) + c = a + (b + c)$.

How to Use the Idea

The associative property of addition can be used to make addend trees. Usually the addend tree will use combinations which add up to a multiple of 10 on at least one side.

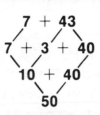

7 + 43
7 + 3 + 40
10 + 40
50

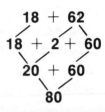

18 + 62
18 + 2 + 60
20 + 60
80

A Fill in the blanks on the addend trees for the following problems.

① 138 + 97
135 + *3* + 97
135 + 100
235

② 723 + 77
723 + 7 + 70
730 + 70
800

③ 242 + 128
240 + 2 + 128
240 + 130
370

④ 594 + 106
594 + 6 + 100
600 + *100*
700

⑤ 254 + 146
250 + 4 + 146
250 + 150
400

⑥ 495 + 215
495 + 5 + 210
500 + 210
710

⑦ 113 + 147
113 + 7 + 140
120 + 140
260

⑧ 182 + 18
180 + 2 + 18
180 + 20
200

B Add each column of numbers as shown, first going down, then checking by going up.

① 8, 4, 7, 9 — down: *12*, *19*, *28*; total *28*; up: *16*, *20*, *28*

② 11, 6, 9, 5 — down: *17*, *26*, *31*; total *31*; up: *14*, *20*, *31*

③ 13, 11, 6, 10 — down: *24*, *30*, *40*; total *40*; up: *16*, *27*, *40*

④ 20, 6, 8, 14 — down: *26*, *34*, *48*; total *48*; up: *22*, *28*, *48*

⑤ 21, 32, 24 — down: *53*, *77*; total *77*; up: *56*, *77*

⑥ 42, 9, 26 — down: *51*, *77*; total *77*; up: *35*, *77*

⑦ 19, 11, 20 — down: *30*, *50*; total *50*; up: *31*, *50*

⑧ 28, 12, 30 — down: *40*, *70*; total *70*; up: *42*, *70*

In *addition*, the associative property means that for any *three* numbers a, b, and c, $(a + b) + c = a + (b + c)$.

Back Page Exercises Create three addend trees.

Using the Associative Property 11

The Idea

In addition, the associative property means that for any three numbers a, b, and c, (a + b) + c = a + (b + c).

How to Use the Idea

The associative property of addition can be used to make addend trees. Usually the addend tree will use combinations which add up to a multiple of 10 on at least one side.

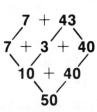

7 + 43
7 + 3 + 40
10 + 40
50

18 + 62
18 + 2 + 60
20 + 60
80

A Fill in the blanks on the addend trees for the following problems.

① 138 + 97
135 + *3* + 97
135 + 100
235

② 723 + 77
723 + 7 + 70
730 + 70
____

③ 242 + 128
240 + 2 + 128
240 + 130
____

④ 594 + 106
594 + 6 + 100
600 + ____
____

⑤ 254 + 146
250 + 4 + 146
250 + 150
____

⑥ 495 + 215
495 + 5 + 210
____ + 210
____

⑦ 113 + 147
____ + 7 + 140
120 + 140
____

⑧ 182 + 18
180 + 2 + 18
180 + 20
____

B Add each column of numbers as shown, first going down, then checking by going up.

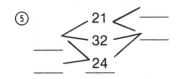

① 8, 4, 7, 9 — going down: *12*, *19*, *28* — going up: *16*, *20*, *28* — total: *28*

② 11, 6, 9, 5 — ____ ____ ____ / ____ ____ ____

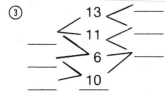

③ 13, 11, 6, 10 — ____ ____ ____ / ____ ____ ____

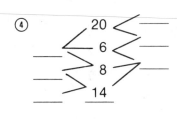

④ 20, 6, 8, 14 — ____ ____ ____ / ____ ____ ____

⑤ 21, 32, 24 — ____ ____ / ____ ____

⑥ 42, 9, 26 — ____ ____ / ____ ____

⑦ 19, 11, 20 — ____ ____ / ____ ____

⑧ 28, 12, 30 — ____ ____ / ____ ____

In ____________________, the associative property means that for any ____________________ numbers a, b, and c, (a + b) + c = a + (b + c).

Back Page Exercises Create three addend trees.

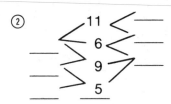

More Commutative Property 13

The Idea

Addition is commutative. This means that a set of numbers can be added in any order without changing the sum.

How to Use the Idea

1 + 2 = 3
2 + 1 = 3

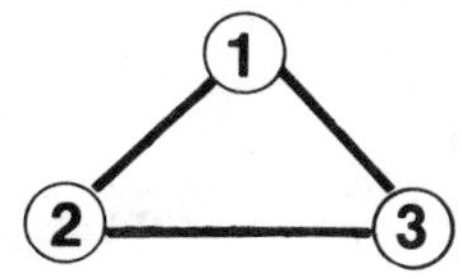

1 + 3 = 4
3 + 1 = 4

2 + 3 = 5
3 + 2 = 5

Write two number addition sentences for each pair of numbers joined by a line segment.

① 2 + 4 = 6; 4 + 2 = 6; 2 + 5 = 7; 5 + 2 = 7

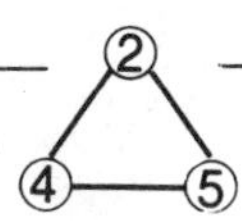

4 + 5 = 9; 5 + 4 = 9

② 2 + 6 = 8; 6 + 2 = 8; 2 + 7 = 9; 7 + 2 = 9

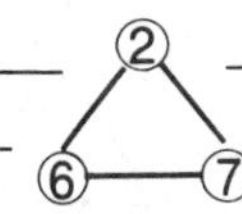

6 + 7 = 13; 7 + 6 = 13

③ 3 + 4 = 7; 4 + 3 = 7; 3 + 6 = 9; 6 + 3 = 9

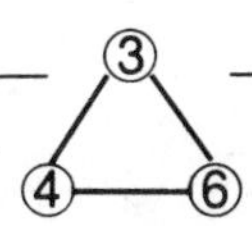

4 + 6 = 10; 6 + 4 = 10

④ 3 + 5 = 8; 5 + 3 = 8; 3 + 8 = 11; 8 + 3 = 11

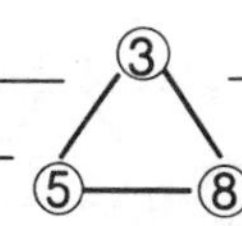

5 + 8 = 13; 8 + 5 = 13

⑤ 4 + 1 = 5; 1 + 4 = 5; 4 + 9 = 13; 9 + 4 = 13

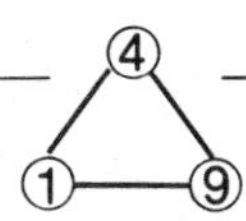

1 + 9 = 10; 9 + 1 = 10

⑥ 4 + 7 = 11; 7 + 4 = 11; 4 + 8 = 12; 8 + 4 = 12

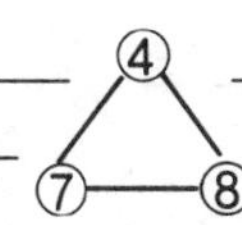

7 + 8 = 15; 8 + 7 = 15

⑦ 5 + 6 = 11; 6 + 5 = 11; 5 + 9 = 14; 9 + 5 = 14

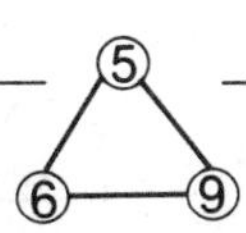

6 + 9 = 15; 9 + 6 = 15

⑧ 6 + 1 = 7; 1 + 6 = 7; 6 + 8 = 14; 8 + 6 = 14

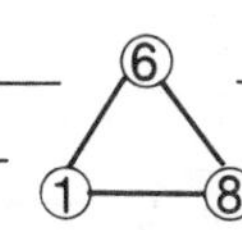

1 + 8 = 9; 8 + 1 = 9

Addition is *commutative*. This means that a *set* of numbers can be added in *any* order without changing the *sum*.

Back Page Exercises Create five problems using the pattern above.

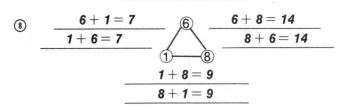

More Commutative Property

The Idea

Addition is commutative. This means that a set of numbers can be added in any order without changing the sum.

How to Use the Idea

1 + 2 = 3
2 + 1 = 3

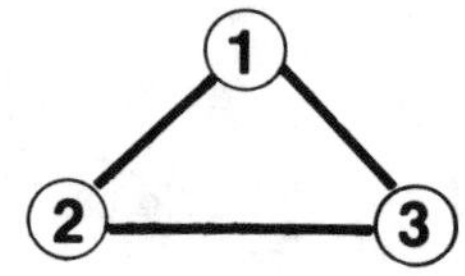

1 + 3 = 4
3 + 1 = 4

2 + 3 = 5
3 + 2 = 5

Write two number addition sentences for each pair of numbers joined by a line segment.

① *2 + 4 = 6* / *4 + 2 = 6*; *2 + 5 = 7* / *5 + 2 = 7*; *4 + 5 = 9* / *5 + 4 = 9*

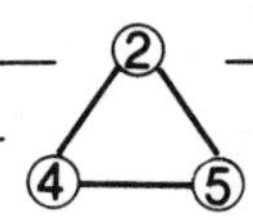

② ______ ______ ______ ______ ______ ______

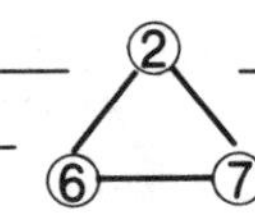

③ ______ ______ ______ ______ ______ ______

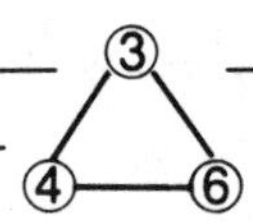

④ ______ ______ ______ ______ ______ ______

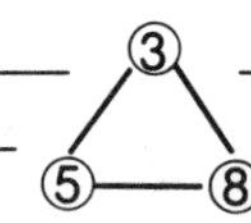

⑤ ______ ______ ______ ______ ______ ______

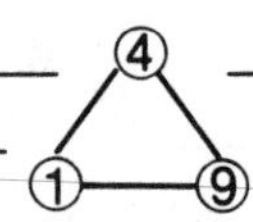

⑥ ______ ______ ______ ______ ______ ______

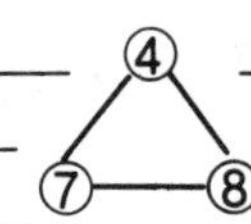

⑦ ______ ______ ______ ______ ______ ______

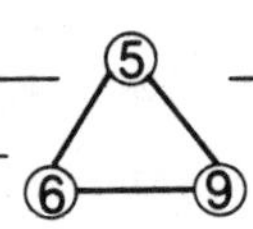

⑧ ______ ______ ______ ______ ______ ______

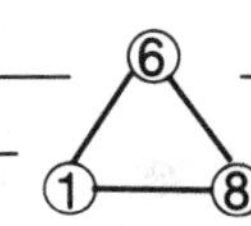

Addition is ______________. This means that a ______________ of numbers can be added in ______________ order without changing the ______________.

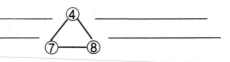

Back Page Exercises Create five problems using the pattern above.

Using the Commutative Property

The Idea

When we add two or more numbers, the order in which we add makes no difference. This is the commutative property of addition.

How to Use the Idea

$8 + 7 + 9 + 4 = 7 + 8 + 4 + 9 = 28$

$100 + 240 + 360 + 80 = 100 + 80 + 360 + 240 = 780$

$31 + 25 + 8 + 14 = 8 + 25 + 14 + 31 = 78$

$90 + 27 + 38 + 23 = 90 + 27 + 23 + 38 = 178$

A Fill in the blanks and find the sums.

① $8 + 4 + 10 + 9 = 4 + 8 + 9 +$ ___*10*___ = ___*31*___

② $14 + 35 + 26 + 20 = 35 +$ ___*14*___ $+ 26 + 20 =$ ___*95*___

③ $22 + 6 + 8 + 14 = 14 + 22 + 8 +$ ___*6*___ = ___*50*___

④ $15 + 39 + 63 + 12 = 15 + 63 + 12 +$ ___*39*___ = ___*129*___

⑤ $113 + 38 + 27 + 12 = 113 + 27 + 12 +$ ___*38*___ = ___*190*___

⑥ $42 + 19 + 28 + 11 = 42 + 28 +$ ___*19*___ $+ 11 =$ ___*100*___

⑦ $26 + 37 + 24 + 38 = 26 + 24 + 37 +$ ___*38*___ = ___*125*___

⑧ $58 + 37 + 12 + 13 = 58 + 12 + 37 +$ ___*13*___ = ___*120*___

⑨ $11 + 28 + 19 + 32 =$ ___*28*___ $+ 11 + 32 + 19 =$ ___*90*___

⑩ $218 + 48 + 12 + 14 = 48 + 12 + 218 +$ ___*14*___ = ___*292*___

B Change the order in the following problems to make adding them easier. Find the sums.

① $18 + 13 + 19 + 12 + 17 + 11 = (18 + 12) + (13 + 17) + (19 + 11) = 30 + 30 + 30 = 90$

② $25 + 16 + 37 + 14 + 15 + 23 = (25 + 15) + (16 + 14) + (37 + 23) = 40 + 30 + 60 = 130$

③ $44 + 18 + 23 + 6 + 22 + 37 = (44 + 6) + (18 + 22) + (23 + 37) = 50 + 40 + 60 = 150$

④ $150 + 40 + 80 + 250 + 60 + 120 = (150 + 250) + (40 + 60) + (80 + 120) = 400 + 100 + 200 = 700$

⑤ $230 + 90 + 40 + 60 + 170 + 10 = (230 + 170) + (90 + 10) + (40 + 60) = 400 + 100 + 100 = 600$

⑥ $80 + 110 + 20 + 90 + 50 + 350 = (80 + 20) + (110 + 90) + (50 + 350) = 100 + 200 + 400 = 700$

⑦ $85 + 215 + 164 + 73 + 17 + 36 = (85 + 215) + (164 + 36) + (73 + 17) = 300 + 200 + 90 = 590$

⑧ $92 + 114 + 28 + 16 + 13 + 7 = (92 + 28) + (114 + 16) + (13 + 7) = 120 + 130 + 20 = 270$

When we ___*add*___ two or more numbers, the ___*order*___ in which we add makes no difference. This is the ___*commutative*___ property of addition.

Back Page Exercises Change the order of the addends in each problem above. Add. Is your answer the same as before?

Using the Commutative Property

The Idea

When we add two or more numbers, the order in which we add makes no difference. This is the commutative property of addition.

How to Use the Idea

$$8 + 7 + 9 + 4 = 7 + 8 + 4 + 9 = 28$$

$$100 + 240 + 360 + 80 = 100 + 80 + 360 + 240 = 780$$

$$31 + 25 + 8 + 14 = 8 + 25 + 14 + 31 = 78$$

$$90 + 27 + 38 + 23 = 90 + 27 + 23 + 38 = 178$$

A Fill in the blanks and find the sums.

① $8 + 4 + 10 + 9 = 4 + 8 + 9 +$ *10* $=$ *31*

② $14 + 35 + 26 + 20 = 35 +$ ____ $+ 26 + 20 =$ ____

③ $22 + 6 + 8 + 14 = 14 + 22 + 8 +$ ____ $=$ ____

④ $15 + 39 + 63 + 12 = 15 + 63 + 12 +$ ____ $=$ ____

⑤ $113 + 38 + 27 + 12 = 113 + 27 + 12 +$ ____ $=$ ____

⑥ $42 + 19 + 28 + 11 = 42 + 28 +$ ____ $+ 11 =$ ____

⑦ $26 + 37 + 24 + 38 = 26 + 24 + 37 +$ ____ $=$ ____

⑧ $58 + 37 + 12 + 13 = 58 + 12 + 37 +$ ____ $=$ ____

⑨ $11 + 28 + 19 + 32 =$ ____ $+ 11 + 32 + 19 =$ ____

⑩ $218 + 48 + 12 + 14 = 48 + 12 + 218 +$ ____ $=$ ____

B Change the order in the following problems to make adding them easier. Find the sums.

① $18 + 13 + 19 + 12 + 17 + 11 =$ *(18 + 12) + (13 + 17) + (19 + 11) = 30 + 30 + 30 = 90*

② $25 + 16 + 37 + 14 + 15 + 23 =$

③ $44 + 18 + 23 + 6 + 22 + 37 =$

④ $150 + 40 + 80 + 250 + 60 + 120 =$

⑤ $230 + 90 + 40 + 60 + 170 + 10 =$

⑥ $80 + 110 + 20 + 90 + 50 + 350 =$

⑦ $85 + 215 + 164 + 73 + 17 + 36 =$

⑧ $92 + 114 + 28 + 16 + 13 + 7 =$

When we ____________ two or more numbers, the ____________ in which we add makes no difference. This is the ____________ property of addition.

Back Page Exercises Change the order of the addends in each problem above. Add. Is your answer the same as before?

Adding Columns

The Idea

Adding columns of numbers is very similar to regular addition. When you add a column of numbers, you must remember to carry if necessary.

How to Use the Idea

324	1,123
598	4,908
+ 601	+ 5,601
1,523	11,632

Find the sums.

①	②	③	④	⑤	⑥	⑦
432	514	726	639	176	222	519
289	373	119	228	824	493	721
+ 113	+ 109	+ 444	+ 417	+ 347	+ 349	+ 393
834	*996*	*1,289*	*1,284*	*1,347*	*1,064*	*1,633*

⑧	⑨	⑩	⑪	⑫	⑬	⑭
811	249	159	502	726	888	187
347	183	426	174	107	291	329
524	372	209	219	229	187	412
+ 123	+ 406	+ 224	+ 263	+ 413	+ 100	+ 194
1,805	*1,210*	*1,018*	*1,158*	*1,475*	*1,466*	*1,122*

⑮	⑯	⑰	⑱	⑲	⑳
1,818	2,703	4,162	5,808	1,776	9,114
2,403	1,826	3,071	3,217	1,986	2,089
+ 7,124	+ 3,081	+ 1,208	+ 1,003	+ 2,001	+ 5,172
11,345	*7,610*	*8,441*	*10,028*	*5,763*	*16,375*

㉑	㉒	㉓	㉔	㉕	㉖
2,093	4,111	5,072	9,126	1,723	2,909
1,986	3,264	1,134	1,555	1,688	3,716
3,124	1,806	2,066	2,431	3,904	829
+ 4,177	+ 2,317	+ 3,208	+ 5,066	+ 2,826	+ 4,183
11,380	*11,498*	*11,480*	*18,178*	*10,141*	*11,637*

___*Adding*___ columns of numbers is very similar to regular addition. When you ___*add*___ a column of numbers, you must remember to ___*carry*___ if necessary.

Back Page Exercises Create ten problems adding columns of numbers.

Adding Columns

15

The Idea

Adding columns of numbers is very similar to regular addition. When you add a column of numbers, you must remember to carry if necessary.

How to Use the Idea

1 1	1 1
324	1,123
598	4,908
+ 601	+ 5,601
1,523	11,632

Find the sums.

①	②	③	④	⑤	⑥	⑦
432	514	726	639	176	222	519
289	373	119	228	824	493	721
+ 113	+ 109	+ 444	+ 417	+ 347	+ 349	+ 393
834						

⑧	⑨	⑩	⑪	⑫	⑬	⑭
811	249	159	502	726	888	187
347	183	426	174	107	291	329
524	372	209	219	229	187	412
+ 123	+ 406	+ 224	+ 263	+ 413	+ 100	+ 194

⑮	⑯	⑰	⑱	⑲	⑳
1,818	2,703	4,162	5,808	1,776	9,114
2,403	1,826	3,071	3,217	1,986	2,089
+ 7,124	+ 3,081	+ 1,208	+ 1,003	+ 2,001	+ 5,172

㉑	㉒	㉓	㉔	㉕	㉖
2,093	4,111	5,072	9,126	1,723	2,909
1,986	3,264	1,134	1,555	1,688	3,716
3,124	1,806	2,066	2,431	3,904	829
+ 4,177	+ 2,317	+ 3,208	+ 5,066	+ 2,826	+ 4,183

________________ columns of numbers is very similar to regular addition. When you ________________ a column of numbers, you must remember to ________________ if necessary.

Back Page Exercises Create ten problems adding columns of numbers.

Three-Digit Subtraction

The Idea

Borrowing is renaming numbers to subtract.

How to Use the Idea

Place value lets us borrow or rename numbers when we subtract. When we borrow one from the hundreds' place to subtract in the tens' place, we are borrowing ten tens. If the digit in the tens' place is a zero and we need to borrow to subtract in the ones' place, then we borrow one one hundred, leave nine tens in the tens' place, and take one ten to the ones' place as ten ones.

a. $\begin{array}{r} 204 \\ -\ 95 \\ \hline \end{array} \begin{array}{l} = \\ = \end{array} \begin{array}{r} 190 + 14 \\ -\ 90 + \ \ 5 \\ \hline 100 + \ \ 9 = 109 \end{array}$

b. $\begin{array}{r} 507 \\ -\ 88 \\ \hline 419 \end{array}$

c. $\begin{array}{r} 684 \\ -\ 193 \\ \hline 491 \end{array}$

Find the remainders. Check each answer with addition.

①	654 − 195	*459*	*195 + 459*	*654*
②	911 − 812	*99*	*812 + 99*	*911*
③	403 − 281	*122*	*281 + 122*	*403*
④	114 − 56	*58*	*56 + 58*	*114*
⑤	555 − 466	*89*	*466 + 89*	*555*
⑥	321 − 122	*199*	*122 + 199*	*321*
⑦	987 − 696	*291*	*696 + 291*	*987*
⑧	267 − 198	*69*	*198 + 69*	*267*
⑨	411 − 213	*198*	*213 + 198*	*411*
⑩	719 − 224	*495*	*224 + 495*	*719*
⑪	841 − 623	*218*	*623 + 218*	*841*
⑫	246 − 168	*78*	*168 + 78*	*246*
⑬	363 − 244	*119*	*244 + 119*	*363*
⑭	701 − 245	*456*	*245 + 456*	*701*
⑮	498 − 299	*199*	*299 + 199*	*498*
⑯	520 − 436	*84*	*436 + 84*	*520*
⑰	920 − 640	*280*	*640 + 280*	*920*
⑱	333 − 241	*92*	*241 + 92*	*333*
⑲	469 − 171	*298*	*171 + 298*	*469*
⑳	702 − 328	*374*	*328 + 374*	*702*
㉑	536 − 244	*292*	*244 + 292*	*536*
㉒	716 − 225	*491*	*225 + 491*	*716*
㉓	823 − 244	*579*	*244 + 579*	*823*
㉔	691 − 287	*404*	*287 + 404*	*691*

Borrowing is ____*renaming*____ numbers to subtract.

Back Page Exercises — **Create ten three-digit subtraction problems. Check with addition.**

Three-Digit Subtraction

The Idea

Borrowing is renaming numbers to subtract.

How to Use the Idea

Place value lets us borrow or rename numbers when we subtract. When we borrow one from the hundreds' place to subtract in the tens' place, we are borrowing ten tens. If the digit in the tens' place is a zero and we need to borrow to subtract in the ones' place, then we borrow one one hundred, leave nine tens in the tens' place, and take one ten to the ones' place as ten ones.

a.
$$\begin{array}{r} 204 \\ -\ 95 \\ \hline \end{array} \begin{array}{l} = \\ = \\ \\ \end{array} \begin{array}{r} 190 + 14 \\ -90 + \ 5 \\ \hline 100 + \ 9 = 109 \end{array}$$

b.
$$\begin{array}{r} 507 \\ -\ 88 \\ \hline 419 \end{array}$$

c.
$$\begin{array}{r} 684 \\ -193 \\ \hline 491 \end{array}$$

Find the remainders. Check each answer with addition.

① 654 − 195 = ***459*** Check: ***195 + 459 = 654***

② 911 − 812

③ 403 − 281

④ 114 − 56

⑤ 555 − 466

⑥ 321 − 122

⑦ 987 − 696

⑧ 267 − 198

⑨ 411 − 213

⑩ 719 − 224

⑪ 841 − 623

⑫ 246 − 168

⑬ 363 − 244

⑭ 701 − 245

⑮ 498 − 299

⑯ 520 − 436

⑰ 920 − 640

⑱ 333 − 241

⑲ 469 − 171

⑳ 702 − 328

㉑ 536 − 244

㉒ 716 − 225

㉓ 823 − 244

㉔ 691 − 287

Borrowing is ____________________ numbers to subtract.

Back Page Exercises Create ten three-digit subtraction problems. Check with addition.

Four-Digit Subtraction

The Idea

Our number system has place value. This means that the position of the digit in the number tells us its value. Each place is worth ten times as much as the place to its right.

How to Use the Idea

When we subtract we do not have to think about what place we are dealing with. If the digit in the minuend is not big enough to subtract the digit under it, then we can borrow 10 from the next place to the left.

2,300	3,793	4,634	5,123
− 1,400	− 1,882	− 2,943	− 3,834
900	1,911	1,691	1,289

Find the remainders. Check using addition.

①	4,320 − 2,716 = *1,604*	*2,716 + 1,604 = 4,320*
②	2,192 − 1,184 = *1,008*	*1,184 + 1,008 = 2,192*
③	7,349 − 6,448 = *901*	*6,448 + 901 = 7,349*
④	6,224 − 3,455 = *2,769*	*3,455 + 2,769 = 6,224*
⑤	9,823 − 7,944 = *1,879*	*7,944 + 1,879 = 9,823*
⑥	6,413 − 3,524 = *2,889*	*3,524 + 2,889 = 6,413*
⑦	5,229 − 4,138 = *1,091*	*4,138 + 1,091 = 5,229*
⑧	4,194 − 3,249 = *945*	*3,249 + 945 = 4,194*
⑨	5,993 − 2,994 = *2,999*	*2,994 + 2,999 = 5,993*
⑩	2,103 − 1,204 = *899*	*1,204 + 899 = 2,103*
⑪	3,906 − 2,805 = *1,101*	*2,805 + 1,101 = 3,906*
⑫	5,398 − 4,299 = *1,099*	*4,299 + 1,099 = 5,398*
⑬	7,392 − 6,293 = *1,099*	*6,293 + 1,099 = 7,392*
⑭	6,449 − 4,963 = *1,486*	*4,963 + 1,486 = 6,449*
⑮	4,983 − 3,874 = *1,109*	*3,874 + 1,109 = 4,983*
⑯	1,186 − 1,139 = *47*	*1,139 + 47 = 1,186*
⑰	5,212 − 3,848 = *1,364*	*3,848 + 1,364 = 5,212*
⑱	7,612 − 2,921 = *4,691*	*2,921 + 4,691 = 7,612*
⑲	3,279 − 1,381 = *1,898*	*1,381 + 1,898 = 3,279*
⑳	4,063 − 2,172 = *1,891*	*2,172 + 1,891 = 4,063*
㉑	2,918 − 1,820 = *1,098*	*1,820 + 1,098 = 2,918*
㉒	6,414 − 3,524 = *2,890*	*3,524 + 2,890 = 6,414*
㉓	8,923 − 7,934 = *989*	*7,934 + 989 = 8,923*
㉔	5,333 − 2,498 = *2,835*	*2,498 + 2,835 = 5,333*
㉕	6,496 − 5,587 = *909*	*5,587 + 909 = 6,496*
㉖	5,961 − 4,872 = *1,089*	*4,872 + 1,089 = 5,961*
㉗	2,389 − 1,498 = *891*	*1,498 + 891 = 2,389*
㉘	8,888 − 7,999 = *889*	*7,999 + 889 = 8,888*

The *position* of the digit in the number tells us its *value*. Each place is worth *ten times* as much as the place to its *right*.

Back Page Exercises Create ten four-digit subtraction problems. Check with addition.

Four-Digit Subtraction

The Idea

Our number system has place value. This means that the position of the digit in the number tells us its value. Each place is worth ten times as much as the place to its right.

How to Use the Idea

When we subtract we do not have to think about what place we are dealing with. If the digit in the minuend is not big enough to subtract the digit under it, then we can borrow 10 from the next place to the left.

2,300	3,793	4,634	5,123
− 1,400	− 1,882	− 2,943	− 3,834
900	1,911	1,691	1,289

Find the remainders. Check using addition.

① 4,320 − 2,716 = ***1,604*** (check: ***2,716 + 1,604 = 4,320***)	② 2,192 − 1,184	③ 7,349 − 6,448	④ 6,224 − 3,455
⑤ 9,823 − 7,944	⑥ 6,413 − 3,524	⑦ 5,229 − 4,138	⑧ 4,194 − 3,249
⑨ 5,993 − 2,994	⑩ 2,103 − 1,204	⑪ 3,906 − 2,805	⑫ 5,398 − 4,299
⑬ 7,392 − 6,293	⑭ 6,449 − 4,963	⑮ 4,983 − 3,874	⑯ 1,186 − 1,139
⑰ 5,212 − 3,848	⑱ 7,612 − 2,921	⑲ 3,279 − 1,381	⑳ 4,063 − 2,172
㉑ 2,918 − 1,820	㉒ 6,414 − 3,524	㉓ 8,923 − 7,934	㉔ 5,333 − 2,498
㉕ 6,496 − 5,587	㉖ 5,961 − 4,872	㉗ 2,389 − 1,498	㉘ 8,888 − 7,999

The ________________ of the digit in the number tells us its ________________.
Each place is worth ________________ as much as the place to its ________________.

Back Page Exercises Create ten four-digit subtraction problems. Check with addition.

Five-Digit Subtraction 18

The Idea

A remainder is the answer to a subtraction problem.

How to Use the Idea

10,672	12,778	81,432
− 9,483	− 11,880	− 68,208
1,189	898	13,224

Find the remainders. Check using addition.

①	73,017	− 69,203	***3,814***	***69,203***	+ ***3,814***	***73,017***
②	44,705	− 23,664	***21,041***	***23,664***	+ ***21,041***	***44,705***
③	55,621	− 43,718	***11,903***	***43,718***	+ ***11,903***	***55,621***
④	61,892	− 48,774	***13,118***	***48,774***	+ ***13,118***	***61,892***
⑤	92,764	− 18,883	***73,881***	***73,881***	+ ***18,883***	***92,764***
⑥	83,113	− 24,205	***58,908***	***24,205***	+ ***58,908***	***83,113***
⑦	49,642	− 29,734	***19,908***	***29,734***	+ ***19,908***	***49,642***
⑧	10,432	− 10,321	***111***	***10,321***	+ ***111***	***10,432***
⑨	70,659	− 43,281	***27,378***	***43,281***	+ ***27,378***	***70,659***
⑩	61,529	− 5,438	***56,091***	***5,438***	+ ***56,091***	***61,529***
⑪	42,691	− 21,692	***20,999***	***21,692***	+ ***20,999***	***42,691***
⑫	57,109	− 41,218	***15,891***	***41,218***	+ ***15,891***	***57,109***
⑬	86,220	− 63,477	***22,743***	***63,477***	+ ***22,743***	***86,220***
⑭	49,067	− 38,174	***10,893***	***38,174***	+ ***10,893***	***49,067***
⑮	31,102	− 18,314	***12,788***	***18,314***	+ ***12,788***	***31,102***
⑯	78,447	− 39,224	***39,223***	***39,224***	+ ***39,223***	***78,447***
⑰	21,008	− 14,123	***6,885***	***14,123***	+ ***6,885***	***21,008***
⑱	19,338	− 9,497	***9,841***	***9,497***	+ ***9,841***	***19,338***
⑲	13,408	− 5,397	***8,011***	***5,397***	+ ***8,011***	***13,408***
⑳	50,069	− 32,178	***17,891***	***32,178***	+ ***17,891***	***50,069***
㉑	30,004	− 11,226	***18,778***	***11,226***	+ ***18,778***	***30,004***
㉒	60,000	− 49,118	***10,882***	***49,118***	+ ***10,882***	***60,000***
㉓	79,176	− 39,721	***39,455***	***39,721***	+ ***39,455***	***79,176***
㉔	12,940	− 10,711	***2,229***	***10,711***	+ ***2,229***	***12,940***

A ***remainder*** is the answer to a subtraction problem.

Back Page Exercises Create ten five-digit subtraction problems. Check with addition.

Five-Digit Subtraction 18

The Idea

A remainder is the answer to a subtraction problem.

How to Use the Idea

10,672 − 9,483 1,189	12,778 − 11,880 898	81,432 − 68,208 13,224

Find the remainders. Check using addition.

① 73,017 − 69,203 ***3,814*** ***69,203*** ***+ 3,814*** ***73,017***	② 44,705 − 23,664	③ 55,621 − 43,718	④ 61,892 − 48,774
⑤ 92,764 − 18,883	⑥ 83,113 − 24,205	⑦ 49,642 − 29,734	⑧ 10,432 − 10,321
⑨ 70,659 − 43,281	⑩ 61,529 − 5,438	⑪ 42,691 − 21,692	⑫ 57,109 − 41,218
⑬ 86,220 − 63,477	⑭ 49,067 − 38,174	⑮ 31,102 − 18,314	⑯ 78,447 − 39,224
⑰ 21,008 − 14,123	⑱ 19,338 − 9,497	⑲ 13,408 − 5,397	⑳ 50,069 − 32,178
㉑ 30,004 − 11,226	㉒ 60,000 − 49,118	㉓ 79,176 − 39,721	㉔ 12,940 − 10,711

A ______________ is the answer to a subtraction problem.

Back Page Exercises Create ten five-digit subtraction problems. Check with addition.

Six-Digit Subtraction

The Idea

Place value tells us how much each digit in a number is worth.

How to Use the Idea

In any subtraction problem, begin with the first column on the right, the ones' column, and deal with each column until the problem is done.

111,671	241,519	735,628
− 98,383	− 134,628	− 426,734
13,288	106,891	308,894

Find the remainders. Check using addition.

①	659,110	***549,223***	②	103,224	***102,453***	③	550,306	***449,218***
	− 549,223	+ ***109,887***		− 102,453	+ ***771***		− 449,218	+ ***101,088***
	109,887	***659,110***		***771***	***103,224***		***101,088***	***550,306***
④	490,626	***312,532***	⑤	272,103	***163,424***	⑥	513,602	***409,713***
	− 312,532	+ ***178,094***		− 163,424	+ ***108,679***		− 409,713	+ ***103,889***
	178,094	***490,626***		***108,679***	***272,103***		***103,889***	***513,602***
⑦	808,239	***721,416***	⑧	920,464	***271,381***	⑨	760,230	***473,079***
	− 721,416	+ ***86,823***		− 271,381	+ ***649,083***		− 473,079	+ ***287,151***
	86,823	***808,239***		***649,083***	***920,464***		***287,151***	***760,230***
⑩	900,401	***297,321***	⑪	270,003	***162,981***	⑫	644,397	***203,408***
	− 297,321	+ ***603,080***		− 162,981	+ ***107,022***		− 203,408	+ ***440,989***
	603,080	***900,401***		***107,022***	***270,003***		***440,989***	***644,397***
⑬	219,305	***108,416***	⑭	623,447	***409,508***	⑮	740,009	***632,118***
	− 108,416	+ ***110,889***		− 409,508	+ ***213,939***		− 632,118	+ ***107,891***
	110,889	***219,305***		***213,939***	***623,447***		***107,891***	***740,009***
⑯	100,000	***69,998***	⑰	426,639	***391,548***	⑱	217,717	***161,628***
	− 69,998	+ ***30,002***		− 391,548	+ ***35,091***		− 161,628	+ ***56,089***
	30,002	***100,000***		***35,091***	***426,639***		***56,089***	***217,717***
⑲	900,000	***652,032***	⑳	527,888	***493,799***	㉑	623,843	***517,209***
	− 652,032	+ ***247,968***		− 493,799	+ ***34,089***		− 517,209	+ ***106,634***
	247,968	***900,000***		***34,089***	***527,888***		***106,634***	***623,843***

Place value tells us how much each digit in a number is worth.

Back Page Exercises **Create ten six-digit subtraction problems. Check with addition.**

Six-Digit Subtraction

The Idea

Place value tells us how much each digit in a number is worth.

How to Use the Idea

In any subtraction problem, begin with the first column on the right, the ones' column, and deal with each column until the problem is done.

$$\begin{array}{r} 111{,}671 \\ -\ 98{,}383 \\ \hline 13{,}288 \end{array} \qquad \begin{array}{r} 241{,}519 \\ -\ 134{,}628 \\ \hline 106{,}891 \end{array} \qquad \begin{array}{r} 735{,}628 \\ -\ 426{,}734 \\ \hline 308{,}894 \end{array}$$

Find the remainders. Check using addition.

① $\begin{array}{r} 659{,}110 \\ -\ 549{,}223 \\ \hline \mathit{109{,}887} \end{array} \quad \begin{array}{r} \mathit{549{,}223} \\ +\ \mathit{109{,}887} \\ \hline \mathit{659{,}110} \end{array}$

② $\begin{array}{r} 103{,}224 \\ -\ 102{,}453 \\ \hline \end{array}$

③ $\begin{array}{r} 550{,}306 \\ -\ 449{,}218 \\ \hline \end{array}$

④ $\begin{array}{r} 490{,}626 \\ -\ 312{,}532 \\ \hline \end{array}$

⑤ $\begin{array}{r} 272{,}103 \\ -\ 163{,}424 \\ \hline \end{array}$

⑥ $\begin{array}{r} 513{,}602 \\ -\ 409{,}713 \\ \hline \end{array}$

⑦ $\begin{array}{r} 808{,}239 \\ -\ 721{,}416 \\ \hline \end{array}$

⑧ $\begin{array}{r} 920{,}464 \\ -\ 271{,}381 \\ \hline \end{array}$

⑨ $\begin{array}{r} 760{,}230 \\ -\ 473{,}079 \\ \hline \end{array}$

⑩ $\begin{array}{r} 900{,}401 \\ -\ 297{,}321 \\ \hline \end{array}$

⑪ $\begin{array}{r} 270{,}003 \\ -\ 162{,}981 \\ \hline \end{array}$

⑫ $\begin{array}{r} 644{,}397 \\ -\ 203{,}408 \\ \hline \end{array}$

⑬ $\begin{array}{r} 219{,}305 \\ -\ 108{,}416 \\ \hline \end{array}$

⑭ $\begin{array}{r} 623{,}447 \\ -\ 409{,}508 \\ \hline \end{array}$

⑮ $\begin{array}{r} 740{,}009 \\ -\ 632{,}118 \\ \hline \end{array}$

⑯ $\begin{array}{r} 100{,}000 \\ -\ 69{,}998 \\ \hline \end{array}$

⑰ $\begin{array}{r} 426{,}639 \\ -\ 391{,}548 \\ \hline \end{array}$

⑱ $\begin{array}{r} 217{,}717 \\ -\ 161{,}628 \\ \hline \end{array}$

⑲ $\begin{array}{r} 900{,}000 \\ -\ 652{,}032 \\ \hline \end{array}$

⑳ $\begin{array}{r} 527{,}888 \\ -\ 493{,}799 \\ \hline \end{array}$

㉑ $\begin{array}{r} 623{,}843 \\ -\ 517{,}209 \\ \hline \end{array}$

_______________ tells us how much each digit in a number is worth.

Back Page Exercises — **Create ten six-digit subtraction problems. Check with addition.**

More Than Six-Digit Subtraction

The Idea

Place value tells us how much each digit in a number is worth.

How to Use the Idea

In any subtraction problem, begin with the first column on the right, the ones' column, and deal with each column until the problem is done.

1,000,000	23,000,321	763,044,577
− 962,700	− 12,106,017	− 204,156,684
37,300	10,894,304	558,887,893

Find the remainders. Check using addition.

①	1,785,420 − 1,641,888 = ***143,532***	***1,641,888 + 143,532 = 1,785,420***
②	2,853,142 − 1,964,227 = ***888,915***	***1,964,227 + 888,915 = 2,853,142***
③	9,461,873 − 8,297,849 = ***1,164,024***	***8,297,849 + 1,164,024 = 9,461,873***
④	7,661,123 − 4,598,819 = ***3,062,304***	***4,598,819 + 3,062,304 = 7,661,123***
⑤	6,114,769 − 2,839,486 = ***3,275,283***	***2,839,486 + 3,275,283 = 6,114,769***
⑥	4,339,228 − 1,229,446 = ***3,109,782***	***1,299,446 + 3,109,782 = 4,339,228***
⑦	21,563,241 − 18,644,983 = ***2,918,258***	***18,644,983 + 2,918,258 = 21,563,241***
⑧	57,286,589 − 46,377,789 = ***10,908,800***	***46,377,789 + 10,908,800 = 57,286,589***
⑨	81,368,739 − 32,481,297 = ***48,887,442***	***32,481,297 + 48,887,442 = 81,368,739***
⑩	37,870,444 − 26,781,531 = ***11,088,913***	***26,781,531 + 11,088,913 = 37,870,444***
⑪	68,946,326 − 29,855,747 = ***39,090,579***	***29,855,747 + 39,090,579 = 68,946,326***
⑫	91,276,326 − 78,388,437 = ***12,887,889***	***78,388,437 + 12,887,889 = 91,276,326***
⑬	213,484,628 − 139,675,749 = ***73,808,879***	***139,675,749 + 73,808,879 = 213,484,628***
⑭	468,715,913 − 271,527,024 = ***197,188,889***	***271,527,024 + 197,188,889 = 468,715,913***
⑮	500,109,876 − 436,218,987 = ***63,890,889***	***436,218,987 + 63,890,889 = 500,109,876***
⑯	735,641,212 − 246,554,329 = ***489,086,883***	***246,554,329 + 489,086,883 = 735,641,212***
⑰	809,506,324 − 621,419,556 = ***188,086,768***	***621,419,556 + 188,086,768 = 809,506,324***
⑱	2,006,543,187 − 917,879,437 = ***1,088,663,750***	***917,879,437 + 1,088,663,750 = 2,006,543,187***

Place value tells us how much each ***digit*** in a number is worth.

Back Page Exercises — Create ten subtraction problems involving more than six digits. Check using addition.

More Than Six-Digit Subtraction

The Idea

Place value tells us how much each digit in a number is worth.

How to Use the Idea

In any subtraction problem, begin with the first column on the right, the ones' column, and deal with each column until the problem is done.

1,000,000	23,000,321	763,044,577
− 962,700	− 12,106,017	− 204,156,684
37,300	10,894,304	558,887,893

Find the remainders. Check using addition.

① 1,785,420 − 1,641,888 = ***143,532*** (check: ***1,641,888 + 143,532 = 1,785,420***)	② 2,853,142 − 1,964,227	③ 9,461,873 − 8,297,849
④ 7,661,123 − 4,598,819	⑤ 6,114,769 − 2,839,486	⑥ 4,339,228 − 1,229,446
⑦ 21,563,241 − 18,644,983	⑧ 57,286,589 − 46,377,789	⑨ 81,368,739 − 32,481,297
⑩ 37,870,444 − 26,781,531	⑪ 68,946,326 − 29,855,747	⑫ 91,276,326 − 78,388,437
⑬ 213,484,628 − 139,675,749	⑭ 468,715,913 − 271,527,024	⑮ 500,109,876 − 436,218,987
⑯ 735,641,212 − 246,554,329	⑰ 809,506,324 − 621,419,556	⑱ 2,006,543,187 − 917,879,437

Place value tells us how much each ______________ in a number is worth.

Back Page Exercises   **Create ten subtraction problems involving more than six digits. Check using addition.**

Subtraction Practice

The Idea

Subtraction is the inverse operation of addition. This means that subtraction undoes what addition does.

How to Use the Idea

841 − 623 = 218
218 + 623 = 841

246 − 168 = 78
78 + 168 = 246

Some of these exercises require borrowing or renaming to subtract. Others do not. Check each problem by addition. If your answer does not check, go back and make sure your borrowing is correct.

①	378 − 286	*92*	*286 + 92*	*378*
②	844 − 233	*611*	*233 + 611*	*844*
③	758 − 661	*97*	*661 + 97*	*758*
④	411 − 286	*125*	*286 + 125*	*411*
⑤	623 − 148	*475*	*148 + 475*	*623*
⑥	525 − 316	*209*	*316 + 209*	*525*
⑦	198 − 39	*159*	*39 + 159*	*198*
⑧	303 − 111	*192*	*111 + 192*	*303*
⑨	460 − 175	*285*	*175 + 285*	*460*
⑩	923 − 267	*656*	*267 + 656*	*923*
⑪	1,076 − 981	*95*	*981 + 95*	*1,076*
⑫	2,287 − 1,164	*1,123*	*1,164 + 1,123*	*2,287*
⑬	4,009 − 1,678	*2,331*	*1,678 + 2,331*	*4,009*
⑭	5,117 − 3,026	*2,091*	*3,026 + 2,091*	*5,117*
⑮	8,700 − 6,432	*2,268*	*6,432 + 2,268*	*8,700*
⑯	9,107 − 2,718	*6,389*	*2,718 + 6,389*	*9,107*
⑰	8,886 − 2,179	*6,707*	*2,179 + 6,707*	*8,886*
⑱	7,912 − 5,554	*2,358*	*5,554 + 2,358*	*7,912*
⑲	6,641 − 1,782	*4,859*	*1,782 + 4,859*	*6,641*
⑳	5,261 − 4,387	*874*	*4,387 + 874*	*5,261*
㉑	9,127 − 3,444	*5,683*	*3,444 + 5,683*	*9,127*
㉒	4,466 − 2,594	*1,872*	*2,594 + 1,872*	*4,466*
㉓	1,066 − 920	*146*	*920 + 146*	*1,066*
㉔	7,923 − 6,813	*1,110*	*6,813 + 1,110*	*7,923*
㉕	51,302 − 46,701	*4,601*	*46,701 + 4,601*	*51,302*
㉖	77,670 − 34,589	*43,081*	*34,589 + 43,081*	*77,670*
㉗	20,042 − 11,961	*8,081*	*11,961 + 8,081*	*20,042*
㉘	91,278 − 81,167	*10,111*	*81,167 + 10,111*	*91,278*

Subtraction is the *inverse* operation of addition.

Back Page Exercises Create twenty subtraction problems. Check with addition.

Subtraction Practice

The Idea

Subtraction is the inverse operation of addition. This means that subtraction undoes what addition does.

How to Use the Idea

841 − 623 = 218	246 − 168 = 78
218 + 623 = 841	78 + 168 = 246

Some of these exercises require borrowing or renaming to subtract. Others do not. Check each problem by addition. If your answer does not check, go back and make sure your borrowing is correct.

① 378 − 286 = ***92*** Check: ***286 + 92 = 378***	② 844 − 233	③ 758 − 661	④ 411 − 286
⑤ 623 − 148	⑥ 525 − 316	⑦ 198 − 39	⑧ 303 − 111
⑨ 460 − 175	⑩ 923 − 267	⑪ 1,076 − 981	⑫ 2,287 − 1,164
⑬ 4,009 − 1,678	⑭ 5,117 − 3,026	⑮ 8,700 − 6,432	⑯ 9,107 − 2,718
⑰ 8,886 − 2,179	⑱ 7,912 − 5,554	⑲ 6,641 − 1,782	⑳ 5,261 − 4,387
㉑ 9,127 − 3,444	㉒ 4,466 − 2,594	㉓ 1,066 − 920	㉔ 7,923 − 6,813
㉕ 51,302 − 46,701	㉖ 77,670 − 34,589	㉗ 20,042 − 11,961	㉘ 91,278 − 81,167

Subtraction is the ____________________ operation of addition.

Back Page Exercises	**Create twenty subtraction problems. Check with addition.**

Multiplication Tables Through Twelve 22

The Idea

Multiplication is a faster way of adding like numbers.

How to Use the Idea

Any number times 1 remains unchanged. The number 1 is called the multiplicative identity element. For example, 6 × 1 = 6. Notice that the answers to multiplying by 2 are the same as counting by 2. 2, 4, 6, 8,... Notice that the answers to multiplying by 5 alternate ending in 5 and 0. 5, 10, 15, 20,... Notice that the digits of the multiples of 9 add up to 9.

Complete the tables.

1 × 1 = ***1***	1 × 7 = ***7***	2 × 1 = ***2***	2 × 7 = ***14***	3 × 1 = ***3***	3 × 7 = ***21***
1 × 2 = ***2***	1 × 8 = ***8***	2 × 2 = ***4***	2 × 8 = ***16***	3 × 2 = ***6***	3 × 8 = ***24***
1 × 3 = ***3***	1 × 9 = ***9***	2 × 3 = ***6***	2 × 9 = ***18***	3 × 3 = ***9***	3 × 9 = ***27***
1 × 4 = ***4***	1 × 10 = ***10***	2 × 4 = ***8***	2 × 10 = ***20***	3 × 4 = ***12***	3 × 10 = ***30***
1 × 5 = ***5***	1 × 11 = ***11***	2 × 5 = ***10***	2 × 11 = ***22***	3 × 5 = ***15***	3 × 11 = ***33***
1 × 6 = ***6***	1 × 12 = ***12***	2 × 6 = ***12***	2 × 12 = ***24***	3 × 6 = ***18***	3 × 12 = ***36***
4 × 1 = ***4***	4 × 7 = ***28***	5 × 1 = ***5***	5 × 7 = ***35***	6 × 1 = ***6***	6 × 7 = ***42***
4 × 2 = ***8***	4 × 8 = ***32***	5 × 2 = ***10***	5 × 8 = ***40***	6 × 2 = ***12***	6 × 8 = ***48***
4 × 3 = ***12***	4 × 9 = ***36***	5 × 3 = ***15***	5 × 9 = ***45***	6 × 3 = ***18***	6 × 9 = ***54***
4 × 4 = ***16***	4 × 10 = ***40***	5 × 4 = ***20***	5 × 10 = ***50***	6 × 4 = ***24***	6 × 10 = ***60***
4 × 5 = ***20***	4 × 11 = ***44***	5 × 5 = ***25***	5 × 11 = ***55***	6 × 5 = ***30***	6 × 11 = ***66***
4 × 6 = ***24***	4 × 12 = ***48***	5 × 6 = ***30***	5 × 12 = ***60***	6 × 6 = ***36***	6 × 12 = ***72***
7 × 1 = ***7***	7 × 7 = ***49***	8 × 1 = ***8***	8 × 7 = ***56***	9 × 1 = ***9***	9 × 7 = ***63***
7 × 2 = ***14***	7 × 8 = ***56***	8 × 2 = ***16***	8 × 8 = ***64***	9 × 2 = ***18***	9 × 8 = ***72***
7 × 3 = ***21***	7 × 9 = ***63***	8 × 3 = ***24***	8 × 9 = ***72***	9 × 3 = ***27***	9 × 9 = ***81***
7 × 4 = ***28***	7 × 10 = ***70***	8 × 4 = ***32***	8 × 10 = ***80***	9 × 4 = ***36***	9 × 10 = ***90***
7 × 5 = ***35***	7 × 11 = ***77***	8 × 5 = ***40***	8 × 11 = ***88***	9 × 5 = ***45***	9 × 11 = ***99***
7 × 6 = ***42***	7 × 12 = ***84***	8 × 6 = ***48***	8 × 12 = ***96***	9 × 6 = ***54***	9 × 12 = ***108***
10 × 1 = ***10***	10 × 7 = ***70***	11 × 1 = ***11***	11 × 7 = ***77***	12 × 1 = ***12***	12 × 7 = ***84***
10 × 2 = ***20***	10 × 8 = ***80***	11 × 2 = ***22***	11 × 8 = ***88***	12 × 2 = ***24***	12 × 8 = ***96***
10 × 3 = ***30***	10 × 9 = ***90***	11 × 3 = ***33***	11 × 9 = ***99***	12 × 3 = ***36***	12 × 9 = ***108***
10 × 4 = ***40***	10 × 10 = ***100***	11 × 4 = ***44***	11 × 10 = ***110***	12 × 4 = ***48***	12 × 10 = ***120***
10 × 5 = ***50***	10 × 11 = ***110***	11 × 5 = ***55***	11 × 11 = ***121***	12 × 5 = ***60***	12 × 11 = ***132***
10 × 6 = ***60***	10 × 12 = ***120***	11 × 6 = ***66***	11 × 12 = ***132***	12 × 6 = ***72***	12 × 12 = ***144***

Multiplication is a faster way of adding like numbers.

Back Page Exercises Create a multiplication table for 13, 14, and 15.

Multiplication Tables Through Twelve

The Idea

Multiplication is a faster way of adding like numbers.

How to Use the Idea

Any number times 1 remains unchanged. The number 1 is called the multiplicative identity element. For example, 6 × 1 = 6. Notice that the answers to multiplying by 2 are the same as counting by 2. 2, 4, 6, 8, . . . Notice that the answers to multiplying by 5 alternate ending in 5 and 0. 5, 10, 15, 20, . . . Notice that the digits of the multiples of 9 add up to 9.

Complete the tables.

1 × 1 = *1*	1 × 7 =	2 × 1 =	2 × 7 =	3 × 1 =	3 × 7 =
1 × 2 =	1 × 8 =	2 × 2 =	2 × 8 =	3 × 2 =	3 × 8 =
1 × 3 =	1 × 9 =	2 × 3 =	2 × 9 =	3 × 3 =	3 × 9 =
1 × 4 =	1 × 10 =	2 × 4 =	2 × 10 =	3 × 4 =	3 × 10 =
1 × 5 =	1 × 11 =	2 × 5 =	2 × 11 =	3 × 5 =	3 × 11 =
1 × 6 =	1 × 12 =	2 × 6 =	2 × 12 =	3 × 6 =	3 × 12 =
4 × 1 =	4 × 7 =	5 × 1 =	5 × 7 =	6 × 1 =	6 × 7 =
4 × 2 =	4 × 8 =	5 × 2 =	5 × 8 =	6 × 2 =	6 × 8 =
4 × 3 =	4 × 9 =	5 × 3 =	5 × 9 =	6 × 3 =	6 × 9 =
4 × 4 =	4 × 10 =	5 × 4 =	5 × 10 =	6 × 4 =	6 × 10 =
4 × 5 =	4 × 11 =	5 × 5 =	5 × 11 =	6 × 5 =	6 × 11 =
4 × 6 =	4 × 12 =	5 × 6 =	5 × 12 =	6 × 6 =	6 × 12 =
7 × 1 =	7 × 7 =	8 × 1 =	8 × 7 =	9 × 1 =	9 × 7 =
7 × 2 =	7 × 8 =	8 × 2 =	8 × 8 =	9 × 2 =	9 × 8 =
7 × 3 =	7 × 9 =	8 × 3 =	8 × 9 =	9 × 3 =	9 × 9 =
7 × 4 =	7 × 10 =	8 × 4 =	8 × 10 =	9 × 4 =	9 × 10 =
7 × 5 =	7 × 11 =	8 × 5 =	8 × 11 =	9 × 5 =	9 × 11 =
7 × 6 =	7 × 12 =	8 × 6 =	8 × 12 =	9 × 6 =	9 × 12 =
10 × 1 =	10 × 7 =	11 × 1 =	11 × 7 =	12 × 1 =	12 × 7 =
10 × 2 =	10 × 8 =	11 × 2 =	11 × 8 =	12 × 2 =	12 × 8 =
10 × 3 =	10 × 9 =	11 × 3 =	11 × 9 =	12 × 3 =	12 × 9 =
10 × 4 =	10 × 10 =	11 × 4 =	11 × 10 =	12 × 4 =	12 × 10 =
10 × 5 =	10 × 11 =	11 × 5 =	11 × 11 =	12 × 5 =	12 × 11 =
10 × 6 =	10 × 12 =	11 × 6 =	11 × 12 =	12 × 6 =	12 × 12 =

__________________ is a faster way of adding like numbers.

Back Page Exercises Create a multiplication table for 13, 14, and 15.

Three-Digit Multiplication

The Idea

Place value tells us what each digit in a number is worth. It also tells us how to multiply with those numbers.

How to Use the Idea

Remember that just as in addition, you must "carry" in multiplication. When you multiply by the tens' digit, you may use "0" as a place holder by the hundreds' digit. Keep your columns straight.

a.
632
× 12
1264 = 2 × 632
632(0) = 10 × 632
7,584

b.
561
× 123
1683 = 3 × 561
1122(0) = 20 × 561
561(00) = 100 × 561
69,003

c.
422
× 235
2110 = 5 × 422
1266(0) = 30 × 422
844(00) = 200 × 422
99,170

Find the products.

1. 760 × 345
3800
3040(0)
2280(00)
262,200

2. 423 × 136
2538
1269(0)
423(00)
57,528

3. 503 × 211
503
503(0)
1006(00)
106,133

4. 819 × 124
3276
1638(0)
819(00)
101,556

5. 412 × 254
1648
2060(0)
824(00)
104,648

6. 673 × 226
4038
1346(0)
1346(00)
152,098

7. 531 × 406
3186
21240(0)
215,586

8. 342 × 276
2052
2394(0)
684(00)
94,392

9. 555 × 247
3885
2220(0)
1110(00)
137,085

10. 963 × 239
8667
2889(0)
1926(00)
230,157

11. 817 × 183
2451
6536(0)
817(00)
149,511

12. 468 × 246
2808
1872(0)
936(00)
115,128

13. 818 × 760
49080
5726(00)
621,680

14. 901 × 109
8109
9010(0)
98,209

15. 664 × 349
5976
2656(0)
1992(00)
231,736

16. 279 × 108
2232
2790(0)
30,132

17. 673 × 240
26920
1346(00)
161,520

18. 886 × 406
5316
35440(0)
359,716

19. 644 × 203
1932
12880(0)
130,732

20. 516 × 620
10320
3096(00)
319,920

Place value tells us what each ___*digit*___ in a number is worth. It also tells us how to ___*multiply*___ with those numbers.

Back Page Exercises Multiply 506 by the multiplier in each problem above.

Three-Digit Multiplication

The Idea

Place value tells us what each digit in a number is worth. It also tells us how to multiply with those numbers.

How to Use the Idea

Remember that just as in addition, you must "carry" in multiplication. When you multiply by the tens' digit, you may use "0" as a place holder by the hundreds' digit. Keep your columns straight.

a.
```
   632
 × 12
------
  1264 = 2 × 632
 632(0) = 10 × 632
------
 7,584
```

b.
```
    561
 × 123
-------
   1683 = 3 × 561
 1122(0) = 20 × 561
 561(00) = 100 × 561
-------
 69,003
```

c.
```
    422
 × 235
-------
   2110 = 5 × 422
 1266(0) = 30 × 422
 844(00) = 200 × 422
-------
 99,170
```

Find the products.

① 760 × 345

```
    760
 × 345
-------
   3800
 3040(0)
2280(00)
-------
262,200
```

② 423 × 136

③ 503 × 211

④ 819 × 124

⑤ 412 × 254

⑥ 673 × 226

⑦ 531 × 406

⑧ 342 × 276

⑨ 555 × 247

⑩ 963 × 239

⑪ 817 × 183

⑫ 468 × 246

⑬ 818 × 760

⑭ 901 × 109

⑮ 664 × 349

⑯ 279 × 108

⑰ 673 × 240

⑱ 886 × 406

⑲ 644 × 203

⑳ 516 × 620

Place value tells us what each ________________ in a number is worth. It also tells us how to ________________ with those numbers.

Back Page Exercises — **Multiply 506 by the multiplier in each problem above.**

Four-Digit Multiplication

The Idea

The answer to a multiplication problem is called the product. When we multiply four-digit numbers, the products are in the millions.

How to Use the Idea

```
   4,657        3,289        2,862
 × 2,124      × 1,234      × 2,244
   18628        13156        11448
   9314         9867        11448
  4657         6578         5724
 9314         3289         5724
 9,891,468    4,058,626    6,422,328
```

Multiply.

```
① 5,068 × 2,312
   10136
   5068
  15204
 10136
 11,717,216

② 6,288 × 3,121
   6288
  12576
  6288
 18864
 19,624,848

③ 7,364 × 1,243
   22092
  29456
 14728
 7364
 9,153,452

④ 8,132 × 2,884
   32528
  65056
 65056
16264
 23,452,688

⑤ 4,486 × 6,702
   8972
 314020
 26916
 30,065,172

⑥ 3,918 × 2,606
   23508
 235080
  7836
 10,210,308

⑦ 4,816 × 3,928
   38528
   9632
  43344
 14448
 18,917,248

⑧ 5,874 × 2,173
   17622
  41118
  5874
 11748
 12,764,202

⑨ 7,826 × 6,312
   15652
   7826
  23478
 46956
 49,397,712

⑩ 9,738 × 8,124
   38952
  19476
   9738
 77904
 79,111,512

⑪ 7,605 × 6,683
   22815
  60840
 45630
45630
 50,824,215

⑫ 9,346 × 7,855
   46730
  46730
 74768
65422
 73,412,830
```

The answer to a multiplication problem is called the ___product___. When we multiply ___four-digit___ numbers, the products are in the ___millions___.

Back Page Exercises Multiply 3,987 by the multiplicand in each problem above.

Four-Digit Multiplication

The Idea

The answer to a multiplication problem is called the product. When we multiply four-digit numbers, the products are in the millions.

How to Use the Idea

```
   4,657        3,289        2,862
 × 2,124      × 1,234      × 2,244
   18628        13156        11448
   9314         9867        11448
  4657         6578        5724
 9314         3289        5724
9,891,468    4,058,626    6,422,328
```

Multiply.

```
①     5,068     ②   6,288     ③   7,364     ④   8,132
    × 2,312       × 3,121       × 1,243       × 2,884
      10136
      5068
    15204
   10136
11,717,216
```

```
⑤     4,486     ⑥   3,918     ⑦   4,816     ⑧   5,874
    × 6,702       × 2,606       × 3,928       × 2,173
```

```
⑨     7,826     ⑩   9,738     ⑪   7,605     ⑫   9,346
    × 6,312       × 8,124       × 6,683       × 7,855
```

The answer to a multiplication problem is called the ______________. When we multiply ______________ numbers, the products are in the ______________.

Back Page Exercises Multiply 3,987 by the multiplicand in each problem above.

The Idea

Place value tells us what each digit in a number is worth.

How to Use the Idea

```
      46,831            31,821            24,101
    × 21,643          × 20,812          × 12,345
      140493             63642            120505
     187324             31821             96404
    280986            254568              72303
   46831             636420              48202
  93662             662,258,652         24101
 1,013,563,333                        297,526,845
```

Multiply.

```
①    50,862       ②    78,341       ③    36,784       ④    43,892
      × 864             × 755             × 917             × 654
     203448            391705            257488            175568
    305172            391705             36784            219460
   406896            548387            331056            263352
  43,944,768        59,147,455        33,730,928        28,705,368

⑤    88,403       ⑥    73,860       ⑦    84,261       ⑧    64,832
    × 1,267           × 2,439           × 3,107           × 2,416
     618821            664740            589827            388992
    530418            221580            842610             64832
   176806            295440            252783            259328
  88403             147720          261,798,927        129664
 112,006,601       180,144,540                        156,634,112

⑨    41,067       ⑩    37,803       ⑪    24,113       ⑫    27,209
   × 10,600          × 12,700          × 13,200          × 14,400
   24640200          26462100           4822600          10883600
  410670            75606             72339            108836
 435,310,200       37803             24113             27209
                  480,098,100       318,291,600       391,809,600
```

Place ____value____ tells us what each digit in a number is ____worth____.

Back Page Exercises Multiply 16,693 by the multiplier in each problem above.

The Idea

Place value tells us what each digit in a number is worth.

How to Use the Idea

```
       46,831           31,821           24,101
    × 21,643         × 20,812         × 12,345
      140493            63642           120505
     187324            31821            96404
    280986           254568            72303
   46831            636420            48202
  93662            662,258,652       24101
1,013,563,333                      297,526,845
```

Multiply.

① 50,862 × 864

```
   50,862
    × 864
   203448
  305172
 406896
43,944,768
```

② 78,341 × 755

③ 36,784 × 917

④ 43,892 × 654

⑤ 88,403 × 1,267

⑥ 73,860 × 2,439

⑦ 84,261 × 3,107

⑧ 64,832 × 2,416

⑨ 41,067 × 10,600

⑩ 37,803 × 12,700

⑪ 24,113 × 13,200

⑫ 27,209 × 14,400

Place ____________ tells us what each digit in a number is ____________.

Back Page Exercises Multiply 16,693 by the multiplier in each problem above.

Using the Associative Property 27

The Idea

The associative property of multiplication holds that the product will be the same regardless of the way in which a series of numbers is grouped.

How to Use the Idea

a. $(6 \times 5) \times 7 = 30 \times 7 = 210$ b. $(8 \times 6) \times 4 = 48 \times 4 = 192$

A Work each problem using the associative property of multiplication.

① $85 \times 2 \times 9 =$
$(85 \times 2) \times 9 = 170 \times 9 = 1{,}530$

② $15 \times 24 \times 39 =$
$(15 \times 24) \times 39 = 360 \times 39 = 14{,}040$

③ $35 \times 4 \times 7 =$
$(35 \times 4) \times 7 = 140 \times 7 = 980$

④ $49 \times 34 \times 15 =$
$49 \times (34 \times 15) = 49 \times 510 = 24{,}990$

⑤ $16 \times 9 \times 5 =$
$(16 \times 9) \times 5 = 144 \times 5 = 720$

⑥ $29 \times 44 \times 25 =$
$29 \times (44 \times 25) = 29 \times 1{,}100 = 31{,}900$

⑦ $22 \times 15 \times 9 =$
$(22 \times 15) \times 9 = 330 \times 9 = 2{,}970$

⑧ $33 \times 27 \times 13 =$
$(33 \times 27) \times 13 = 891 \times 13 = 11{,}583$

B When multiplying larger numbers, it is easier to multiply by putting one number under another. Find the product of each set of numbers below. Choose either the first or the third number of each set to multiply with the middle number to make the set of numbers easier to multiply.

① 50, 63, 48

63	3,150
× 50	× 48
3,150	25200
	12600
	151,200

② 89, 61, 54

89	5,429
× 61	× 54
89	21716
534	27145
5,429	293,166

③ 75, 20, 46

75	1,500
× 20	× 46
1,500	9000
	6000
	69,000

④ 91, 35, 60

91	3,185
× 35	× 60
455	191,100
273	
3,185	

⑤ 150, 45, 34

45	1,530
× 34	× 150
180	76500
135	1530
1,530	229,500

⑥ 17, 270, 54

270	14,580
× 54	× 17
1080	102060
1350	14580
14,580	247,860

⑦ 38, 165, 57

165	6,270
× 38	× 57
1320	43890
495	31350
6,270	357,390

⑧ 79, 45, 44

45	1,980
× 44	× 79
180	17820
180	13860
1,980	156,420

The ___*associative*___ property of multiplication holds that the ___*product*___ will be the same regardless of the way in which a ___*series*___ of numbers is grouped.

Back Page Exercises Multiply the problems in exercise B in a different order.

Using the Associative Property

The Idea

The associative property of multiplication holds that the product will be the same regardless of the way in which a series of numbers is grouped.

How to Use the Idea

a. $(6 \times 5) \times 7 = 30 \times 7 = 210$ b. $(8 \times 6) \times 4 = 48 \times 4 = 192$

A **Work each problem using the associative property of multiplication.**

① $85 \times 2 \times 9 =$
$(85 \times 2) \times 9 = 170 \times 9 = 1{,}530$

② $15 \times 24 \times 39 =$

③ $35 \times 4 \times 7 =$

④ $49 \times 34 \times 15 =$

⑤ $16 \times 9 \times 5 =$

⑥ $29 \times 44 \times 25 =$

⑦ $22 \times 15 \times 9 =$

⑧ $33 \times 27 \times 13 =$

B **When multiplying larger numbers, it is easier to multiply by putting one number under another. Find the product of each set of numbers below. Choose either the first or the third number of each set to multiply with the middle number to make the set of numbers easier to multiply.**

① 50, 63, 48

63 × 50 = 3,150

3,150 × 48: 25200 + 12600 = 151,200

② 89, 61, 54

③ 75, 20, 46

④ 91, 35, 60

⑤ 150, 45, 34

⑥ 17, 270, 54

⑦ 38, 165, 57

⑧ 79, 45, 44

The ____________ property of multiplication holds that the ____________ will be the same regardless of the way in which a ____________ of numbers is grouped.

Back Page Exercises Multiply the problems in exercise B in a different order.

Using the Commutative Property

The Idea

The commutative property of multiplication holds that the product will be the same regardless of the order in which the numbers are multiplied.

How to Use the Idea

When we have a multiplication problem with three or more factors, we may find it easier to change the order of the factors. It is easy, for instance, to multiply by a one digit number, or by a multiple of 10.

$20 \times 14 \times 3 \times 5 = (20 \times 3) \times (14 \times 5) = 60 \times 70 = 4{,}200$

Work the problems using the commutative property to make each problem easier.

① $6 \times 8 \times 27 \times 25 =$ *$(6 \times 27) \times (8 \times 25) = 162 \times 200 = 32{,}400$*

② $15 \times 9 \times 4 \times 14 =$ *$(15 \times 4) \times 9 \times 14 = 60 \times (9 \times 14) = 60 \times 126 = 7{,}560$*

③ $35 \times 3 \times 4 \times 3 =$ *$(35 \times 4) \times (3 \times 3) = 140 \times 9 = 1{,}260$*

④ $17 \times 4 \times 7 \times 15 =$ *$(17 \times 7) \times (4 \times 15) = 119 \times 60 = 7{,}140$*

⑤ $13 \times 5 \times 7 \times 2 =$ *$13 \times (5 \times 2) \times 7 = (13 \times 10) \times 7 = 130 \times 7 = 910$*

⑥ $16 \times 17 \times 5 \times 3 =$ *$(16 \times 5) \times (17 \times 3) = 80 \times 51 = 4{,}080$*

⑦ $17 \times 18 \times 7 \times 5 =$ *$(17 \times 7) \times (18 \times 5) = 119 \times 90 = 10{,}710$*

⑧ $21 \times 12 \times 3 \times 5 =$ *$(21 \times 3) \times (12 \times 5) = 63 \times 60 = 3{,}780$*

⑨ $22 \times 6 \times 7 \times 5 =$ *$(22 \times 7) \times (6 \times 5) = 154 \times 30 = 4{,}620$*

⑩ $7 \times 2 \times 18 \times 5 =$ *$(7 \times 2) \times (18 \times 5) = 14 \times 90 = 1{,}260$*

⑪ $4 \times 17 \times 2 \times 6 =$ *$(4 \times 17) \times 2 \times 6 = (68 \times 2) \times 6 = 136 \times 6 = 816$*

⑫ $9 \times 3 \times 8 \times 3 =$ *$9 \times (3 \times 3) \times 8 = (9 \times 9) \times 8 = 81 \times 8 = 648$*

⑬ $45 \times 3 \times 6 \times 7 =$ *$(45 \times 6) \times 3 \times 7 = (270 \times 3) \times 7 = 810 \times 7 = 5{,}670$*

⑭ $28 \times 9 \times 5 \times 3 =$ *$(28 \times 5) \times 9 \times 3 = (140 \times 9) \times 3 = 1{,}260 \times 3 = 3{,}780$*

The *commutative property* of multiplication holds that the product will be the same *regardless* of the order in which the numbers are *multiplied*.

Back Page Exercises — **Change the order of the numbers in the above problems and find the products.**

Using the Commutative Property

The Idea

The commutative property of multiplication holds that the product will be the same regardless of the order in which the numbers are multiplied.

How to Use the Idea

When we have a multiplication problem with three or more factors, we may find it easier to change the order of the factors. It is easy, for instance, to multiply by a one digit number, or by a multiple of 10.

$20 \times 14 \times 3 \times 5 = (20 \times 3) \times (14 \times 5) = 60 \times 70 = 4{,}200$

Work the problems using the commutative property to make each problem easier.

① $6 \times 8 \times 27 \times 25 =$ *$(6 \times 27) \times (8 \times 25) = 162 \times 200 = 32{,}400$*

② $15 \times 9 \times 4 \times 14 =$

③ $35 \times 3 \times 4 \times 3 =$

④ $17 \times 4 \times 7 \times 15 =$

⑤ $13 \times 5 \times 7 \times 2 =$

⑥ $16 \times 17 \times 5 \times 3 =$

⑦ $17 \times 18 \times 7 \times 5 =$

⑧ $21 \times 12 \times 3 \times 5 =$

⑨ $22 \times 6 \times 7 \times 5 =$

⑩ $7 \times 2 \times 18 \times 5 =$

⑪ $4 \times 17 \times 2 \times 6 =$

⑫ $9 \times 3 \times 8 \times 3 =$

⑬ $45 \times 3 \times 6 \times 7 =$

⑭ $28 \times 9 \times 5 \times 3 =$

The ______________________ of multiplication holds that the product will be the same ______________________ of the order in which the numbers are ______________________.

Back Page Exercises	**Change the order of the numbers in the above problems and find the products.**

Using the Distributive Property

The Idea

The distributive property of multiplication holds that the product of a number and a sum is equal to the sum of the two products.

How to Use the Idea

We can use the distributive property to help multiply larger numbers quickly.

$25 \times 25 = 25 \times (20 + 5) = (25 \times 20) + (25 \times 5) = 500 + 125 = 625$

$45 \times 56 = 45 \times (50 + 6) = (45 \times 50) + (45 \times 6) = 2{,}250 + 270 = 2{,}520$

✱ **Use the distributive property to find the products.**

① $16 \times 16 =$ *$16 \times (10 + 6) = (16 \times 10) + (16 \times 6) = 160 + 96 = 256$*

② $15 \times 29 =$ *$15 \times (20 + 9) = 300 + 135 = 435$*

③ $14 \times 23 =$ *$14 \times (20 + 3) = 280 + 42 = 322$*

④ $22 \times 22 =$ *$22 \times (20 + 2) = 440 + 44 = 484$*

⑤ $13 \times 13 =$ *$13 \times (10 + 3) = 130 + 39 = 169$*

⑥ $25 \times 35 =$ *$25 \times (30 + 5) = 750 + 125 = 875$*

⑦ $17 \times 34 =$ *$17 \times (30 + 4) = 510 + 68 = 578$*

⑧ $23 \times 23 =$ *$23 \times (20 + 3) = 460 + 69 = 529$*

⑨ $15 \times 15 =$ *$15 \times (10 + 5) = 150 + 75 = 225$*

⑩ $64 \times 62 =$ *$64 \times (60 + 2) = 3{,}840 + 128 = 3{,}968$*

⑪ $21 \times 19 =$ *$21 \times (10 + 9) = 210 + 189 = 399$*

⑫ $24 \times 24 =$ *$24 \times (20 + 4) = 480 + 96 = 576$*

⑬ $14 \times 14 =$ *$14 \times (10 + 4) = 140 + 56 = 196$*

⑭ $51 \times 53 =$ *$51 \times (50 + 3) = 2{,}550 + 153 = 2{,}703$*

⑮ $26 \times 29 =$ *$26 \times (20 + 9) = 520 + 234 = 754$*

⑯ $26 \times 26 =$ *$26 \times (20 + 6) = 520 + 156 = 676$*

⑰ $17 \times 17 =$ *$17 \times (10 + 7) = 170 + 119 = 289$*

⑱ $43 \times 46 =$ *$43 \times (40 + 6) = 1{,}720 + 258 = 1{,}978$*

⑲ $24 \times 37 =$ *$24 \times (30 + 7) = 720 + 168 = 888$*

⑳ $27 \times 27 =$ *$27 \times (20 + 7) = 540 + 189 = 729$*

The ***distributive property*** of multiplication holds that the product of a ***number*** and a sum is ***equal*** to the ***sum*** of the ***two products***.

Back Page Exercises Create ten problems using the distributive property.

Using the Distributive Property

The Idea

The distributive property of multiplication holds that the product of a number and a sum is equal to the sum of the two products.

How to Use the Idea

We can use the distributive property to help multiply larger numbers quickly.

$$25 \times 25 = 25 \times (20 + 5) = (25 \times 20) + (25 \times 5) = 500 + 125 = 625$$

$$45 \times 56 = 45 \times (50 + 6) = (45 \times 50) + (45 \times 6) = 2{,}250 + 270 = 2{,}520$$

Use the distributive property to find the products.

① $16 \times 16 =$
$16 \times (10 + 6) = (16 \times 10) + (16 \times 6) =$
$160 + 96 = 256$

② $15 \times 29 =$

③ $14 \times 23 =$

④ $22 \times 22 =$

⑤ $13 \times 13 =$

⑥ $25 \times 35 =$

⑦ $17 \times 34 =$

⑧ $23 \times 23 =$

⑨ $15 \times 15 =$

⑩ $64 \times 62 =$

⑪ $21 \times 19 =$

⑫ $24 \times 24 =$

⑬ $14 \times 14 =$

⑭ $51 \times 53 =$

⑮ $26 \times 29 =$

⑯ $26 \times 26 =$

⑰ $17 \times 17 =$

⑱ $43 \times 46 =$

⑲ $24 \times 37 =$

⑳ $27 \times 27 =$

The ______________________ of multiplication holds that the product of a ______________________ and a sum is ______________________ to the ______________________ of the ______________________.

Back Page Exercises Create ten problems using the distributive property.

Products

The Idea

The answer to a multiplication problem is called the product. The numbers multiplied together are called factors.

How to Use the Idea

Remember: Always complete the work inside the parentheses first.

a. $(3 \times 4) \times (5 \times 6) = 12 \times 30 = 360$ — 360 is the product

b. $(8 + 7) \times (6 - 4) = 15 \times 2 = 30$ — 30 is the product

c. $(18 - 9) \times (14 - 7) = 9 \times 7 = 63$ — 63 is the product

Find the products.

1. $(4 \times 6) \times (5 \times 1) = \mathit{24} \times \mathit{5} = \mathit{120}$
2. $(17 - 3) \times (27 + 23) = \mathit{14} \times \mathit{50} = \mathit{700}$
3. $(18 \times 5) \times (6 \times 2) = \mathit{90} \times \mathit{12} = \mathit{1,080}$
4. $(28 + 32) \times (42 - 14) = \mathit{60} \times \mathit{28} = \mathit{1,680}$
5. $(14 \times 6) \times (8 \times 5) = \mathit{84} \times \mathit{40} = \mathit{3,360}$
6. $(36 + 12) \times (64 + 36) = \mathit{48} \times \mathit{100} = \mathit{4,800}$
7. $(8 \times 15) \times (3 \times 3) = \mathit{120} \times \mathit{9} = \mathit{1,080}$
8. $(56 + 12) \times (29 - 22) = \mathit{68} \times \mathit{7} = \mathit{476}$
9. $(6 \times 25) \times (5 \times 2) = \mathit{150} \times \mathit{10} = \mathit{1,500}$
10. $(114 + 23) \times (37 - 29) = \mathit{137} \times \mathit{8} = \mathit{1,096}$
11. $(18 - 12) \times (17 - 7) = \mathit{6} \times \mathit{10} = \mathit{60}$
12. $(9 + 6) \times (9 - 4) \times (5 \times 2) = \mathit{15} \times \mathit{5} \times \mathit{10} = \mathit{750}$
13. $(36 - 11) \times (16 - 8) = \mathit{25} \times \mathit{8} = \mathit{200}$
14. $(17 - 5) \times (19 - 14) \times (8 - 4) = \mathit{12} \times \mathit{5} \times \mathit{4} = \mathit{240}$
15. $(15 + 10) \times (17 - 8) = \mathit{25} \times \mathit{9} = \mathit{225}$
16. $(24 + 6) \times (27 - 26) \times (14 + 5) = \mathit{30} \times \mathit{1} \times \mathit{19} = \mathit{570}$
17. $(16 + 14) \times (25 + 10) = \mathit{30} \times \mathit{35} = \mathit{1,050}$
18. $(27 + 6) \times (7 + 3) \times (9 - 4) = \mathit{33} \times \mathit{10} \times \mathit{5} = \mathit{1,650}$
19. $(55 - 30) \times (6 + 14) = \mathit{25} \times \mathit{20} = \mathit{500}$
20. $(47 + 13) \times (27 - 15) \times (18 - 11) = \mathit{60} \times \mathit{12} \times \mathit{7} = \mathit{5,040}$
21. $(18 + 12) \times (37 - 13) = \mathit{30} \times \mathit{24} = \mathit{720}$
22. $(26 - 14) \times (65 + 5) \times (16 - 8) = \mathit{12} \times \mathit{70} \times \mathit{8} = \mathit{6,720}$
23. $(22 + 17) \times (35 + 15) = \mathit{39} \times \mathit{50} = \mathit{1,950}$
24. $(73 + 7) \times (16 + 4) \times (73 - 43) = \mathit{80} \times \mathit{20} \times \mathit{30} = \mathit{48,000}$
25. $(24 - 4) \times (49 - 23) = \mathit{20} \times \mathit{26} = \mathit{520}$
26. $(42 + 58) \times (17 + 3) \times (16 - 9) = \mathit{100} \times \mathit{20} \times \mathit{7} = \mathit{14,000}$
27. $(37 - 13) \times (46 + 14) = \mathit{24} \times \mathit{60} = \mathit{1,440}$
28. $(19 + 11) \times (17 + 3) \times (15 + 3) = \mathit{30} \times \mathit{20} \times \mathit{18} = \mathit{10,800}$

The ___*answer*___ to a multiplication problem is called the ___*product*___. The ___*numbers*___ multiplied together are called ___*factors*___.

Back Page Exercises Create ten problems similar to those above.

Products

The Idea

The answer to a multiplication problem is called the product. The numbers multiplied together are called factors.

How to Use the Idea

Remember: Always complete the work inside the parentheses first.

a. $(3 \times 4) \times (5 \times 6) = 12 \times 30 = 360$ — 360 is the product
b. $(8 + 7) \times (6 - 4) = 15 \times 2 = 30$ — 30 is the product
c. $(18 - 9) \times (14 - 7) = 9 \times 7 = 63$ — 63 is the product

Find the products.

1. $(4 \times 6) \times (5 \times 1) = \mathbf{24} \times \mathbf{5} = \mathbf{120}$
2. $(17 - 3) \times (27 + 23) =$
3. $(18 \times 5) \times (6 \times 2) =$
4. $(28 + 32) \times (42 - 14) =$
5. $(14 \times 6) \times (8 \times 5) =$
6. $(36 + 12) \times (64 + 36) =$
7. $(8 \times 15) \times (3 \times 3) =$
8. $(56 + 12) \times (29 - 22) =$
9. $(6 \times 25) \times (5 \times 2) =$
10. $(114 + 23) \times (37 - 29) =$
11. $(18 - 12) \times (17 - 7) =$
12. $(9 + 6) \times (9 - 4) \times (5 \times 2) =$
13. $(36 - 11) \times (16 - 8) =$
14. $(17 - 5) \times (19 - 14) \times (8 - 4) =$
15. $(15 + 10) \times (17 - 8) =$
16. $(24 + 6) \times (27 - 26) \times (14 + 5) =$
17. $(16 + 14) \times (25 + 10) =$
18. $(27 + 6) \times (7 + 3) \times (9 - 4) =$
19. $(55 - 30) \times (6 + 14) =$
20. $(47 + 13) \times (27 - 15) \times (18 - 11) =$
21. $(18 + 12) \times (37 - 13) =$
22. $(26 - 14) \times (65 + 5) \times (16 - 8) =$
23. $(22 + 17) \times (35 + 15) =$
24. $(73 + 7) \times (16 + 4) \times (73 - 43) =$
25. $(24 - 4) \times (49 - 23) =$
26. $(42 + 58) \times (17 + 3) \times (16 - 9) =$
27. $(37 - 13) \times (46 + 14) =$
28. $(19 + 11) \times (17 + 3) \times (15 + 3) =$

The ______________ to a multiplication problem is called the ______________. The ______________ multiplied together are called ______________.

Back Page Exercises Create ten problems similar to those above.

Simple Division

The Idea

Division is the method by which we determine how many times one number contains another.

How to Use the Idea

For any three numbers a, b, and c, if $a \neq 0$ and $a \times b = c$, then $b = \frac{c}{a}$ or $c \div a = b$. We cannot divide by zero. The answer to a division problem is called a quotient.

There are two ways to write a division problem.

$3\overline{)15}$ $15 \div 3$

Find the quotients. Write out each problem as you would read it aloud.

① $4\overline{)20}$ = *5* — *20 divided by 4 equals 5*

② $144 \div 12 =$ ***12*** — *144 divided by 12 equals 12*

③ $21 \div 3 =$ ***7*** — *21 divided by 3 equals 7*

④ $40 \div 8 =$ ***5*** — *40 divided by 8 equals 5*

⑤ $36 \div 6 =$ ***6*** — *36 divided by 6 equals 6*

⑥ $5\overline{)40}$ = *8* — *40 divided by 5 equals 8*

⑦ $2\overline{)14}$ = *7* — *14 divided by 2 equals 7*

⑧ $12\overline{)60}$ = *5* — *60 divided by 12 equals 5*

⑨ $7\overline{)35}$ = *5* — *35 divided by 7 equals 5*

⑩ $81 \div 9 =$ ***9*** — *81 divided by 9 equals 9*

⑪ $64 \div 8 =$ ***8*** — *64 divided by 8 equals 8*

⑫ $28 \div 7 =$ ***4*** — *28 divided by 7 equals 4*

⑬ $72 \div 9 =$ ***8*** — *72 divided by 9 equals 8*

⑭ $30 \div 6 =$ ***5*** — *30 divided by 6 equals 5*

Division is the method by which we determine how many times one number contains another.

Back Page Exercises Divide 2 into 26, 36, 46, 56, 76, 86, and 96. Divide 3 into 33, 45, 51, 63, 75, 81, and 96.

Simple Division

The Idea

Division is the method by which we determine how many times one number contains another.

How to Use the Idea

For any three numbers a, b, and c, if $a \neq 0$ and $a \times b = c$, then $b = \frac{c}{a}$ or $c \div a = b$. We cannot divide by zero. The answer to a division problem is called a quotient.

There are two ways to write a division problem.

$3\overline{)15}$ $15 \div 3$

Find the quotients. Write out each problem as you would read it aloud.

① $4\overline{)20}$ = 5 — *20 divided by 4 equals 5*

② $144 \div 12 =$ __________

③ $21 \div 3 =$ __________

④ $40 \div 8 =$ __________

⑤ $36 \div 6 =$ __________

⑥ $5\overline{)40}$ __________

⑦ $2\overline{)14}$ __________

⑧ $12\overline{)60}$ __________

⑨ $7\overline{)35}$ __________

⑩ $81 \div 9 =$ __________

⑪ $64 \div 8 =$ __________

⑫ $28 \div 7 =$ __________

⑬ $72 \div 9 =$ __________

⑭ $30 \div 6 =$ __________

________________ is the method by which we determine how many times one number contains another.

Back Page Exercises Divide 2 into 26, 36, 46, 56, 76, 86, and 96. Divide 3 into 33, 45, 51, 63, 75, 81, and 96.

Long Division

The Idea

Division is said to be the inverse operation of multiplication; that is, division undoes what multiplication does.

How to Use the Idea

Long division uses multiplication and subtraction.

Step 1

```
    9
8 )728
   72
```

$72 \div 8 = 9$

$72 = 8 \times 9$

Step 2

```
   91
8 )728
   72
    8
    8
```

$8 \div 8 = 1$ $\quad$ $728 \div 8 = 91$

$8 = 8 \times 1$ $\quad$ $91 \times 8 = 728$

Find the quotients.

```
① 25 )575    ② 12 )264    ③ 9 )378    ④ 14 )294
   23           22          42           21
   50           24          36           28
   75           24          18           14
   75           24          18           14

⑤ 30 )2,760  ⑥ 17 )357    ⑦ 45) 945   ⑧ 36 )756
   92           21          21           21
   270          34          90           72
   60           17          45           36
   60           17          45           36

⑨ 11 )451    ⑩ 15 )765    ⑪ 16 )848   ⑫ 35 )770
   41           51          53           22
   44           75          80           70
   11           15          48           70
   11           15          48           70

⑬ 320 )5,120 ⑭ 15 )7,635  ⑮ 250 )5,250 ⑯ 31 )6,479
   16           509         21           209
   320          75          500          62
   1920         135         250          279
   1920         135         250          279
```

Division is said to be the *inverse* operation of multiplication; that is, division *undoes* what multiplication does.

Back Page Exercises Divide 62 into 19,220; 11 into 649; and 36 into 1, 944.

Long Division

The Idea

Division is said to be the inverse operation of multiplication; that is, division undoes what multiplication does.

How to Use the Idea

Long division uses multiplication and subtraction.

Step 1

```
    9
8 )728
   72
   --
```

$72 \div 8 = 9$

$72 = 8 \times 9$

Step 2

```
   91
8 )728
   72
   --
    8
    8
    -
```

$8 \div 8 = 1$

$8 = 8 \times 1$

$728 \div 8 = 91$

$91 \times 8 = 728$

Find the quotients.

①
```
    23
25 )575
    50
    --
     75
     75
     --
```

② 12) 264

③ 9) 378

④ 14) 294

⑤ 30) 2,760

⑥ 17) 357

⑦ 45) 945

⑧ 36) 756

⑨ 11) 451

⑩ 15) 765

⑪ 16) 848

⑫ 35) 770

⑬ 320) 5,120

⑭ 15) 7,635

⑮ 250) 5,250

⑯ 31) 6,479

________________ is said to be the ________________ operation of multiplication; that is, division ________________ what multiplication does.

Back Page Exercises **Divide 62 into 19,220; 11 into 649; and 36 into 1, 944.**

Averages

The Idea

The average of a set of numbers is the quotient we get by dividing the sum of the members of the set by the number of members in the set.

How to Use the Idea

a. {4, 7, 9, 13, 17} $4 + 7 + 9 + 13 + 17 = 50$. There are 5 members of the set. $50 \div 5 = 10 =$ the average.

b. {20, 30, 70, 80} $20 + 30 + 70 + 80 = 200$. There are 4 members of the set. $200 \div 4 = 50 =$ the average.

Find the average of each set of numbers.

① {1, 2, 3, 4, 5}	$1 + 2 + 3 + 4 + 5 = 15$	$15 \div 5 = 3$
② {2, 4, 6, 8, 10}	$2 + 4 + 6 + 8 + 10 = 30$	$30 \div 5 = 6$
③ {20, 25, 35, 40}	$20 + 25 + 35 + 40 = 120$	$120 \div 4 = 30$
④ {120, 360, 240}	$120 + 360 + 240 = 720$	$720 \div 3 = 240$
⑤ {96, 98, 85, 95, 91}	$96 + 98 + 85 + 95 + 91 = 465$	$465 \div 5 = 93$
⑥ {7, 68, 43, 17, 25}	$7 + 68 + 43 + 17 + 25 = 160$	$160 \div 5 = 32$
⑦ {14, 18, 26, 30, 34, 40}	$14 + 18 + 26 + 30 + 34 + 40 = 162$	$162 \div 6 = 27$
⑧ {5, 38, 22, 65, 30}	$5 + 38 + 22 + 65 + 30 = 160$	$160 \div 5 = 32$
⑨ {1, 2, 3, 4, 5, 6, 7, 8, 9}	$1 + 2 + 3 + 4 + 5 + 6 + 7 + 8 + 9 = 45$	$45 \div 9 = 5$
⑩ {4, 9, 13, 26}	$4 + 9 + 13 + 26 = 52$	$52 \div 4 = 13$
⑪ {9, 14, 17, 20}	$9 + 14 + 17 + 20 = 60$	$60 \div 4 = 15$
⑫ {19, 23, 31, 35, 42}	$19 + 23 + 31 + 35 + 42 = 150$	$150 \div 5 = 30$
⑬ {6, 16, 26, 36}	$6 + 16 + 26 + 36 = 84$	$84 \div 4 = 21$
⑭ {1, 3, 5, 7, 9, 11}	$1 + 3 + 5 + 7 + 9 + 11 = 36$	$36 \div 6 = 6$
⑮ {1, 3, 5, 7, 9}	$1 + 3 + 5 + 7 + 9 = 25$	$25 \div 5 = 5$
⑯ {17, 33, 61, 55, 44}	$17 + 33 + 61 + 55 + 44 = 210$	$210 \div 5 = 42$

The ___*average*___ of a set of numbers is the ___*quotient*___ we get by dividing the ___*sum*___ of the members of the ___*set*___ by the ___*number*___ of members in the set.

Back Page Exercises Find the average of your classmates' ages.

Averages

The Idea

The average of a set of numbers is the quotient we get by dividing the sum of the members of the set by the number of members in the set.

How to Use the Idea

a. {4, 7, 9, 13, 17} $4 + 7 + 9 + 13 + 17 = 50$. There are 5 members of the set.
$50 \div 5 = 10 =$ the average.

b. {20, 30, 70, 80} $20 + 30 + 70 + 80 = 200$. There are 4 members of the set.
$200 \div 4 = 50 =$ the average.

Find the average of each set of numbers.

① {1, 2, 3, 4, 5} *$1 + 2 + 3 + 4 + 5 = 15$* *$15 \div 5 = 3$*

② {2, 4, 6, 8, 10}

③ {20, 25, 35, 40}

④ {120, 360, 240}

⑤ {96, 98, 85, 95, 91}

⑥ {7, 68, 43, 17, 25}

⑦ {14, 18, 26, 30, 34, 40}

⑧ {5, 38, 22, 65, 30}

⑨ {1, 2, 3, 4, 5, 6, 7, 8, 9}

⑩ {4, 9, 13, 26}

⑪ {9, 14, 17, 20}

⑫ {19, 23, 31, 35, 42}

⑬ {6, 16, 26, 36}

⑭ {1, 3, 5, 7, 9, 11}

⑮ {1, 3, 5, 7, 9}

⑯ {17, 33, 61, 55, 44}

The ____________ of a set of numbers is the ____________ we get by dividing the ____________ of the members of the ____________ by the ____________ of members in the set.

Back Page Exercises Find the average of your classmates' ages.

Remainders

36

The Idea

When the divisior (the number that does the dividing) does not divide equally into the dividend (the number which gets divided), the answer has a remainder as well as the quotient. The remainder is smaller than the divisor.

How to Use the Idea

a. 2 R2
3) 8
6
2

b. 2 R1
26) 53
52
1

c. 2 R3
18) 39
36
3

d. 6 R43
100) 643
600
43

Find the quotients. Show remainders.

① *90 R3*
8) 723
72
3

② *92 R3*
5) 463
45
13
10
3

③ *62 R1*
7) 435
42
15
14
1

④ *180 R2*
3) 542
3
24
24
2

⑤ *206 R3*
4) 827
8
27
24
3

⑥ *148 R5*
6) 893
6
29
24
53
48
5

⑦ *195 R1*
2) 391
2
19
18
11
10
1

⑧ *41 R5*
9) 374
36
14
9
5

⑨ *21*
12) 252
24
12
12

⑩ *31*
19) 589
57
19
19

⑪ *21 R1*
23) 484
46
24
23
1

⑫ *22 R2*
16) 354
32
34
32
2

When the ___*divisor*___ does not divide equally into the ___*dividend*___, the answer has a ___*remainder*___ as well as the quotient.

Back Page Exercises — **Create ten division problems showing remainders.**

Remainders

The Idea

When the divisior (the number that does the dividing) does not divide equally into the dividend (the number which gets divided), the answer has a remainder as well as the quotient. The remainder is smaller than the divisor.

How to Use the Idea

a. $3\overline{)8}$ = 2 R2; 6; 2

b. $26\overline{)53}$ = 2 R1; 52; 1

c. $18\overline{)39}$ = 2 R3; 36; 3

d. $100\overline{)643}$ = 6 R43; 600; 43

Find the quotients. Show remainders.

① $8\overline{)723}$ — *90 R3*; *72*; *3*

② $5\overline{)463}$

③ $7\overline{)435}$

④ $3\overline{)542}$

⑤ $4\overline{)827}$

⑥ $6\overline{)893}$

⑦ $2\overline{)391}$

⑧ $9\overline{)374}$

⑨ $12\overline{)252}$

⑩ $19\overline{)589}$

⑪ $23\overline{)484}$

⑫ $16\overline{)354}$

When the ________________ does not divide equally into the ________________, the answer has a ________________ as well as the quotient.

Back Page Exercises Create ten division problems showing remainders.

Dividing Lesser by Greater

The Idea

When we divide a lesser number by a greater number, the quotient is a number less than 1. We use a decimal point to show this.

How to Use the Idea

Keep the decimal points in line.

a. $\frac{2}{5} = 5\overline{)2.0}$ = .4; 20

b. $\frac{3}{6} = 6\overline{)3.0}$ = .5; 30

c. $\frac{5}{8} = 8\overline{)5.000}$ = .625; 48, 20, 16, 40, 40

d. $14 \div 20 = 20\overline{)14.0}$ = .7; 140

Find the decimal quotients.

1. $\frac{6}{8} =$ *.75* — *8)6.00; 56; 40; 40*
2. $\frac{7}{10} =$ *.7* — *10)7.0; 70*
3. $\frac{7}{8} =$ *.875* — *8)7.000; 64; 60; 56; 40; 40*
4. $\frac{25}{40} =$ *.625* — *40)25.000; 240; 100; 80; 200; 200*
5. $\frac{9}{36} =$ *.25* — *36)9.00; 72; 180; 180*
6. $\frac{1}{4} =$ *.25* — *4)1.00; 8; 20; 20*
7. $\frac{16}{20} =$ *.8* — *20)16.0; 160*
8. $\frac{9}{18} =$ *.5* — *18)9.0; 90*
9. $17 \div 34 =$ *.5* — *34)17.0; 170*
10. $28 \div 56 =$ *.5* — *56)28.0; 280*
11. $15 \div 75 =$ *.2* — *75)15.0; 150*
12. $9 \div 45 =$ *.2* — *45)9.0; 90*
13. $18 \div 72 =$ *.25* — *72)18.00; 144; 360; 360*
14. $54 \div 72 =$ *.75* — *72)54.00; 504; 360; 360*
15. $16 \div 64 =$ *.25* — *64)16.00; 128; 320; 320*
16. $48 \div 60 =$ *.8* — *60)48.0; 480*
17. $13 \div 65 =$ *.2* — *65)13.0; 130*
18. $9 \div 72 =$ *.125* — *72)9.000; 72; 180; 144; 360; 360*
19. $4 \div 64 =$ *.0625* — *64)4.0000; 384; 160; 128; 320; 320*
20. $\frac{21}{28} =$ *.75* — *28)21.00; 196; 140; 140*

When we divide a *lesser* number by a *greater* number, the *quotient* is a number less than 1. We use a *decimal point* to show this.

Back Page Exercises Divide 56 into 15, 49 into 14, and 32 into 7.

Dividing Lesser by Greater

The Idea

When we divide a lesser number by a greater number, the quotient is a number less than 1. We use a decimal point to show this.

How to Use the Idea

Keep the decimal points in line.

a. $\frac{2}{5} = 5\overline{)2.0}$ → .4 (20)

b. $\frac{3}{6} = 6\overline{)3.0}$ → .5 (30)

c. $\frac{5}{8} = 8\overline{)5.000}$ → .625 (48, 20, 16, 40, 40)

d. $14 \div 20 = 20\overline{)14.0}$ → .7 (140)

Find the decimal quotients.

1. $\frac{6}{8} = 8\overline{)6.00}$ → .75 (56, 40, 40)
2. $\frac{7}{10} =$
3. $\frac{7}{8} =$
4. $\frac{25}{40} =$
5. $\frac{9}{36} =$
6. $\frac{1}{4} =$
7. $\frac{16}{20} =$
8. $\frac{9}{18} =$
9. $17 \div 34 =$
10. $28 \div 56 =$
11. $15 \div 75 =$
12. $9 \div 45 =$
13. $18 \div 72 =$
14. $54 \div 72 =$
15. $16 \div 64 =$
16. $48 \div 60 =$
17. $13 \div 65 =$
18. $9 \div 72 =$
19. $4 \div 64 =$
20. $\frac{21}{28} =$

When we divide a __________ number by a __________ number, the __________ is a number less than 1. We use a __________ to show this.

Back Page Exercises Divide 56 into 15, 49 into 14, and 32 into 7.

Quotients

The Idea

A quotient is the answer to a division problem.

How to Use the Idea

Some problems require us to use decimal places or to show a remainder.

4.6	7.5	1 R2
5) 23.0	6) 45.0	8) 10
20	42	8
30	30	2
30	30	

A Use decimal places, if necessary, to find the quotients.

① *2.5*
4) 10.*0*
8
20
20

② *5.2*
5) 26.*0*
25
10
10

③ *3.3*
10) 33.*0*
30
30
30

④ *.2*
30) 6.*0*
60

⑤ *10*
8) 80
8
0
0

⑥ *3.25*
36) 117.*00*
108
90
72
180
180

⑦ *2.24*
25) 56.*00*
50
60
50
100
100

⑧ *7.2*
50) 360.*0*
350
100
100

⑨ *.2*
60) 12.*0*
120

⑩ *2.5*
12) 30.*0*
24
60
60

B Find the quotients. Show remainders.

① *2 R2*
4) 10
8
2

② *5 R1*
5) 26
25
1

③ *3 R3*
10) 33
30
3

④ *1 R8*
30) 38
30
8

⑤ *3 R3*
24) 75
72
3

⑥ *2 R1*
17) 35
34
1

⑦ *20 R3*
25) 503
50
3
0
3

⑧ *47 R7*
9) 430
36
70
63
7

⑨ *40 R12*
15) 612
60
12
0
12

⑩ *32 R58*
101) 3,290
303
260
202
58

A *quotient* is the answer to a *division* problem.

Back Page Exercises Create ten division problems showing a remainder.

Quotients

The Idea

A quotient is the answer to a division problem.

How to Use the Idea

Some problems require us to use decimal places or to show a remainder.

$$\begin{array}{r} 4.6 \\ 5\overline{)23.0} \\ \underline{20} \\ 3\,0 \\ \underline{3\,0} \end{array} \qquad \begin{array}{r} 7.5 \\ 6\overline{)45.0} \\ \underline{42} \\ 3\,0 \\ \underline{3\,0} \end{array} \qquad \begin{array}{r} 1\text{ R2} \\ 8\overline{)10}\phantom{\text{ R2}} \\ \underline{8}\phantom{\text{ R2}} \\ 2\phantom{\text{ R2}} \end{array}$$

A Use decimal places, if necessary, to find the quotients.

① $\begin{array}{r} 2.5 \\ 4\overline{)10.0} \\ \underline{8} \\ 2\,0 \\ \underline{2\,0} \end{array}$

② $5\overline{)26}$

③ $10\overline{)33}$

④ $30\overline{)6}$

⑤ $8\overline{)80}$

⑥ $36\overline{)117}$

⑦ $25\overline{)56}$

⑧ $50\overline{)360}$

⑨ $60\overline{)12}$

⑩ $12\overline{)30}$

B Find the quotients. Show remainders.

① $\begin{array}{r} 2\text{ R2} \\ 4\overline{)10}\phantom{\text{ R2}} \\ \underline{8}\phantom{\text{ R2}} \\ 2\phantom{\text{ R2}} \end{array}$

② $5\overline{)26}$

③ $10\overline{)33}$

④ $30\overline{)38}$

⑤ $24\overline{)75}$

⑥ $17\overline{)35}$

⑦ $25\overline{)503}$

⑧ $9\overline{)430}$

⑨ $15\overline{)612}$

⑩ $101\overline{)3{,}290}$

A ____________________ is the answer to a ____________________ problem.

Back Page Exercises — **Create ten division problems showing a remainder.**

Factoring

The Idea

Numbers that are multiplied together are called factors. When we factor a number, we find what sets of numbers are multiplied together to make that number.

How to Use the Idea

If the number is prime, like 7, there is only one set of factors. 7 = 7 × 1. If the number is composite, like 12, there are two or more sets.
12 = 12 × 1 = 6 × 2 = 4 × 3.

Write all sets of factors for each number. Then write the set of prime factors for each number.

	ALL FACTORS	PRIME FACTORS
①	24 = *(24 × 1) = (12 × 2) = (8 × 3) = (6 × 4)*	*(2 × 2 × 2 × 3)*
②	6 = *(1 × 6) = (2 × 3)*	*(2 × 3)*
③	8 = *(1 × 8) = (2 × 4)*	*(2 × 2 × 2)*
④	9 = *(1 × 9) = (3 × 3)*	*(3 × 3)*
⑤	11 = *(1 × 11)*	*(1 × 11)*
⑥	15 = *(1 × 15) = (3 × 5)*	*(3 × 5)*
⑦	25 = *(1 × 25) = (5 × 5)*	*(5 × 5)*
⑧	49 = *(1 × 49) = (7 × 7)*	*(7 × 7)*
⑨	48 = *(1 × 48) = (2 × 24) = (3 × 16) = (4 × 12) = (6 × 8)*	*(2 × 2 × 2 × 2 × 3)*
⑩	64 = *(1 × 64) = (2 × 32) = (4 × 16) = (8 × 8)*	*(2 × 2 × 2 × 2 × 2 × 2)*
⑪	45 = *(1 × 45) = (3 × 15) = (5 × 9)*	*(3 × 3 × 5)*
⑫	54 = *(1 × 54) = (2 × 27) = (3 × 18) = (6 × 9)*	*(2 × 3 × 3 × 3)*
⑬	100 = *(1 × 100) = (2 × 50) = (4 × 25) = (5 × 20) = (10 × 10)*	*(2 × 2 × 5 × 5)*
⑭	120 = *(1 × 120) = (2 × 60) = (3 × 40) = (4 × 30) = (5 × 24) = (6 × 20) = (8 × 15) = (10 × 12)*	*(2 × 2 × 2 × 3 × 5)*

Numbers that are multiplied together are called *factors*.

Back Page Exercises **Factor the following: 26, 39, 42, 61, 150, 173, and 200.**

Factoring

The Idea

Numbers that are multiplied together are called factors. When we factor a number, we find what sets of numbers are multiplied together to make that number.

How to Use the Idea

If the number is prime, like 7, there is only one set of factors. 7 = 7 × 1. If the number is composite, like 12, there are two or more sets.
12 = 12 × 1 = 6 × 2 = 4 × 3.

Write all sets of factors for each number. Then write the set of prime factors for each number.

ALL FACTORS | PRIME FACTORS

① 24 = *(24 × 1)* = *(12 × 2)* = *(8 × 3)* = *(6 × 4)* *(2 × 2 × 2 × 3)*

② 6 =

③ 8 =

④ 9 =

⑤ 11 =

⑥ 15 =

⑦ 25 =

⑧ 49 =

⑨ 48 =

⑩ 64 =

⑪ 45 =

⑫ 54 =

⑬ 100 =

⑭ 120 =

__________________ that are multiplied together are called __________________.

Back Page Exercises **Factor the following: 26, 39, 42, 61, 150, 173, and 200.**

Common Factors 40

The Idea

A number which is a factor for each of two or more numbers is called a common factor of those numbers.

How to Use the Idea

a. 18, 24 $18 = \underline{2} \times \underline{3} \times 3$
$24 = 2 \times 2 \times \underline{2} \times \underline{3}$

b. 10, 25 $10 = 2 \times \underline{5}$
$25 = 5 \times \underline{5}$

c. 6, 36 $6 = \underline{2} \times \underline{3}$
$36 = \underline{2} \times 2 \times \underline{3} \times 3$

A Find the prime factors. Underline the common factors.

① 25, 30 $25 = 5 \times \underline{5}$
$30 = 2 \times 3 \times \underline{5}$

② 30, 36 $30 = \underline{2} \times \underline{3} \times 5$
$36 = 2 \times \underline{2} \times \underline{3} \times 3$

③ 8, 10 $8 = \underline{2} \times 2 \times 2$
$10 = \underline{2} \times 5$

④ 18, 27 $18 = 2 \times \underline{3} \times \underline{3}$
$27 = 3 \times \underline{3} \times \underline{3}$

⑤ 20, 32 $20 = \underline{2} \times \underline{2} \times 5$
$32 = \underline{2} \times \underline{2} \times 2 \times 2 \times 2$

⑥ 16, 24 $16 = \underline{2} \times \underline{2} \times \underline{2} \times 2$
$24 = \underline{2} \times \underline{2} \times \underline{2} \times 3$

⑦ 32, 40 $32 = \underline{2} \times \underline{2} \times \underline{2} \times 2 \times 2$
$40 = \underline{2} \times \underline{2} \times \underline{2} \times 5$

⑧ 15, 18 $15 = \underline{3} \times 5$
$18 = 2 \times \underline{3} \times 3$

⑨ 21, 35 $21 = 3 \times \underline{7}$
$35 = 5 \times \underline{7}$

⑩ 28, 40 $28 = \underline{2} \times \underline{2} \times 7$
$40 = \underline{2} \times \underline{2} \times 2 \times 5$

B Find the prime factors. Underline the common factors. Multiply the common factors to find the greatest common factor.

① 14, 18 $14 = \underline{2} \times 7$
$18 = \underline{2} \times 3 \times 3$
greatest common factor is *2*

② 30, 36 $30 = \underline{2} \times \underline{3} \times 5$
$36 = 2 \times \underline{2} \times \underline{3} \times 3$
greatest common factor is *6*

③ 25, 50 $25 = \underline{5} \times \underline{5}$
$50 = \underline{5} \times \underline{5} \times 2$
greatest common factor is *25*

④ 28, 30 $28 = \underline{2} \times 2 \times 7$
$30 = \underline{2} \times 3 \times 5$
greatest common factor is *2*

⑤ 32, 48 $32 = \underline{2} \times \underline{2} \times \underline{2} \times \underline{2} \times 2$
$48 = \underline{2} \times \underline{2} \times \underline{2} \times \underline{2} \times 3$
greatest common factor is *16*

⑥ 24, 42 $24 = 2 \times 2 \times \underline{2} \times \underline{3}$
$42 = \underline{2} \times \underline{3} \times 7$
greatest common factor is *6*

⑦ 13, 39 $13 = 1 \times \underline{13}$
$39 = 3 \times \underline{13}$
greatest common factor is *13*

⑧ 45, 70 $45 = 3 \times 3 \times \underline{5}$
$70 = 2 \times 7 \times \underline{5}$
greatest common factor is *5*

A *number* which is a factor for each of two or more numbers is called a *common factor* of those numbers.

Back Page Exercises Find the common factors of the following: 9 and 27, 26 and 94, 32 and 57, 48 and 86, 52 and 104.

Common Factors

The Idea

A number which is a factor for each of two or more numbers is called a common factor of those numbers.

How to Use the Idea

a. 18, 24 — $18 = \underline{2} \times \underline{3} \times 3$, $24 = 2 \times 2 \times \underline{2} \times \underline{3}$

b. 10, 25 — $10 = 2 \times \underline{5}$, $25 = 5 \times \underline{5}$

c. 6, 36 — $6 = \underline{2} \times \underline{3}$, $36 = \underline{2} \times 2 \times \underline{3} \times 3$

A Find the prime factors. Underline the common factors.

① 25, 30 — $25 = 5 \times \underline{5}$, $30 = 2 \times 3 \times \underline{5}$

② 30, 36

③ 8, 10

④ 18, 27

⑤ 20, 32

⑥ 16, 24

⑦ 32, 40

⑧ 15, 18

⑨ 21, 35

⑩ 28, 40

B Find the prime factors. Underline the common factors. Multiply the common factors to find the greatest common factor.

① 14, 18 — $14 = \underline{2} \times 7$, $18 = \underline{2} \times 3 \times 3$

greatest common factor is 2

② 30, 36

greatest common factor is ______

③ 25, 50

greatest common factor is ______

④ 28, 30

greatest common factor is ______

⑤ 32, 48

greatest common factor is ______

⑥ 24, 42

greatest common factor is ______

⑦ 13, 39

greatest common factor is ______

⑧ 45, 70

greatest common factor is ______

A ______________ which is a factor for each of two or more numbers is called a ______________ of those numbers.

Back Page Exercises Find the common factors of the following: 9 and 27, 26 and 94, 32 and 57, 48 and 86, 52 and 104.

Fractions

The Idea

A fraction is a numerical representation of some portion of a whole.

How to Use the Idea

a. 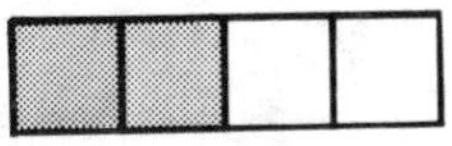 2/4 b. 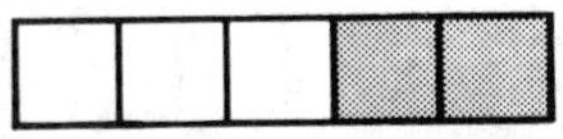 2/5 c. 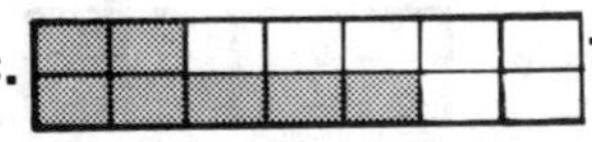 7/14

A Write the fraction which each figure represents. Some figures have more than one answer.

①  1/2

②  3/4

③ 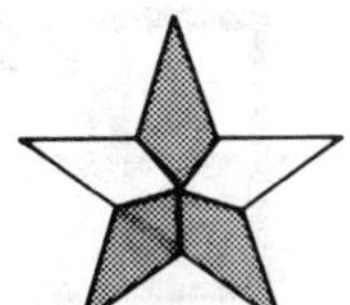 3/5

④ 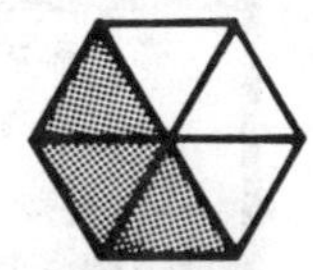 3/6 or 1/2

⑤ 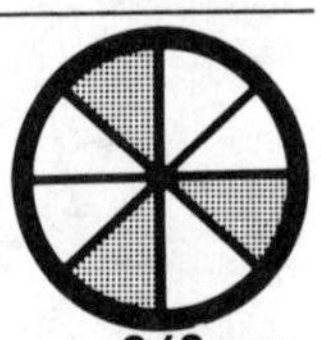 3/8

⑥  1/2

⑦ 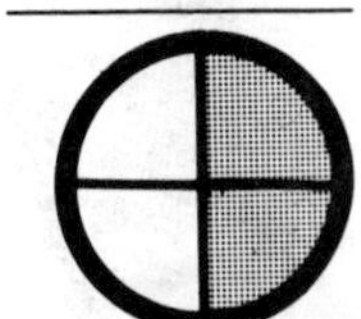 2/4 or 1/2

⑧ 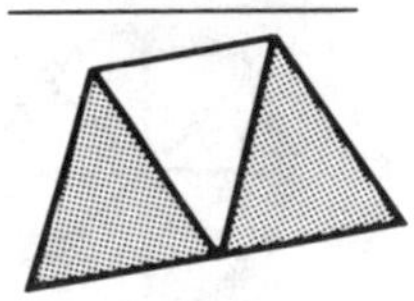 2/3

⑨  6/12 or 1/2

⑩ 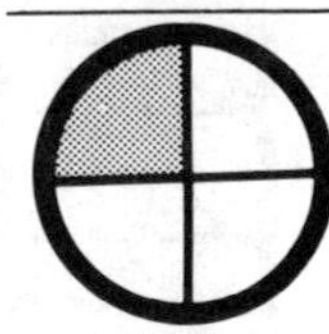 1/4

⑪  8/16 or 1/2

⑫  6/10 or 3/5

B Shade each figure to show the fraction.

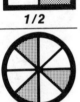

① 1/4 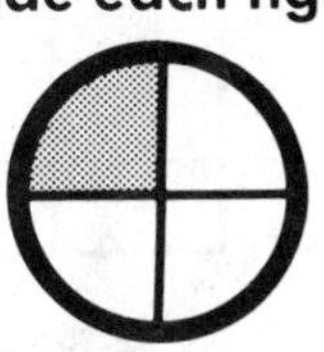

② 1/4 

③ 1/2 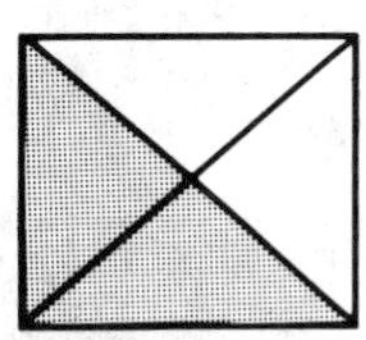

④ 2/6 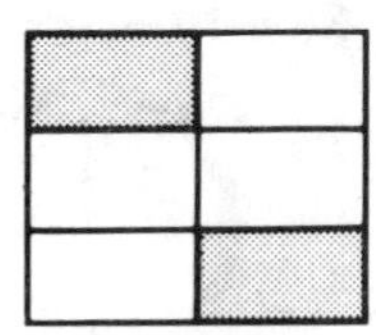

⑤ 1/3 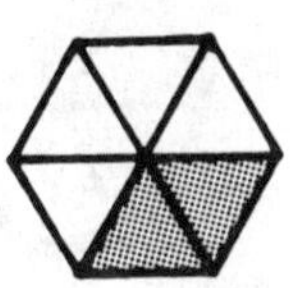

⑥ 3/8 

⑦ 3/15 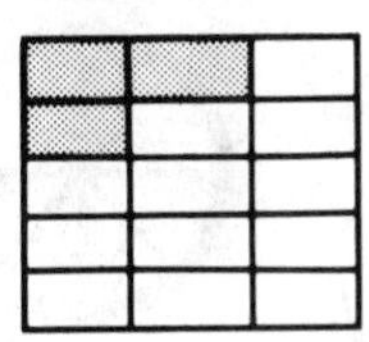

⑧ 1/3 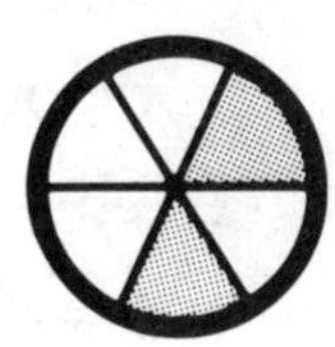

A ___*fraction*___ is a numerical representation of some portion of a ___*whole*___.

Back Page Exercises Draw a different picture to represent each fraction in exercise B.

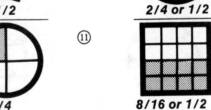

The Idea

A fraction is a numerical representation of some portion of a whole.

How to Use the Idea

a. 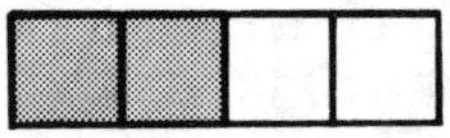 2/4 b. 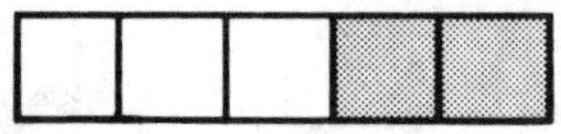 2/5 c. 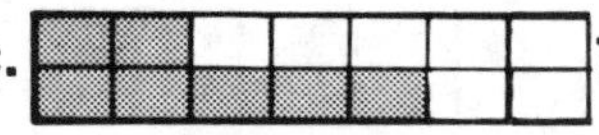 7/14

A Write the fraction which each figure represents. Some figures have more than one answer.

① 
1/2

② 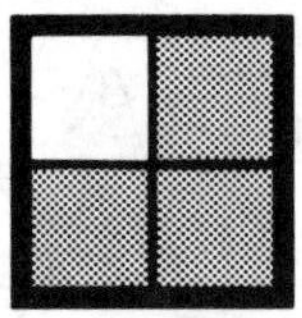

③ 

④ 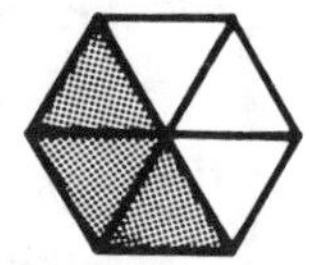

⑤ 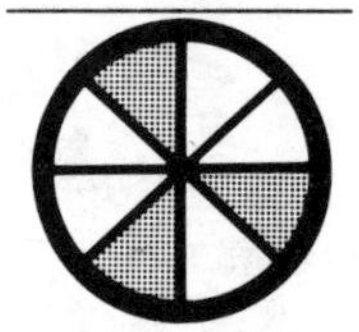

⑥ 

⑦ 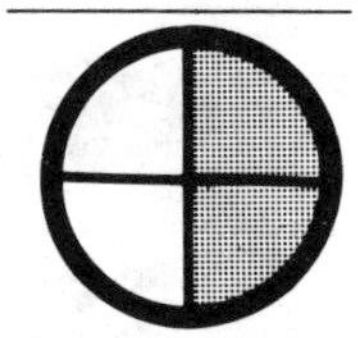

⑧ 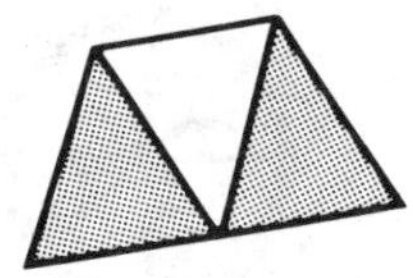

⑨ 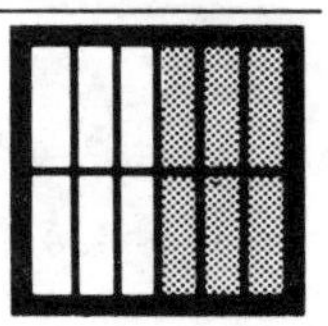

⑩ 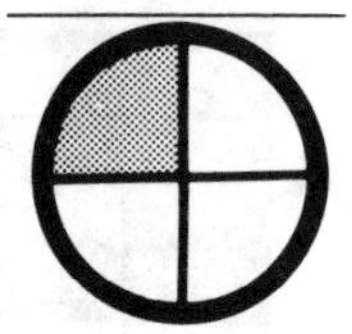

⑪ 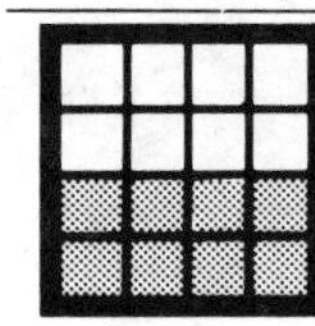

⑫ 

B Shade each figure to show the fraction.

① 1/4 

② 1/4 

③ 1/2 

④ 2/6 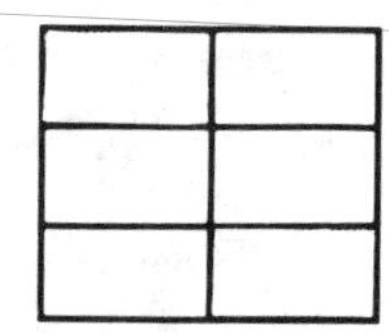

⑤ 1/3 

⑥ 3/8 

⑦ 3/15 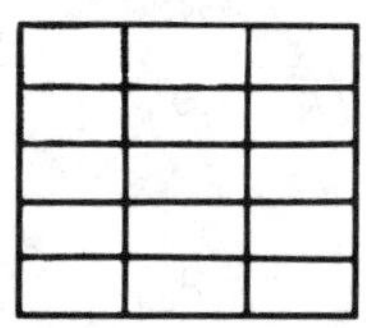

⑧ 1/3 

A ____________ is a numerical representation of some portion of a ____________ .

Back Page Exercises Draw a different picture to represent each fraction in exercise B.

Remainders as Fractions 42

The Idea

A remainder written as a fraction shows the remainder divided by the divisor.

How to Use the Idea

a. 2 3/7
7) 17
14
3

b. 4 3/4
4) 19
16
3

c. 6 1/6
6) 37
36
1

d. 4 1/12
12) 49
48
1

Underline the divisors. Find the quotients. Show remainders as fractions.

① 49 1/5
5) 246
20
46
45
1

② 40 10/12
12) 490
48
10
0
10

③ 88 2/6
6) 530
48
50
48
2

④ 24 10/24
24) 586
48
106
96
10

⑤ 151 5/50
50) 7,555
50
255
250
55
50
5

⑥ 144 28/63
63) 9,100
63
280
252
280
252
28

⑦ 4 20/75
75) 320
300
20

⑧ 81 40/80
80) 6,520
640
120
80
40

⑨ 91 44/91
91) 8,325
819
135
91
44

⑩ 204 8/36
36) 7,352
72
152
144
8

⑪ 70 50/60
60) 4,250
420
50
0
50

⑫ 118 40/55
55) 6,530
55
103
55
480
440
40

A ___*remainder*___ written as a fraction shows the remainder divided by the ___*divisor*___.

Back Page Exercises — **Create ten division problems showing remainders as fractions.**

Remainders as Fractions

The Idea

A remainder written as a fraction shows the remainder divided by the divisor.

How to Use the Idea

a. 7) 17 = 2 3/7
   14
   3

b. 4) 19 = 4 3/4
   16
   3

c. 6) 37 = 6 1/6
   36
   1

d. 12) 49 = 4 1/12
   48
   1

Underline the divisors. Find the quotients. Show remainders as fractions.

1. 5) 246 = *49 1/5*
   20
   46
   45
   1
2. 12) 490
3. 6) 530
4. 24) 586
5. 50) 7,555
6. 63) 9,100
7. 75) 320
8. 80) 6,520
9. 91) 8,325
10. 36) 7,352
11. 60) 4,250
12. 55) 6,530

A ________________ written as a fraction shows the remainder divided by the ________________.

Back Page Exercises Create ten division problems showing remainders as fractions.

Common Denominators

The Idea

A common denominator of two fractions is a number which is divisible by both denominators.

How to Use the Idea

We cannot add or subtract fractions unless they have the same denominators. Fractions A and B share a common denominator 3. To find the least common denominator of A, B, and C, determine the least common multiple of the three denominators. In this case, 6 is the lowest multiple. ($3 \times 2 = 6$ and $6 \times 1 = 6$) Fractions D, E, and F are expressed with least common denominators.

A. 2/3 B. 1/3 C. 1/6 D. 4/6 E. 2/6 F. 1/6

Find a common denominator for each set of fractions.

① 1/2, 1/4
multiples of 2 *2, 4, 6, 8*
multiples of 4 *4, 8*
common denominator *8*

② 1/2, 1/3
multiples of 2 *2, 4, 6*
multiples of 3 *3, 6*
common denominator *6*

③ 1/3, 1/4
multiples of 3 *3, 6, 9, 12*
multiples of 4 *4, 8, 12*
common denominator *12*

④ 2/5, 1/4
multiples of 5 *5, 10, 15, 20*
multiples of 4 *4, 8, 12, 16, 20*
common denominator *20*

⑤ 5/6, 1/8
multiples of 6 *6, 12, 18, 24*
multiples of 8 *8, 16, 24*
common denominator *24*

⑥ 1/3, 1/5
multiples of 3 *3, 6, 9, 12, 15*
multiples of 5 *5, 10, 15*
common denominator *15*

⑦ 3/5, 1/2
multiples of 5 *5, 10*
multiples of 2 *2, 4, 6, 8, 10*
common denominator *10*

⑧ 1/2, 1/7
multiples of 2 *2, 4, 6, 8, 10, 12, 14*
multiples of 7 *7, 14*
common denominator *14*

⑨ 1/3, 1/6
multiples of 3 *3, 6*
multiples of 6 *6*
common denominator *6*

⑩ 1/3, 1/7
multiples of 3 *3, 6, 9, 12, 18, 21*
multiples of 7 *7, 14, 21*
common denominator *21*

⑪ 1/4, 1/8
multiples of 4 *4, 8*
multiples of 8 *8*
common denominator *8*

⑫ 1/4, 1/6
multiples of 4 *4, 8, 12*
multiples of 6 *6, 12*
common denominator *12*

A *common denominator* of two fractions is a number which is divisible by both *denominators*.

Back Page Exercises Find the common denominators of the following: 1/8 and 1/23, 2/4 and 3/16, and 9/26 and 1/13.

Common Denominators

The Idea

A common denominator of two fractions is a number which is divisible by both denominators.

How to Use the Idea

We cannot add or subtract fractions unless they have the same denominators. Fractions A and B share a common denominator 3. To find the least common denominator of A, B, and C, determine the least common multiple of the three denominators. In this case, 6 is the lowest multiple. (3 × 2 = 6 and 6 × 1 = 6) Fractions D, E, and F are expressed with least common denominators.

A. 2/3 B. 1/3 C. 1/6 D. 4/6 E. 2/6 F. 1/6

Find a common denominator for each set of fractions.

① 1/2, 1/4 multiples of 2 *2, 4, 6, 8* ______
multiples of 4 ______
common denominator ______

② 1/2, 1/3 multiples of 2 ______
multiples of 3 ______
common denominator ______

③ 1/3, 1/4 multiples of 3 ______
multiples of 4 ______
common denominator ______

④ 2/5, 1/4 multiples of 5 ______
multiples of 4 ______
common denominator ______

⑤ 5/6, 1/8 multiples of 6 ______
multiples of 8 ______
common denominator ______

⑥ 1/3, 1/5 multiples of 3 ______
multiples of 5 ______
common denominator ______

⑦ 3/5, 1/2 multiples of 5 ______
multiples of 2 ______
common denominator ______

⑧ 1/2, 1/7 multiples of 2 ______
multiples of 7 ______
common denominator ______

⑨ 1/3, 1/6 multiples of 3 ______
multiples of 6 ______
common denominator ______

⑩ 1/3, 1/7 multiples of 3 ______
multiples of 7 ______
common denominator ______

⑪ 1/4, 1/8 multiples of 4 ______
multiples of 8 ______
common denominator ______

⑫ 1/4, 1/6 multiples of 4 ______
multiples of 6 ______
common denominator ______

A __________ of two fractions is a number which is divisible by both __________ .

Back Page Exercises Find the common denominators of the following: 1/8 and 1/23, 2/4 and 3/16, and 9/26 and 1/13.

Adding Fractions

The Idea

A common denominator of two fractions is a number which is divisible by both denominators.

How to Use the Idea

In finding the common denominator of 1/2 and 1/4, notice that 4 is a multiple of 2. This means that the number multiplied by 2 to equal 4 can be multiplied by both the 1 and the 2 in 1/2 to make 1/2 and 1/4 have common denominators. 1/2 × 2/2 = 2/4 Now we can add 2/4 to 1/4 and find the sum of 3/4.

Find a common denominator for each problem; then add.

① $\frac{1}{8} + \frac{1}{3} = \frac{3}{24} + \frac{8}{24} = \frac{11}{24}$

② $\frac{2}{5} + \frac{1}{10} = \frac{4}{10} + \frac{1}{10} = \frac{5}{10} = \frac{1}{2}$

③ $\frac{1}{3} + \frac{1}{6} = \frac{2}{6} + \frac{1}{6} = \frac{3}{6} = \frac{1}{2}$

④ $\frac{1}{4} + \frac{1}{6} = \frac{3}{12} + \frac{2}{12} = \frac{5}{12}$

⑤ $\frac{1}{4} + \frac{1}{3} = \frac{3}{12} + \frac{4}{12} = \frac{7}{12}$

⑥ $\frac{2}{7} + \frac{3}{5} = \frac{10}{35} + \frac{21}{35} = \frac{31}{35}$

⑦ $\frac{1}{2} + \frac{1}{7} = \frac{7}{14} + \frac{2}{14} = \frac{9}{14}$

⑧ $\frac{3}{8} + \frac{1}{2} = \frac{3}{8} + \frac{4}{8} = \frac{7}{8}$

⑨ $\frac{1}{7} + \frac{1}{3} = \frac{3}{21} + \frac{7}{21} = \frac{10}{21}$

⑩ $\frac{2}{5} + \frac{3}{8} = \frac{16}{40} + \frac{15}{40} = \frac{31}{40}$

⑪ $\frac{1}{8} + \frac{1}{6} = \frac{3}{24} + \frac{4}{24} = \frac{7}{24}$

⑫ $\frac{1}{4} + \frac{1}{16} = \frac{4}{16} + \frac{1}{16} = \frac{5}{16}$

⑬ $\frac{1}{2} + \frac{1}{9} = \frac{9}{18} + \frac{2}{18} = \frac{11}{18}$

⑭ $\frac{3}{7} + \frac{1}{3} = \frac{9}{21} + \frac{7}{21} = \frac{16}{21}$

⑮ $\frac{1}{5} + \frac{1}{9} = \frac{9}{45} + \frac{5}{45} = \frac{14}{45}$

⑯ $\frac{1}{8} + \frac{5}{24} = \frac{3}{24} + \frac{5}{24} = \frac{8}{24} = \frac{1}{3}$

⑰ $\frac{2}{3} + \frac{1}{6} = \frac{4}{6} + \frac{1}{6} = \frac{5}{6}$

⑱ $\frac{3}{20} + \frac{1}{10} = \frac{3}{20} + \frac{2}{20} = \frac{5}{20} = \frac{1}{4}$

A ___*common denominator*___ of two fractions is a number which is divisible by both ___*denominators*___.

Back Page Exercises Create ten problems adding fractions.

Adding Fractions

The Idea

A common denominator of two fractions is a number which is divisible by both denominators.

How to Use the Idea

In finding the common denominator of 1/2 and 1/4, notice that 4 is a multiple of 2. This means that the number multiplied by 2 to equal 4 can be multiplied by both the 1 and the 2 in 1/2 to make 1/2 and 1/4 have common denominators. 1/2 × 2/2 = 2/4 Now we can add 2/4 to 1/4 and find the sum of 3/4.

Find a common denominator for each problem; then add.

① $\frac{1}{8} + \frac{1}{3} = \frac{3}{24} + \frac{8}{24} = \frac{11}{24}$

② $\frac{2}{5} + \frac{1}{10} =$

③ $\frac{1}{3} + \frac{1}{6} =$

④ $\frac{1}{4} + \frac{1}{6} =$

⑤ $\frac{1}{4} + \frac{1}{3} =$

⑥ $\frac{2}{7} + \frac{3}{5} =$

⑦ $\frac{1}{2} + \frac{1}{7} =$

⑧ $\frac{3}{8} + \frac{1}{2} =$

⑨ $\frac{1}{7} + \frac{1}{3} =$

⑩ $\frac{2}{5} + \frac{3}{8} =$

⑪ $\frac{1}{8} + \frac{1}{6} =$

⑫ $\frac{1}{4} + \frac{1}{16} =$

⑬ $\frac{1}{2} + \frac{1}{9} =$

⑭ $\frac{3}{7} + \frac{1}{3} =$

⑮ $\frac{1}{5} + \frac{1}{9} =$

⑯ $\frac{1}{8} + \frac{5}{24} =$

⑰ $\frac{2}{3} + \frac{1}{6} =$

⑱ $\frac{3}{20} + \frac{1}{10} =$

A ________________ of two fractions is a number which is divisible by both ________________.

Back Page Exercises Create ten problems adding fractions.

Adding Columns of Fractions

The Idea

A common denominator is a number which is divisible by all denominators of a set of two or more fractions.

How to Use the Idea

We can add a column of fractions only if they have a common denominator.

$$\begin{array}{rl} \frac{1}{2} = & \frac{15}{30} \\ \frac{1}{3} = & \frac{10}{30} \\ +\frac{2}{5} = & \frac{12}{30} \\ \hline & \frac{37}{30} = 1\frac{7}{30} \end{array} \qquad \begin{array}{rl} \frac{1}{5} = & \frac{12}{60} \\ \frac{2}{3} = & \frac{40}{60} \\ +\frac{1}{4} & \frac{15}{60} \\ \hline & \frac{67}{60} = 1\frac{7}{60} \end{array}$$

Add. Reduce fractions to lowest terms.

① $\frac{1}{6} = \frac{2}{12}$, $\frac{1}{4} = \frac{3}{12}$, $+\frac{1}{2} = \frac{6}{12}$; $\frac{11}{12}$

② $\frac{1}{7} = \frac{4}{28}$, $\frac{1}{4} = \frac{7}{28}$, $+\frac{1}{2} = \frac{14}{28}$; $\frac{25}{28}$

③ $\frac{1}{4} = \frac{4}{16}$, $\frac{1}{8} = \frac{2}{16}$, $+\frac{13}{16} = \frac{13}{16}$; $\frac{19}{16} = 1\frac{3}{16}$

④ $\frac{2}{3} = \frac{8}{12}$, $\frac{3}{4} = \frac{9}{12}$, $+\frac{1}{12} = \frac{1}{12}$; $\frac{18}{12} = 1\frac{6}{12} = 1\frac{1}{2}$

⑤ $\frac{3}{40} = \frac{3}{40}$, $\frac{3}{8} = \frac{15}{40}$, $\frac{5}{10} = \frac{20}{40}$, $+\frac{1}{40} = \frac{1}{40}$; $\frac{39}{40}$

⑥ $\frac{5}{8} = \frac{15}{24}$, $\frac{1}{2} = \frac{12}{24}$, $\frac{2}{3} = \frac{16}{24}$, $+\frac{1}{6} = \frac{4}{24}$; $\frac{47}{24} = 1\frac{23}{24}$

⑦ $\frac{3}{25} = \frac{12}{100}$, $\frac{7}{10} = \frac{70}{100}$, $\frac{1}{5} = \frac{20}{100}$, $+\frac{1}{4} = \frac{25}{100}$; $\frac{127}{100} = 1\frac{27}{100}$

⑧ $\frac{5}{9} = \frac{20}{36}$, $\frac{3}{4} = \frac{27}{36}$, $\frac{7}{12} = \frac{21}{36}$, $+\frac{1}{18} = \frac{2}{36}$; $\frac{70}{36} = 1\frac{34}{36} = 1\frac{17}{18}$

⑨ $\frac{1}{4} = \frac{10}{40}$, $\frac{1}{5} = \frac{8}{40}$, $\frac{1}{8} = \frac{5}{40}$, $+\frac{1}{10} = \frac{4}{40}$; $\frac{27}{40}$

⑩ $\frac{5}{12} = \frac{10}{24}$, $\frac{1}{8} = \frac{3}{24}$, $\frac{1}{3} = \frac{8}{24}$, $+\frac{1}{6} = \frac{4}{24}$; $\frac{25}{24} = 1\frac{1}{24}$

⑪ $\frac{1}{2} = \frac{30}{60}$, $\frac{1}{3} = \frac{20}{60}$, $\frac{1}{4} = \frac{15}{60}$, $+\frac{1}{5} = \frac{12}{60}$; $\frac{77}{60} = 1\frac{17}{60}$

⑫ $\frac{2}{3} = \frac{30}{45}$, $\frac{2}{5} = \frac{18}{45}$, $\frac{1}{9} = \frac{5}{45}$, $+\frac{4}{15} = \frac{12}{45}$; $\frac{65}{45} = 1\frac{20}{45} = 1\frac{4}{9}$

A common denominator is a number which is *divisible* by all denominators of a *set* of two or more *fractions*.

Back Page Exercises Create ten problems adding fractions with five fractions in each column.

Adding Columns of Fractions

The Idea

A common denominator is a number which is divisible by all denominators of a set of two or more fractions.

How to Use the Idea

We can add a column of fractions only if they have a common denominator.

$$\begin{array}{r} \frac{1}{2} = \frac{15}{30} \\ \frac{1}{3} = \frac{10}{30} \\ +\frac{2}{5} = \frac{12}{30} \\ \hline \frac{37}{30} = 1\frac{7}{30} \end{array} \qquad \begin{array}{r} \frac{1}{5} = \frac{12}{60} \\ \frac{2}{3} = \frac{40}{60} \\ +\frac{1}{4} = \frac{15}{60} \\ \hline \frac{67}{60} = 1\frac{7}{60} \end{array}$$

Add. Reduce fractions to lowest terms.

① $\frac{1}{6} = \frac{2}{12}$, $\frac{1}{4} = \frac{3}{12}$, $+\frac{1}{2} = \frac{6}{12}$; $\frac{11}{12}$

② $\frac{1}{7} =$, $\frac{1}{4} =$, $+\frac{1}{2} =$

③ $\frac{1}{4} =$, $\frac{1}{8} =$, $+\frac{13}{16} =$

④ $\frac{2}{3} =$, $\frac{3}{4} =$, $+\frac{1}{12} =$

⑤ $\frac{3}{40} =$, $\frac{3}{8} =$, $\frac{5}{10} =$, $+\frac{1}{40} =$

⑥ $\frac{5}{8} =$, $\frac{1}{2} =$, $\frac{2}{3} =$, $+\frac{1}{6} =$

⑦ $\frac{3}{25} =$, $\frac{7}{10} =$, $\frac{1}{5} =$, $+\frac{1}{4} =$

⑧ $\frac{5}{9} =$, $\frac{3}{4} =$, $\frac{7}{12} =$, $+\frac{1}{18} =$

⑨ $\frac{1}{4} =$, $\frac{1}{5} =$, $\frac{1}{8} =$, $+\frac{1}{10} =$

⑩ $\frac{5}{12} =$, $\frac{1}{8} =$, $\frac{1}{3} =$, $+\frac{1}{6} =$

⑪ $\frac{1}{2} =$, $\frac{1}{3} =$, $\frac{1}{4} =$, $+\frac{1}{5} =$

⑫ $\frac{2}{3} =$, $\frac{2}{5} =$, $\frac{1}{9} =$, $+\frac{4}{15} =$

A common denominator is a number which is ______________ by all denominators of a ______________ of two or more ______________.

Back Page Exercises Create ten problems adding fractions with five fractions in each column.

Subtracting Fractions 46

The Idea

A common denominator of two fractions is a number which is divisible by both denominators.

How to Use the Idea

To subtract one fraction from another, the fractions must have a common denominator. As oranges cannot be subtracted from apples, fourths cannot be subtracted from thirds, but fourths and thirds can change into twelfths and be subtracted.

$$\begin{array}{r} \frac{1}{3} = \frac{4}{12} \\ -\frac{1}{4} = \frac{3}{12} \\ \hline \frac{1}{12} \end{array}$$

Find a common denominator for each pair of fractions and then subtract.

① $\frac{7}{12} = \frac{7}{12}$, $-\frac{1}{4} = \frac{3}{12}$, $\frac{4}{12} = \frac{1}{3}$

② $\frac{6}{7} = \frac{60}{70}$, $-\frac{1}{10} = \frac{7}{70}$, $\frac{53}{70}$

③ $\frac{4}{5} = \frac{32}{40}$, $-\frac{1}{8} = \frac{5}{40}$, $\frac{27}{40}$

④ $\frac{9}{10} = \frac{18}{20}$, $-\frac{1}{4} = \frac{5}{20}$, $\frac{13}{20}$

⑤ $\frac{4}{7} = \frac{20}{35}$, $-\frac{2}{5} = \frac{14}{35}$, $\frac{6}{35}$

⑥ $\frac{3}{8} = \frac{21}{56}$, $-\frac{1}{7} = \frac{8}{56}$, $\frac{13}{56}$

⑦ $\frac{1}{3} = \frac{8}{24}$, $-\frac{1}{8} = \frac{3}{24}$, $\frac{5}{24}$

⑧ $\frac{2}{3} = \frac{14}{21}$, $-\frac{4}{7} = \frac{12}{21}$, $\frac{2}{21}$

⑨ $\frac{1}{8} = \frac{3}{24}$, $-\frac{1}{12} = \frac{2}{24}$, $\frac{1}{24}$

⑩ $\frac{1}{5} = \frac{9}{45}$, $-\frac{1}{9} = \frac{5}{45}$, $\frac{4}{45}$

⑪ $\frac{1}{6} = \frac{3}{18}$, $-\frac{1}{9} = \frac{2}{18}$, $\frac{1}{18}$

⑫ $\frac{1}{8} = \frac{5}{40}$, $-\frac{1}{10} = \frac{4}{40}$, $\frac{1}{40}$

⑬ $\frac{1}{6} = \frac{5}{30}$, $-\frac{1}{10} \quad \frac{3}{30}$, $\frac{2}{30} = \frac{1}{15}$

⑭ $\frac{1}{4} = \frac{9}{36}$, $-\frac{1}{9} = \frac{4}{36}$, $\frac{5}{36}$

⑮ $\frac{3}{4} = \frac{6}{8}$, $-\frac{5}{8} = \frac{5}{8}$, $\frac{1}{8}$

⑯ $\frac{3}{7} = \frac{15}{35}$, $-\frac{1}{5} = \frac{7}{35}$, $\frac{8}{35}$

⑰ $\frac{2}{5} = \frac{6}{15}$, $-\frac{1}{3} = \frac{5}{15}$, $\frac{1}{15}$

⑱ $\frac{4}{9} = \frac{16}{36}$, $-\frac{1}{4} = \frac{9}{36}$, $\frac{7}{36}$

⑲ $\frac{8}{15} = \frac{8}{15}$, $-\frac{1}{5} = \frac{3}{15}$, $\frac{5}{15} = \frac{1}{3}$

⑳ $\frac{3}{10} = \frac{3}{10}$, $-\frac{1}{5} = \frac{2}{10}$, $\frac{1}{10}$

A ___*common*___ denominator of two fractions is a number which is divisible by ___*both*___ denominators.

Back Page Exercises Subtract 1/2 from 9/12, 5/6 from 10/36, 3/8 from 15/17, and 6/12 from 12/24.

Subtracting Fractions

The Idea

A common denominator of two fractions is a number which is divisible by both denominators.

How to Use the Idea

To subtract one fraction from another, the fractions must have a common denominator. As oranges cannot be subtracted from apples, fourths cannot be subtracted from thirds, but fourths and thirds can change into twelfths and be subtracted.

$$\frac{1}{3} = \frac{4}{12}$$
$$-\frac{1}{4} = \frac{3}{12}$$
$$\frac{1}{12}$$

Find a common denominator for each pair of fractions and then subtract.

① $\frac{7}{12} = \frac{7}{12}$, $-\frac{1}{4} = \frac{3}{12}$, $\frac{4}{12} = \frac{1}{3}$

② $\frac{6}{7} =$, $-\frac{1}{10} =$

③ $\frac{4}{5} =$, $-\frac{1}{8} =$

④ $\frac{9}{10} =$, $-\frac{1}{4} =$

⑤ $\frac{4}{7} =$, $-\frac{2}{5} =$

⑥ $\frac{3}{8} =$, $-\frac{1}{7} =$

⑦ $\frac{1}{3} =$, $-\frac{1}{8} =$

⑧ $\frac{2}{3} =$, $-\frac{4}{7} =$

⑨ $\frac{1}{8} =$, $-\frac{1}{12} =$

⑩ $\frac{1}{5} =$, $-\frac{1}{9} =$

⑪ $\frac{1}{6} =$, $-\frac{1}{9} =$

⑫ $\frac{1}{8} =$, $-\frac{1}{10} =$

⑬ $\frac{1}{6} =$, $-\frac{1}{10}$

⑭ $\frac{1}{4} =$, $-\frac{1}{9} =$

⑮ $\frac{3}{4} =$, $-\frac{5}{8} =$

⑯ $\frac{3}{7} =$, $-\frac{1}{5} =$

⑰ $\frac{2}{5} =$, $-\frac{1}{3} =$

⑱ $\frac{4}{9} =$, $-\frac{1}{4} =$

⑲ $\frac{8}{15} =$, $-\frac{1}{5} =$

⑳ $\frac{3}{10} =$, $-\frac{1}{5} =$

A ______________ denominator of two fractions is a number which is divisible by ______________ denominators.

Back Page Exercises Subtract 1/2 from 9/12, 5/6 from 10/36, 3/8 from 15/17, and 6/12 from 12/24.

Multiplying Fractions

The Idea

A fraction is a numerical representation of some portion of a whole.

How to Use the Idea

To multiply fractions, find the product of the numerators. This is the numerator of the product. The denominator of the product is the product of the denominators. When fractions are multiplied you are dividing something into smaller pieces.

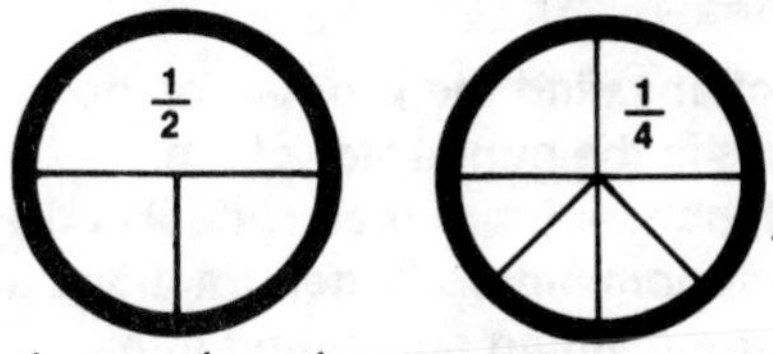

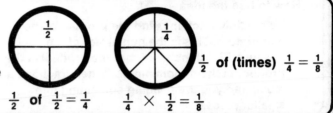

$\frac{1}{2}$ of $\frac{1}{2} = \frac{1}{4}$ $\quad$ $\frac{1}{4} \times \frac{1}{2} = \frac{1}{8}$ $\quad$ $\frac{1}{2}$ of (times) $\frac{1}{4} = \frac{1}{8}$

Find the products.

1. $\frac{2}{3} \times \frac{4}{5} = \frac{2 \times 4}{3 \times 5} = \frac{8}{15}$
2. $\frac{1}{8} \times \frac{2}{5} = \frac{2}{40} = \frac{1}{20}$
3. $\frac{1}{9} \times \frac{3}{7} = \frac{3}{63} = \frac{1}{21}$
4. $\frac{3}{8} \times \frac{1}{2} = \frac{3}{16}$
5. $\frac{1}{4} \times \frac{1}{3} = \frac{1}{12}$
6. $\frac{1}{5} \times \frac{1}{6} = \frac{1}{30}$
7. $\frac{4}{5} \times \frac{1}{7} = \frac{4}{35}$
8. $\frac{1}{10} \times \frac{3}{4} = \frac{3}{40}$
9. $\frac{2}{7} \times \frac{1}{3} = \frac{2}{21}$
10. $\frac{1}{16} \times \frac{3}{4} = \frac{3}{64}$
11. $\frac{2}{9} \times \frac{1}{3} = \frac{2}{27}$
12. $\frac{1}{4} \times \frac{1}{7} = \frac{1}{28}$
13. $\frac{2}{11} \times \frac{1}{3} = \frac{2}{33}$
14. $\frac{1}{5} \times \frac{3}{4} = \frac{3}{20}$
15. $\frac{3}{5} \times \frac{3}{5} = \frac{9}{25}$
16. $\frac{1}{4} \times \frac{3}{10} = \frac{3}{40}$
17. $\frac{1}{2} \times \frac{1}{2} = \frac{1}{4}$
18. $\frac{1}{4} \times \frac{3}{8} = \frac{3}{32}$
19. $\frac{2}{5} \times \frac{8}{9} = \frac{16}{45}$
20. $\frac{3}{10} \times \frac{1}{2} = \frac{3}{20}$
21. $\frac{5}{8} \times \frac{1}{3} = \frac{5}{24}$
22. $\frac{1}{2} \times \frac{1}{8} = \frac{1}{16}$
23. $\frac{3}{4} \times \frac{1}{2} = \frac{3}{8}$
24. $\frac{9}{10} \times \frac{2}{5} = \frac{18}{50} = \frac{9}{25}$
25. $\frac{7}{8} \times \frac{1}{2} = \frac{7}{16}$
26. $\frac{7}{9} \times \frac{4}{5} = \frac{28}{45}$
27. $\frac{1}{3} \times \frac{1}{3} = \frac{1}{9}$
28. $\frac{1}{2} \times \frac{3}{10} = \frac{3}{20}$
29. $\frac{1}{4} \times \frac{1}{4} = \frac{1}{16}$
30. $\frac{1}{8} \times \frac{1}{2} = \frac{1}{16}$
31. $\frac{1}{2} \times \frac{1}{1} = \frac{1}{2}$
32. $\frac{1}{2} \times \frac{2}{1} = \frac{2}{2} = 1$
33. $\frac{4}{9} \times \frac{2}{5} = \frac{8}{45}$
34. $\frac{5}{8} \times \frac{1}{1} = \frac{5}{8}$
35. $\frac{9}{16} \times \frac{3}{4} = \frac{27}{64}$
36. $\frac{1}{3} \times \frac{2}{2} = \frac{2}{6} = \frac{1}{3}$

A ____*fraction*____ is a numerical representation of some ____*portion*____ of a whole.

Back Page Exercises Create ten problems multiplying fractions.

Multiplying Fractions

The Idea

A fraction is a numerical representation of some portion of a whole.

How to Use the Idea

To multiply fractions, find the product of the numerators. This is the numerator of the product. The denominator of the product is the product of the denominators. When fractions are multiplied you are dividing something into smaller pieces.

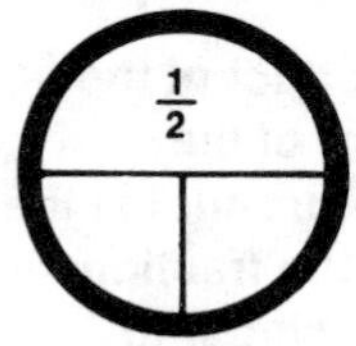

$\frac{1}{2}$ of $\frac{1}{2} = \frac{1}{4}$

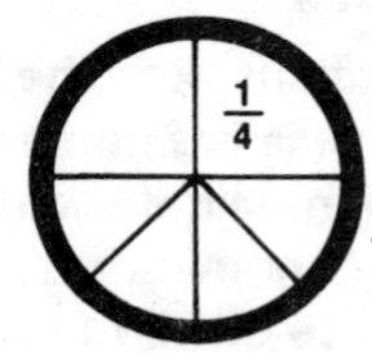

$\frac{1}{4} \times \frac{1}{2} = \frac{1}{8}$

$\frac{1}{2}$ of (times) $\frac{1}{4} = \frac{1}{8}$

Find the products.

(1) $\frac{2}{3} \times \frac{4}{5} = \frac{2 \times 4}{3 \times 5} = \frac{8}{15}$
(2) $\frac{1}{8} \times \frac{2}{5} = \quad =$
(3) $\frac{1}{9} \times \frac{3}{7} = \quad =$
(4) $\frac{3}{8} \times \frac{1}{2} =$

(5) $\frac{1}{4} \times \frac{1}{3} =$
(6) $\frac{1}{5} \times \frac{1}{6} =$
(7) $\frac{4}{5} \times \frac{1}{7} =$
(8) $\frac{1}{10} \times \frac{3}{4} =$

(9) $\frac{2}{7} \times \frac{1}{3} =$
(10) $\frac{1}{16} \times \frac{3}{4} =$
(11) $\frac{2}{9} \times \frac{1}{3} =$
(12) $\frac{1}{4} \times \frac{1}{7} =$

(13) $\frac{2}{11} \times \frac{1}{3} =$
(14) $\frac{1}{5} \times \frac{3}{4} =$
(15) $\frac{3}{5} \times \frac{3}{5} =$
(16) $\frac{1}{4} \times \frac{3}{10} =$

(17) $\frac{1}{2} \times \frac{1}{2} =$
(18) $\frac{1}{4} \times \frac{3}{8} =$
(19) $\frac{2}{5} \times \frac{8}{9} =$
(20) $\frac{3}{10} \times \frac{1}{2} =$

(21) $\frac{5}{8} \times \frac{1}{3} =$
(22) $\frac{1}{2} \times \frac{1}{8} =$
(23) $\frac{3}{4} \times \frac{1}{2} =$
(24) $\frac{9}{10} \times \frac{2}{5} = \quad =$

(25) $\frac{7}{8} \times \frac{1}{2} =$
(26) $\frac{7}{9} \times \frac{4}{5} =$
(27) $\frac{1}{3} \times \frac{1}{3} =$
(28) $\frac{1}{2} \times \frac{3}{10} =$

(29) $\frac{1}{4} \times \frac{1}{4} =$
(30) $\frac{1}{8} \times \frac{1}{2} =$
(31) $\frac{1}{2} \times \frac{1}{1} =$
(32) $\frac{1}{2} \times \frac{2}{1} = \quad =$

(33) $\frac{4}{9} \times \frac{2}{5} =$
(34) $\frac{5}{8} \times \frac{1}{1} =$
(35) $\frac{9}{16} \times \frac{3}{4} =$
(36) $\frac{1}{3} \times \frac{2}{2} = \quad =$

A ______________________ is a numerical representation of some ______________________ of a whole.

Back Page Exercises **Create ten problems multiplying fractions.**

Dividing Fractions

The Idea

Dividing by a fraction is the same as multiplying by its reciprocal.

How to Use the Idea

To divide by a fraction, invert the fraction and multiply.

$9 \div \frac{2}{3} = \frac{9}{1} \times \frac{3}{2} = \frac{27}{2} = 13\frac{1}{2}$ $10 \div \frac{1}{5} = \frac{10}{1} \times \frac{5}{1} = 50$ $6 \div \frac{3}{4} = \frac{6}{1} \times \frac{4}{3} = \frac{24}{3} = 8$

Divide.

① $8 \div \frac{4}{5} = \frac{8}{1} \times \frac{5}{4} = \frac{40}{4} = 10$

② $6 \div \frac{3}{8} = \frac{6}{1} \times \frac{8}{3} = \frac{48}{3} = 16$

③ $3 \div \frac{1}{6} = \frac{3}{1} \times \frac{6}{1} = 18$

④ $16 \div \frac{4}{5} = \frac{16}{1} \times \frac{5}{4} = \frac{80}{4} = 20$

⑤ $5 \div \frac{1}{4} = \frac{5}{1} \times \frac{4}{1} = 20$

⑥ $4 \div \frac{4}{5} = \frac{4}{1} \times \frac{5}{4} = \frac{20}{4} = 5$

⑦ $4 \div \frac{2}{7} = \frac{4}{1} \times \frac{7}{2} = \frac{28}{2} = 14$

⑧ $9 \div \frac{1}{2} = \frac{9}{1} \times \frac{2}{1} = 18$

⑨ $9 \div \frac{3}{4} = \frac{9}{1} \times \frac{4}{3} = \frac{36}{3} = 12$

⑩ $3\frac{1}{2} \div \frac{1}{2} = \frac{7}{2} \times \frac{2}{1} = \frac{14}{2} = 7$

⑪ $10 \div \frac{5}{2} = \frac{10}{1} \times \frac{2}{5} = \frac{20}{5} = 4$

⑫ $6\frac{3}{5} \div \frac{3}{5} = \frac{33}{5} \times \frac{5}{3} = \frac{165}{15} = 11$

⑬ $12 \div \frac{1}{12} = \frac{12}{1} \times \frac{12}{1} = 144$

⑭ $2\frac{1}{4} \div \frac{3}{8} = \frac{9}{4} \times \frac{8}{3} = \frac{72}{12} = 6$

⑮ $15 \div \frac{3}{5} = \frac{15}{1} \times \frac{5}{3} = \frac{75}{3} = 25$

⑯ $5\frac{2}{3} \div \frac{5}{6} = \frac{17}{3} \times \frac{6}{5} = \frac{102}{15} = 6\frac{12}{15} = 6\frac{4}{5}$

⑰ $2 \div \frac{2}{7} = \frac{2}{1} \times \frac{7}{2} = \frac{14}{2} = 7$

⑱ $1\frac{7}{8} \div \frac{1}{8} = \frac{15}{8} \times \frac{8}{1} = \frac{120}{8} = 15$

Dividing by a fraction is the same as multiplying by its ***reciprocal***.

Back Page Exercises — Create ten problems dividing fractions.

Dividing Fractions

The Idea

Dividing by a fraction is the same as multiplying by its reciprocal.

How to Use the Idea

To divide by a fraction, invert the fraction and multiply.

$9 \div \frac{2}{3} = \frac{9}{1} \times \frac{3}{2} = \frac{27}{2} = 13\frac{1}{2}$ $10 \div \frac{1}{5} = \frac{10}{1} \times \frac{5}{1} = 50$ $6 \div \frac{3}{4} = \frac{6}{1} \times \frac{4}{3} = \frac{24}{3} = 8$

Divide.

1. $8 \div \frac{4}{5} = \frac{8}{1} \times \frac{5}{4} = \frac{40}{4} = 10$
2. $6 \div \frac{3}{8} =$
3. $3 \div \frac{1}{6} =$
4. $16 \div \frac{4}{5} =$
5. $5 \div \frac{1}{4} =$
6. $4 \div \frac{4}{5} =$
7. $4 \div \frac{2}{7} =$
8. $9 \div \frac{1}{2} =$
9. $9 \div \frac{3}{4} =$
10. $3\frac{1}{2} \div \frac{1}{2} =$
11. $10 \div \frac{5}{2} =$
12. $6\frac{3}{5} \div \frac{3}{5} =$
13. $12 \div \frac{1}{12} =$
14. $2\frac{1}{4} \div \frac{3}{8} =$
15. $15 \div \frac{3}{5} =$
16. $5\frac{2}{3} \div \frac{5}{6} =$
17. $2 \div \frac{2}{7} =$
18. $1\frac{7}{8} \div \frac{1}{8} =$

Dividing by a fraction is the same as multiplying by its ____________________.

Back Page Exercises Create ten problems dividing fractions.

Reciprocals

The Idea

If the product of two numbers is one, the numbers are said to be reciprocals of each other.

How to Use the Idea

$$3 \times \frac{1}{3} = \frac{3}{3} = 1$$

Three is the reciprocal of $\frac{1}{3}$, and $\frac{1}{3}$ is the reciprocal of three. For two numbers to be reciprocals, the numerator of the first must be the same number as the denominator of the second. The denominator of the first must be the same number as the numerator of the second.

A Show that each pair of numbers is reciprocal.

1. $\frac{1}{2} \times \frac{2}{1} =$ $\frac{2}{2} = 1$ The reciprocal of $\frac{1}{2}$ is 2. The reciprocal of 2 is $\frac{1}{2}$.
2. $\frac{5}{1} \times \frac{1}{5} =$ $\frac{5}{5} = 1$ The reciprocal of 5 is $\frac{1}{5}$. The reciprocal of $\frac{1}{5}$ is 5.
3. $\frac{1}{4} \times \frac{4}{1} =$ $\frac{4}{4} = 1$ The reciprocal of $\frac{1}{4}$ is 4. The reciprocal of 4 is $\frac{1}{4}$.
4. $\frac{25}{1} \times \frac{1}{25} =$ $\frac{25}{25} = 1$ The reciprocal of 25 is $\frac{1}{25}$. The reciprocal of $\frac{1}{25}$ is 25.
5. $\frac{100}{1} \times \frac{1}{100} =$ $\frac{100}{100} = 1$ The reciprocal of 100 is $\frac{1}{100}$. The reciprocal of $\frac{1}{100}$ is 100.
6. $\frac{1}{18} \times \frac{18}{1} =$ $\frac{18}{18} = 1$ The reciprocal of $\frac{1}{18}$ is 18. The reciprocal of 18 is $\frac{1}{18}$.
7. $\frac{3}{2} \times \frac{2}{3} =$ $\frac{6}{6} = 1$ The reciprocal of $\frac{3}{2}$ is $\frac{2}{3}$. The reciprocal of $\frac{2}{3}$ is $\frac{3}{2}$.
8. $\frac{4}{5} \times \frac{5}{4} =$ $\frac{20}{20} = 1$ The reciprocal of $\frac{4}{5}$ is $\frac{5}{4}$. The reciprocal of $\frac{5}{4}$ is $\frac{4}{5}$.
9. $\frac{9}{10} \times \frac{10}{9} =$ $\frac{90}{90} = 1$ The reciprocal of $\frac{9}{10}$ is $\frac{10}{9}$. The reciprocal of $\frac{10}{9}$ is $\frac{9}{10}$.
10. $\frac{15}{4} \times \frac{4}{15} =$ $\frac{60}{60} = 1$ The reciprocal of $\frac{15}{4}$ is $\frac{4}{15}$. The reciprocal of $\frac{4}{15}$ is $\frac{15}{4}$.

B Name the reciprocal of each number.

1. $\frac{1}{2}$	2	2. $\frac{14}{13}$	$\frac{13}{14}$	3. $\frac{17}{15}$	$\frac{15}{17}$	4. $\frac{7}{9}$	$\frac{9}{7}$
5. $\frac{3}{4}$	$\frac{4}{3}$	6. $\frac{25}{24}$	$\frac{24}{25}$	7. 12	$\frac{1}{12}$	8. 10	$\frac{1}{10}$
9. $\frac{6}{5}$	$\frac{5}{6}$	10. $\frac{15}{11}$	$\frac{11}{15}$	11. $\frac{40}{39}$	$\frac{39}{40}$	12. $\frac{5}{8}$	$\frac{8}{5}$
13. $\frac{12}{7}$	$\frac{7}{12}$	14. 6	$\frac{1}{6}$	15. $\frac{1}{3}$	3	16. $\frac{1}{12}$	12

If the product of two numbers is *one*, the numbers are said to be *reciprocals* of each other.

Back Page Exercises Find the reciprocals of the following: 3, 3/8, 9/13, 4/17, 62, 31/43, 99/102, 78, and 15/78.

Reciprocals

The Idea

If the product of two numbers is one, the numbers are said to be reciprocals of each other.

How to Use the Idea

$$3 \times \frac{1}{3} = \frac{3}{3} = 1$$

Three is the reciprocal of $\frac{1}{3}$, and $\frac{1}{3}$ is the reciprocal of three. For two numbers to be reciprocals, the numerator of the first must be the same number as the denominator of the second. The denominator of the first must be the same number as the numerator of the second.

A Show that each pair of numbers is reciprocal.

1. $\frac{1}{2} \times \frac{2}{1} =$ $\frac{2}{2} = 1$ The reciprocal of $\frac{1}{2}$ is 2. The reciprocal of 2 is $\frac{1}{2}$.
2. $\frac{5}{1} \times \frac{1}{5} =$ ______ The reciprocal of 5 is ______. The reciprocal of $\frac{1}{5}$ is ______.
3. $\frac{1}{4} \times \frac{4}{1} =$ ______ The reciprocal of $\frac{1}{4}$ is ______. The reciprocal of 4 is ______.
4. $\frac{25}{1} \times \frac{1}{25} =$ ______ The reciprocal of 25 is ______. The reciprocal of $\frac{1}{25}$ is ______.
5. $\frac{100}{1} \times \frac{1}{100} =$ ______ The reciprocal of 100 is ______. The reciprocal of $\frac{1}{100}$ is ______.
6. $\frac{1}{18} \times \frac{18}{1} =$ ______ The reciprocal of $\frac{1}{18}$ is ______. The reciprocal of 18 is ______.
7. $\frac{3}{2} \times \frac{2}{3} =$ ______ The reciprocal of $\frac{3}{2}$ is ______. The reciprocal of $\frac{2}{3}$ is ______.
8. $\frac{4}{5} \times \frac{5}{4} =$ ______ The reciprocal of $\frac{4}{5}$ is ______. The reciprocal of $\frac{5}{4}$ is ______.
9. $\frac{9}{10} \times \frac{10}{9} =$ ______ The reciprocal of $\frac{9}{10}$ is ______. The reciprocal of $\frac{10}{9}$ is ______.
10. $\frac{15}{4} \times \frac{4}{15} =$ ______ The reciprocal of $\frac{15}{4}$ is ______. The reciprocal of $\frac{4}{15}$ is ______.

B Name the reciprocal of each number.

1. $\frac{1}{2}$ 2	2. $\frac{14}{13}$ ______	3. $\frac{17}{15}$ ______	4. $\frac{7}{9}$ ______
5. $\frac{3}{4}$ ______	6. $\frac{25}{24}$ ______	7. 12 ______	8. 10 ______
9. $\frac{6}{5}$ ______	10. $\frac{15}{11}$ ______	11. $\frac{40}{39}$ ______	12. $\frac{5}{8}$ ______
13. $\frac{12}{7}$ ______	14. 6 ______	15. $\frac{1}{3}$ ______	16. $\frac{1}{12}$ ______

If the product of two numbers is ______, the numbers are said to be ______ of each other.

Back Page Exercises Find the reciprocals of the following: 3, 3/8, 9/13, 4/17, 62, 31/43, 99/102, 78, and 15/78.

Mixed Numbers 50

The Idea

A mixed number is a whole number and a fraction together. A mixed number can be changed into an improper fraction, in which the numerator is larger than the denominator. And, an improper fraction can be written as a mixed number.

How to Use the Idea

a. $2\frac{1}{2} = \frac{(2 \times 2) + 1}{2} = \frac{5}{2}$

b. $\frac{7}{3} = 2\frac{1}{3}$

A Change each mixed number to a improper fraction.

1. $1\frac{1}{2} = \frac{3}{2}$
2. $1\frac{1}{3} = \frac{4}{3}$
3. $1\frac{2}{3} = \frac{5}{3}$
4. $3\frac{2}{3} = \frac{11}{3}$
5. $4\frac{1}{5} = \frac{21}{5}$
6. $2\frac{1}{4} = \frac{9}{4}$
7. $5\frac{1}{2} = \frac{11}{2}$
8. $3\frac{1}{5} = \frac{16}{5}$
9. $4\frac{1}{2} = \frac{9}{2}$
10. $1\frac{1}{10} = \frac{11}{10}$
11. $2\frac{5}{6} = \frac{17}{6}$
12. $6\frac{1}{3} = \frac{19}{3}$
13. $7\frac{3}{5} = \frac{38}{5}$
14. $4\frac{5}{6} = \frac{29}{6}$
15. $1\frac{7}{8} = \frac{15}{8}$
16. $3\frac{9}{10} = \frac{39}{10}$
17. $4\frac{4}{5} = \frac{24}{5}$
18. $1\frac{5}{6} = \frac{11}{6}$
19. $3\frac{5}{12} = \frac{41}{12}$
20. $2\frac{7}{8} = \frac{23}{8}$
21. $3\frac{1}{8} = \frac{25}{8}$
22. $5\frac{4}{5} = \frac{29}{5}$
23. $20\frac{1}{4} = \frac{81}{4}$
24. $15\frac{2}{3} = \frac{47}{3}$
25. $10\frac{9}{10} = \frac{109}{10}$
26. $4\frac{6}{7} = \frac{34}{7}$
27. $5\frac{7}{8} = \frac{47}{8}$
28. $3\frac{1}{8} = \frac{25}{8}$

B Change each improper fraction to a mixed number.

1. $\frac{5}{2} = 2\frac{1}{2}$
2. $\frac{6}{5} = 1\frac{1}{5}$
3. $\frac{7}{3} = 2\frac{1}{3}$
4. $\frac{5}{4} = 1\frac{1}{4}$
5. $\frac{3}{2} = 1\frac{1}{2}$
6. $\frac{8}{5} = 1\frac{3}{5}$
7. $\frac{10}{9} = 1\frac{1}{9}$
8. $\frac{4}{3} = 1\frac{1}{3}$
9. $\frac{9}{8} = 1\frac{1}{8}$
10. $\frac{7}{2} = 3\frac{1}{2}$
11. $\frac{8}{3} = 2\frac{2}{3}$
12. $\frac{9}{4} = 2\frac{1}{4}$
13. $\frac{11}{5} = 2\frac{1}{5}$
14. $\frac{17}{6} = 2\frac{5}{6}$
15. $\frac{21}{20} = 1\frac{1}{20}$
16. $\frac{23}{20} = 1\frac{3}{20}$
17. $\frac{8}{5} = 1\frac{3}{5}$
18. $\frac{7}{6} = 1\frac{1}{6}$
19. $\frac{10}{3} = 3\frac{1}{3}$
20. $\frac{15}{7} = 2\frac{1}{7}$
21. $\frac{16}{5} = 3\frac{1}{5}$
22. $\frac{23}{10} = 2\frac{3}{10}$
23. $\frac{6}{2} = 3$
24. $\frac{21}{7} = 3$
25. $\frac{16}{3} = 5\frac{1}{3}$
26. $\frac{16}{4} = 4$
27. $\frac{100}{33} = 3\frac{1}{33}$
28. $\frac{50}{7} = 7\frac{1}{7}$

A ___*mixed*___ number is a whole number and a fraction together.

Back Page Exercises Write ten mixed numbers. Change them to improper fractions. Write ten improper fractions. Change them into mixed numbers.

Mixed Numbers

The Idea

A mixed number is a whole number and a fraction together. A mixed number can be changed into an improper fraction, in which the numerator is larger than the denominator. And, an improper fraction can be written as a mixed number.

How to Use the Idea a. $2\frac{1}{2} = \frac{(2 \times 2) + 1}{2} = \frac{5}{2}$ b. $\frac{7}{3} = 2\frac{1}{3}$

A Change each mixed number to a improper fraction.

① $1\frac{1}{2} = \frac{3}{2}$	⑧ $3\frac{1}{5} =$	⑮ $1\frac{7}{8} =$	㉒ $5\frac{4}{5} =$
② $1\frac{1}{3} =$	⑨ $4\frac{1}{2} =$	⑯ $3\frac{9}{10} =$	㉓ $20\frac{1}{4} =$
③ $1\frac{2}{3} =$	⑩ $1\frac{1}{10} =$	⑰ $4\frac{4}{5} =$	㉔ $15\frac{2}{3} =$
④ $3\frac{2}{3} =$	⑪ $2\frac{5}{6} =$	⑱ $1\frac{5}{6} =$	㉕ $10\frac{9}{10} =$
⑤ $4\frac{1}{5} =$	⑫ $6\frac{1}{3} =$	⑲ $3\frac{5}{12} =$	㉖ $4\frac{6}{7} =$
⑥ $2\frac{1}{4} =$	⑬ $7\frac{3}{5} =$	⑳ $2\frac{7}{8} =$	㉗ $5\frac{7}{8} =$
⑦ $5\frac{1}{2} =$	⑭ $4\frac{5}{6} =$	㉑ $3\frac{1}{8} =$	㉘ $3\frac{1}{8} =$

B Change each improper fraction to a mixed number.

① $\frac{5}{2} = 2\frac{1}{2}$	⑧ $\frac{4}{3} =$	⑮ $\frac{21}{20} =$	㉒ $\frac{23}{10} =$
② $\frac{6}{5} =$	⑨ $\frac{9}{8} =$	⑯ $\frac{23}{20} =$	㉓ $\frac{6}{2} =$
③ $\frac{7}{3} =$	⑩ $\frac{7}{2} =$	⑰ $\frac{8}{5} =$	㉔ $\frac{21}{7} =$
④ $\frac{5}{4} =$	⑪ $\frac{8}{3} =$	⑱ $\frac{7}{6} =$	㉕ $\frac{16}{3} =$
⑤ $\frac{3}{2} =$	⑫ $\frac{9}{4} =$	⑲ $\frac{10}{3} =$	㉖ $\frac{16}{4} =$
⑥ $\frac{8}{5} =$	⑬ $\frac{11}{5} =$	⑳ $\frac{15}{7} =$	㉗ $\frac{100}{33} =$
⑦ $\frac{10}{9} =$	⑭ $\frac{17}{6} =$	㉑ $\frac{16}{5} =$	㉘ $\frac{50}{7} =$

A ________________ number is a whole number and a fraction together.

Back Page Exercises Write ten mixed numbers. Change them to improper fractions. Write ten improper fractions. Change them into mixed numbers.

The Idea

To add mixed numbers, we must find a common denominator. A common denominator is a number which is divisible by all the denominators in the problem.

How to Use the Idea

a. $$\begin{aligned} 1\tfrac{1}{2} &= 1\tfrac{2}{4} \\ +2\tfrac{1}{4} &= 2\tfrac{1}{4} \\ \hline & 3\tfrac{3}{4} \end{aligned}$$

b. $$\begin{aligned} 3\tfrac{3}{5} &= 3\tfrac{12}{20} \\ +1\tfrac{3}{4} &= 1\tfrac{15}{20} \\ \hline & 4\tfrac{27}{20} = 5\tfrac{7}{20} \end{aligned}$$

c. $$\begin{aligned} 16\tfrac{1}{3} &= 16\tfrac{8}{24} \\ +\ 4\tfrac{1}{8} &= 4\tfrac{3}{24} \\ \hline & 20\tfrac{11}{24} \end{aligned}$$

Find the sums.

① $$\begin{aligned} 2\tfrac{1}{4} &= 2\tfrac{3}{12} \\ +1\tfrac{1}{6} &= 1\tfrac{2}{12} \\ \hline & 3\tfrac{5}{12} \end{aligned}$$

② $$\begin{aligned} 6\tfrac{1}{5} &= 6\tfrac{2}{10} \\ +3\tfrac{1}{2} &= 3\tfrac{5}{10} \\ \hline & 9\tfrac{7}{10} \end{aligned}$$

③ $$\begin{aligned} 1\tfrac{1}{6} &= 1\tfrac{5}{30} \\ +2\tfrac{1}{5} &= 2\tfrac{6}{30} \\ \hline & 3\tfrac{11}{30} \end{aligned}$$

④ $$\begin{aligned} 5\tfrac{2}{5} &= 5\tfrac{6}{15} \\ +6\tfrac{2}{3} &= 6\tfrac{10}{15} \\ \hline & 11\tfrac{16}{15} = 12\tfrac{1}{15} \end{aligned}$$

⑤ $$\begin{aligned} 6\tfrac{1}{25} &= 6\tfrac{2}{50} \\ +9\tfrac{3}{10} &= 9\tfrac{15}{50} \\ \hline & 15\tfrac{17}{50} \end{aligned}$$

⑥ $$\begin{aligned} 18\tfrac{1}{6} &= 18\tfrac{2}{12} \\ +\ 7\tfrac{3}{4} &= 7\tfrac{9}{12} \\ \hline & 25\tfrac{11}{12} \end{aligned}$$

⑦ $$\begin{aligned} 21\tfrac{3}{20} &= 21\tfrac{9}{60} \\ +14\tfrac{2}{15} &= 14\tfrac{8}{60} \\ \hline & 35\tfrac{17}{60} \end{aligned}$$

⑧ $$\begin{aligned} 16\tfrac{1}{2} &= 16\tfrac{5}{10} \\ +31\tfrac{3}{10} &= 31\tfrac{3}{10} \\ \hline & 47\tfrac{8}{10} = 47\tfrac{4}{5} \end{aligned}$$

⑨ $$\begin{aligned} 1\tfrac{1}{4} &= 1\tfrac{3}{12} \\ 2\tfrac{1}{3} &= 2\tfrac{4}{12} \\ +6\tfrac{1}{2} &= 6\tfrac{6}{12} \\ \hline & 9\tfrac{13}{12} = 10\tfrac{1}{12} \end{aligned}$$

⑩ $$\begin{aligned} 7\tfrac{1}{6} &= 7\tfrac{5}{30} \\ 2\tfrac{2}{5} &= 2\tfrac{12}{30} \\ +1\tfrac{1}{3} &= 1\tfrac{10}{30} \\ \hline & 10\tfrac{27}{30} = 10\tfrac{9}{10} \end{aligned}$$

⑪ $$\begin{aligned} 14\tfrac{1}{7} &= 14\tfrac{6}{42} \\ 2\tfrac{2}{3} &= 2\tfrac{28}{42} \\ +\ 8\tfrac{1}{2} &= 8\tfrac{21}{42} \\ \hline & 24\tfrac{55}{42} = 25\tfrac{13}{42} \end{aligned}$$

⑫ $$\begin{aligned} 4\tfrac{1}{6} &= 4\tfrac{2}{12} \\ 2\tfrac{1}{4} &= 2\tfrac{3}{12} \\ +3\tfrac{1}{12} &= 3\tfrac{1}{12} \\ \hline & 9\tfrac{6}{12} = 9\tfrac{1}{2} \end{aligned}$$

⑬ $$\begin{aligned} 16\tfrac{1}{5} &= 16\tfrac{14}{70} \\ 4\tfrac{2}{7} &= 4\tfrac{20}{70} \\ 5\tfrac{1}{2} &= 5\tfrac{35}{70} \\ +\ 3\tfrac{3}{14} &= 3\tfrac{15}{70} \\ \hline & 28\tfrac{84}{70} = 29\tfrac{1}{5} \end{aligned}$$

⑭ $$\begin{aligned} 7\tfrac{8}{9} &= 7\tfrac{32}{36} \\ 1\tfrac{1}{2} &= 1\tfrac{18}{36} \\ 3\tfrac{3}{4} &= 3\tfrac{27}{36} \\ +2\tfrac{1}{6} &= 2\tfrac{6}{36} \\ \hline & 13\tfrac{83}{36} = 15\tfrac{11}{36} \end{aligned}$$

⑮ $$\begin{aligned} 3\tfrac{1}{10} &= 3\tfrac{5}{50} \\ 2\tfrac{1}{5} &= 2\tfrac{10}{50} \\ 5\tfrac{1}{2} &= 5\tfrac{25}{50} \\ +6\tfrac{1}{25} &= 6\tfrac{2}{50} \\ \hline & 16\tfrac{42}{50} = 16\tfrac{21}{25} \end{aligned}$$

⑯ $$\begin{aligned} 6\tfrac{1}{10} &= 6\tfrac{10}{100} \\ 3\tfrac{1}{4} &= 3\tfrac{25}{100} \\ 5\tfrac{3}{25} &= 5\tfrac{12}{100} \\ +12\tfrac{1}{2} &= 12\tfrac{50}{100} \\ \hline & 26\tfrac{97}{100} \end{aligned}$$

A *common denominator* is a number which is divisible by *all* the denominators in the problem.

Back Page Exercises Create ten problems adding mixed numbers.

Adding Mixed Numbers

The Idea

To add mixed numbers, we must find a common denominator. A common denominator is a number which is divisible by all the denominators in the problem.

How to Use the Idea

a. $1\frac{1}{2} = 1\frac{2}{4}$
$+2\frac{1}{4} = 2\frac{1}{4}$
$3\frac{3}{4}$

b. $3\frac{3}{5} = 3\frac{12}{20}$
$+1\frac{3}{4} = 1\frac{15}{20}$
$4\frac{27}{20} = 5\frac{7}{20}$

c. $16\frac{1}{3} = 16\frac{8}{24}$
$+\ 4\frac{1}{8} = 4\frac{3}{24}$
$20\frac{11}{24}$

Find the sums.

① $2\frac{1}{4} = 2\frac{3}{12}$
$+1\frac{1}{6} = 1\frac{2}{12}$
$3\frac{5}{12}$

② $6\frac{1}{5} =$
$+3\frac{1}{2} =$

③ $1\frac{1}{6} =$
$+2\frac{1}{5} =$

④ $5\frac{2}{5} =$
$+6\frac{2}{3} =$

⑤ $6\frac{1}{25} =$
$+9\frac{3}{10} =$

⑥ $18\frac{1}{6} =$
$+\ 7\frac{3}{4} =$

⑦ $21\frac{3}{20} =$
$+14\frac{2}{15} =$

⑧ $16\frac{1}{2} =$
$+31\frac{3}{10} =$

⑨ $1\frac{1}{4} =$
$2\frac{1}{3} =$
$+6\frac{1}{2} =$

⑩ $7\frac{1}{6} =$
$2\frac{2}{5} =$
$+1\frac{1}{3} =$

⑪ $14\frac{1}{7} =$
$2\frac{2}{3} =$
$+\ 8\frac{1}{2} =$

⑫ $4\frac{1}{6} =$
$2\frac{1}{4} =$
$+3\frac{1}{12} =$

⑬ $16\frac{1}{5} =$
$4\frac{2}{7} =$
$5\frac{1}{2} =$
$+\ 3\frac{3}{14} =$

⑭ $7\frac{8}{9} =$
$1\frac{1}{2} =$
$3\frac{3}{4} =$
$+2\frac{1}{6} =$

⑮ $3\frac{1}{10} =$
$2\frac{1}{5} =$
$5\frac{1}{2} =$
$+6\frac{1}{25} =$

⑯ $6\frac{1}{10} =$
$3\frac{1}{4} =$
$5\frac{3}{25} =$
$+12\frac{1}{2} =$

A ______________________ is a number which is divisible by ______________________ the denominators in the problem.

Back Page Exercises Create ten problems adding mixed numbers.

Subtracting Mixed Numbers

The Idea

A common denominator is a number which is divisible by the denominators of both fractions. If the fraction to be subtracted is a larger fraction, then we must borrow from the whole number.

How to Use the Idea

$$\begin{array}{r} 4\frac{1}{2} = 4\frac{2}{4} \\ -1\frac{1}{4} = 1\frac{1}{4} \\ \hline 3\frac{1}{4} \end{array}$$

$$\begin{array}{r} 6\frac{1}{3} = 6\frac{2}{6} = 5 + \frac{6}{6} + \frac{2}{6} = 5\frac{8}{6} \\ -4\frac{5}{6} = 4\frac{5}{6} = 4\frac{5}{6} \qquad\qquad = 4\frac{5}{6} \\ \hline 1\frac{3}{6} = 1\frac{1}{2} \end{array}$$

Find the remainders.

① $5\frac{3}{4} = 5\frac{3}{4}$, $-3\frac{1}{2} = 3\frac{2}{4}$, $2\frac{1}{4}$

② $6\frac{2}{5} = 6\frac{4}{10}$, $-3\frac{3}{10} = 3\frac{3}{10}$, $3\frac{1}{10}$

③ $9\frac{5}{6} = 9\frac{5}{6}$, $-7\frac{1}{3} = 7\frac{2}{6}$, $2\frac{3}{6} = 2\frac{1}{2}$

④ $4\frac{7}{8} = 4\frac{7}{8}$, $-2\frac{1}{2} = 2\frac{4}{8}$, $2\frac{3}{8}$

⑤ $4\frac{3}{16} = 4\frac{3}{16}$, $-2\frac{1}{8} = 2\frac{2}{16}$, $2\frac{1}{16}$

⑥ $7\frac{3}{4} = 7\frac{9}{12}$, $-2\frac{1}{3} = 2\frac{4}{12}$, $5\frac{5}{12}$

⑦ $16\frac{9}{10} = 16\frac{9}{10}$, $-3\frac{2}{5} = 3\frac{4}{10}$, $13\frac{5}{10} = 13\frac{1}{2}$

⑧ $4\frac{5}{8} = 4\frac{15}{24}$, $-2\frac{1}{3} = 2\frac{8}{24}$, $2\frac{7}{24}$

⑨ $10\frac{7}{10} = 10\frac{14}{20}$, $-2\frac{1}{4} = 2\frac{5}{20}$, $8\frac{9}{20}$

⑩ $17\frac{11}{12} = 17\frac{11}{12}$, $-11\frac{5}{6} = 11\frac{10}{12}$, $6\frac{1}{12}$

⑪ $24\frac{2}{7} = 24\frac{8}{28}$, $-13\frac{1}{4} = 13\frac{7}{28}$, $11\frac{1}{28}$

⑫ $15\frac{1}{3} = 15\frac{4}{12}$, $-3\frac{1}{12} = 3\frac{1}{12}$, $12\frac{3}{12} = 12\frac{1}{4}$

⑬ $67\frac{1}{4} = 67\frac{3}{12} = 66\frac{15}{12}$, $-60\frac{1}{3} = 60\frac{4}{12} = 60\frac{4}{12}$, $6\frac{11}{12}$

⑭ $23\frac{1}{6} = 23\frac{4}{24} = 22\frac{28}{24}$, $-18\frac{3}{8} = 18\frac{9}{24} = 18\frac{9}{24}$, $4\frac{19}{24}$

⑮ $29\frac{1}{2} = 29\frac{5}{10} = 28\frac{15}{10}$, $-14\frac{3}{5} = 14\frac{6}{10} = 14\frac{6}{10}$, $14\frac{9}{10}$

A common denominator is a number divisible by ___*both*___ denominators.

Back Page Exercises Create ten problems subtracting mixed numbers.

Subtracting Mixed Numbers

The Idea

A common denominator is a number which is divisible by the denominators of both fractions. If the fraction to be subtracted is a larger fraction, then we must borrow from the whole number.

How to Use the Idea

$$\begin{array}{r} 4\frac{1}{2} = 4\frac{2}{4} \\ -1\frac{1}{4} = 1\frac{1}{4} \\ \hline 3\frac{1}{4} \end{array}$$

$$\begin{array}{r} 6\frac{1}{3} = 6\frac{2}{6} = 5 + \frac{6}{6} + \frac{2}{6} = 5\frac{8}{6} \\ -4\frac{5}{6} = 4\frac{5}{6} = 4\frac{5}{6} \qquad = 4\frac{5}{6} \\ \hline 1\frac{3}{6} = 1\frac{1}{2} \end{array}$$

Find the remainders.

① $5\frac{3}{4} = 5\frac{3}{4}$; $-3\frac{1}{2} = 3\frac{2}{4}$; $2\frac{1}{4}$

② $6\frac{2}{5} =$; $-3\frac{3}{10} =$

③ $9\frac{5}{6} =$; $-7\frac{1}{3} =$

④ $4\frac{7}{8} =$; $-2\frac{1}{2} =$

⑤ $4\frac{3}{16} =$; $-2\frac{1}{8} =$

⑥ $7\frac{3}{4} =$; $-2\frac{1}{3} =$

⑦ $16\frac{9}{10} =$; $-3\frac{2}{5} =$

⑧ $4\frac{5}{8} =$; $-2\frac{1}{3} =$

⑨ $10\frac{7}{10} =$; $-2\frac{1}{4} =$

⑩ $17\frac{11}{12} =$; $-11\frac{5}{6} =$

⑪ $24\frac{2}{7} =$; $-13\frac{1}{4} =$

⑫ $15\frac{1}{3} =$; $-3\frac{1}{12} =$

⑬ $67\frac{1}{4} = \quad =$; $-60\frac{1}{3} = \_\_\_ =$

⑭ $23\frac{1}{6} = \quad =$; $-18\frac{3}{8} = \_\_\_ =$

⑮ $29\frac{1}{2} = \quad =$; $-14\frac{3}{5} = \_\_\_ =$

A common denominator is a number divisible by ______________ denominators.

Back Page Exercises Create ten problems subtracting mixed numbers.

Multiplying Mixed Numbers

The Idea

A mixed number is made of both a whole number and a fraction.

How to Use the Idea

When we multiply mixed numbers, it is easiest to change mixed numbers to improper fractions. Then we multiply numerator times numerator and denominator times denominator. There is a shortcut to multiplying fractions. If one of the numerators has a factor in common with a denominator, we can divide by that factor.

$$1\frac{1}{3} \times 2\frac{2}{5} = \frac{4}{\underset{1}{\cancel{3}}} \times \frac{\overset{4}{\cancel{12}}}{5} = \frac{16}{5} = 3\frac{1}{5}$$

$$3\frac{1}{2} \times 1\frac{1}{7} = \frac{\overset{1}{\cancel{7}}}{\underset{1}{\cancel{2}}} \times \frac{\overset{4}{\cancel{8}}}{\underset{1}{\cancel{7}}} = 4$$

Find the products.

① $5\frac{1}{6} \times 1\frac{2}{3} = \frac{31}{6} \times \frac{5}{3} = \frac{155}{18} = 8\frac{11}{18}$

② $2\frac{2}{7} \times 1\frac{1}{4} = \frac{\overset{4}{\cancel{16}}}{7} \times \frac{5}{\underset{1}{\cancel{4}}} = \frac{20}{7} = 2\frac{6}{7}$

③ $2\frac{2}{5} \times 3\frac{1}{3} = \frac{\overset{4}{\cancel{12}}}{\underset{1}{\cancel{5}}} \times \frac{\overset{2}{\cancel{10}}}{\underset{1}{\cancel{3}}} = 8$

④ $6\frac{2}{3} \times 1\frac{1}{10} = \frac{\overset{2}{\cancel{20}}}{3} \times \frac{11}{\underset{1}{\cancel{10}}} = \frac{22}{3} = 7\frac{1}{3}$

⑤ $4\frac{1}{2} \times 1\frac{1}{5} = \frac{9}{\underset{1}{\cancel{2}}} \times \frac{\overset{3}{\cancel{6}}}{5} = \frac{27}{5} = 5\frac{2}{5}$

⑥ $1\frac{3}{4} \times 1\frac{1}{7} = \frac{\overset{1}{\cancel{7}}}{\underset{1}{\cancel{4}}} \times \frac{\overset{2}{\cancel{8}}}{\underset{1}{\cancel{7}}} = 2$

⑦ $5\frac{1}{3} \times 1\frac{1}{8} = \frac{\overset{2}{\cancel{16}}}{\underset{1}{\cancel{3}}} \times \frac{\overset{3}{\cancel{9}}}{\underset{1}{\cancel{8}}} = 6$

⑧ $1\frac{1}{3} \times 1\frac{1}{3} = \frac{4}{3} \times \frac{4}{3} = \frac{16}{9} = 1\frac{7}{9}$

⑨ $4\frac{2}{3} \times 3 = \frac{14}{\underset{1}{\cancel{3}}} \times \frac{\overset{1}{\cancel{3}}}{1} = 14$

⑩ $1\frac{1}{5} \times 1\frac{1}{5} = \frac{6}{5} \times \frac{6}{5} = \frac{36}{25} = 1\frac{11}{25}$

⑪ $2\frac{1}{10} \times 1\frac{2}{3} = \frac{\overset{7}{\cancel{21}}}{\underset{2}{\cancel{10}}} \times \frac{\overset{1}{\cancel{5}}}{\underset{1}{\cancel{3}}} = \frac{7}{2} = 3\frac{1}{2}$

⑫ $4 \times 2\frac{2}{3} = \frac{4}{1} \times \frac{8}{3} = \frac{32}{3} = 10\frac{2}{3}$

⑬ $3\frac{1}{4} \times 2\frac{1}{2} = \frac{13}{4} \times \frac{5}{2} = \frac{65}{8} = 8\frac{1}{8}$

⑭ $5\frac{1}{4} \times 2 = \frac{21}{\underset{2}{\cancel{4}}} \times \frac{\overset{1}{\cancel{2}}}{1} = \frac{21}{2} = 10\frac{1}{2}$

⑮ $1\frac{1}{2} \times 1\frac{1}{2} = \frac{3}{2} \times \frac{3}{2} = \frac{9}{4} = 2\frac{1}{4}$

⑯ $3\frac{1}{3} \times 1\frac{3}{10} = \frac{\overset{1}{\cancel{10}}}{3} \times \frac{13}{\underset{1}{\cancel{10}}} = \frac{13}{3} = 4\frac{1}{3}$

A *mixed* number is made of both a *whole* number and a *fraction*.

Back Page Exercises Create ten problems similar to those above. Work them.

Multiplying Mixed Numbers

The Idea

A mixed number is made of both a whole number and a fraction.

How to Use the Idea

When we multiply mixed numbers, it is easiest to change mixed numbers to improper fractions. Then we multiply numerator times numerator and denominator times denominator. There is a shortcut to multiplying fractions. If one of the numerators has a factor in common with a denominator, we can divide by that factor.

$$1\frac{1}{3} \times 2\frac{2}{5} = \frac{4}{\cancel{3}_1} \times \frac{\cancel{12}^4}{5} = \frac{16}{5} = 3\frac{1}{5}$$

$$3\frac{1}{2} \times 1\frac{1}{7} = \frac{\cancel{7}^1}{\cancel{2}_1} \times \frac{\cancel{8}^4}{\cancel{7}_1} = 4$$

Find the products.

① $5\frac{1}{6} \times 1\frac{2}{3} = \frac{31}{6} \times \frac{5}{3} = \frac{155}{18} = 8\frac{11}{18}$

② $2\frac{2}{7} \times 1\frac{1}{4} =$

③ $2\frac{2}{5} \times 3\frac{1}{3} =$

④ $6\frac{2}{3} \times 1\frac{1}{10} =$

⑤ $4\frac{1}{2} \times 1\frac{1}{5} =$

⑥ $1\frac{3}{4} \times 1\frac{1}{7} =$

⑦ $5\frac{1}{3} \times 1\frac{1}{8} =$

⑧ $1\frac{1}{3} \times 1\frac{1}{3} =$

⑨ $4\frac{2}{3} \times 3 =$

⑩ $1\frac{1}{5} \times 1\frac{1}{5} =$

⑪ $2\frac{1}{10} \times 1\frac{2}{3} =$

⑫ $4 \times 2\frac{2}{3} =$

⑬ $3\frac{1}{4} \times 2\frac{1}{2} =$

⑭ $5\frac{1}{4} \times 2 =$

⑮ $1\frac{1}{2} \times 1\frac{1}{2} =$

⑯ $3\frac{1}{3} \times 1\frac{3}{10} =$

A ______________________ number is made of both a ____________________ number and a ____________________.

Back Page Exercises Create ten problems similar to those above. Work them.

Dividing Mixed Numbers

The Idea

An improper fraction has a numerator that is larger than its denominator.

How to Use the Idea

To divide with mixed numbers, we change them to improper fractions, then invert the divisor and multiply.

$$1\frac{3}{5} \div 1\frac{1}{10} = \frac{8}{5} \div \frac{11}{10} = \frac{8}{5} \times \frac{10}{11} = \frac{8}{5} \times \frac{2 \times 5}{11} = \frac{8}{1} \times \frac{2}{11} = \frac{16}{11} = 1\frac{5}{11}$$

$$1\frac{2}{3} \div 2\frac{1}{2} = \frac{5}{3} \div \frac{5}{2} = \frac{5}{3} \times \frac{2}{5} = \frac{\overset{1}{\cancel{5}} \times 2}{3 \times \underset{1}{\cancel{5}}} = \frac{2}{3}$$

Find the quotients.

① $4\frac{1}{2} \div 2\frac{2}{5} = \frac{9}{2} \div \frac{12}{5} = \frac{9}{2} \times \frac{5}{12} = \frac{\overset{3}{\cancel{9}} \times 5}{2 \times \underset{4}{\cancel{12}}} = \frac{15}{8} = 1\frac{7}{8}$

② $2\frac{2}{5} \div 4\frac{1}{2} = \frac{12}{5} \div \frac{9}{2} = \frac{\overset{4}{\cancel{12}}}{5} \times \frac{2}{\underset{3}{\cancel{9}}} = \frac{8}{15}$

③ $1\frac{1}{2} \div 1\frac{1}{2} = \frac{3}{2} \div \frac{3}{2} = \frac{\overset{1}{\cancel{3}}}{\underset{1}{\cancel{2}}} \times \frac{\overset{1}{\cancel{2}}}{\underset{1}{\cancel{3}}} = 1$

④ $2\frac{2}{3} \div 1\frac{3}{5} = \frac{8}{3} \div \frac{8}{5} = \frac{\overset{1}{\cancel{8}}}{3} \times \frac{5}{\underset{1}{\cancel{8}}} = \frac{5}{3} = 1\frac{2}{3}$

⑤ $1\frac{3}{5} \div 2\frac{2}{3} = \frac{8}{5} \div \frac{8}{3} = \frac{\overset{1}{\cancel{8}}}{5} \times \frac{3}{\underset{1}{\cancel{8}}} = \frac{3}{5}$

⑥ $3\frac{3}{4} \div 1\frac{1}{5} = \frac{15}{4} \div \frac{6}{5} = \frac{\overset{5}{\cancel{15}}}{4} \times \frac{5}{\underset{2}{\cancel{6}}} = \frac{25}{8} = 3\frac{1}{8}$

⑦ $2\frac{1}{5} \div 1\frac{1}{3} = \frac{11}{5} \div \frac{4}{3} = \frac{11}{5} \times \frac{3}{4} = \frac{33}{20} = 1\frac{13}{20}$

⑧ $1\frac{1}{3} \div 2\frac{1}{5} = \frac{4}{3} \div \frac{11}{5} = \frac{4}{3} \times \frac{5}{11} = \frac{20}{33}$

⑨ $5\frac{1}{5} \div 1\frac{1}{2} = \frac{26}{5} \div \frac{3}{2} = \frac{26}{5} \times \frac{2}{3} = \frac{52}{15} = 3\frac{7}{15}$

⑩ $1\frac{1}{2} \div 5\frac{1}{5} = \frac{3}{2} \div \frac{26}{5} = \frac{3}{2} \times \frac{5}{26} = \frac{15}{52}$

⑪ $2\frac{2}{3} \div 2\frac{3}{4} = \frac{8}{3} \div \frac{11}{4} = \frac{8}{3} \times \frac{4}{11} = \frac{32}{33}$

⑫ $4\frac{1}{5} \div 3\frac{1}{3} = \frac{21}{5} \div \frac{10}{3} = \frac{21}{5} \times \frac{3}{10} = \frac{63}{50} = 1\frac{13}{50}$

An ___*improper*___ fraction has a ___*numerator*___ that is larger than its ___*denominator*___.

Back Page Exercises Create ten problems similar to those above. Work them.

Dividing Mixed Numbers

The Idea

An improper fraction has a numerator that is larger than its denominator.

How to Use the Idea

To divide with mixed numbers, we change them to improper fractions, then invert the divisor and multiply.

$$1\frac{3}{5} \div 1\frac{1}{10} = \frac{8}{5} \div \frac{11}{10} = \frac{8}{5} \times \frac{10}{11} = \frac{8}{5} \times \frac{2 \times 5}{11} = \frac{8}{1} \times \frac{2}{11} = \frac{16}{11} = 1\frac{5}{11}$$

$$1\frac{2}{3} \div 2\frac{1}{2} = \frac{5}{3} \div \frac{5}{2} = \frac{5}{3} \times \frac{2}{5} = \frac{\overset{1}{\cancel{5}} \times 2}{3 \times \underset{1}{\cancel{5}}} = \frac{2}{3}$$

Find the quotients.

① $4\frac{1}{2} \div 2\frac{2}{5} = \frac{9}{2} \div \frac{12}{5} = \frac{9}{2} \times \frac{5}{12} = \frac{\overset{3}{\cancel{9}} \times 5}{2 \times \underset{4}{\cancel{12}}} = \frac{15}{8} = 1\frac{7}{8}$

② $2\frac{2}{5} \div 4\frac{1}{2} =$

③ $1\frac{1}{2} \div 1\frac{1}{2} =$

④ $2\frac{2}{3} \div 1\frac{3}{5} =$

⑤ $1\frac{3}{5} \div 2\frac{2}{3} =$

⑥ $3\frac{3}{4} \div 1\frac{1}{5} =$

⑦ $2\frac{1}{5} \div 1\frac{1}{3} =$

⑧ $1\frac{1}{3} \div 2\frac{1}{5} =$

⑨ $5\frac{1}{5} \div 1\frac{1}{2} =$

⑩ $1\frac{1}{2} \div 5\frac{1}{5} =$

⑪ $2\frac{2}{3} \div 2\frac{3}{4} =$

⑫ $4\frac{1}{5} \div 3\frac{1}{3} =$

An ______________ fraction has a ______________ that is larger than its ______________.

Back Page Exercises Create ten problems similar to those above. Work them.

Decimal Number Place Value

The Idea

Place value is the property of our number system which tells us by the position of a digit what its value in the number is. As we move to the left from the decimal point, the value of each place is higher. As we move to the right from the decimal point, the value of each place is smaller. To the right of the decimal point, we are talking about fractional parts of the number 1.

How to Use the Idea

The number on the chart is read as 23 and 456 thousandths. We can also write it as 2 × 10 + 3 × 1 + 4/10 + 5/100 + 6/1,000. If we change the fractions to a common denominator of 1,000, we have 400/1,000 + 50/1,000 + 6/1,000 = 456/1,000, which is how we read the number.

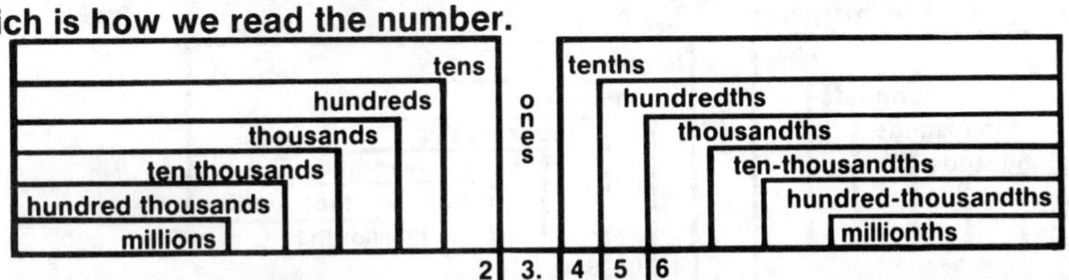

Write each member to show the place values.

① 871.2386 = *8 × 100 + 7 × 10 + 1 + 2/10 + 3/100 + 8/1,000 + 6/10,000*

② 1,289.3014 = *1 × 1,000 + 2 × 100 + 8 × 10 + 9 + 3/10 + 0/100 + 1/1,000 + 4/10,000*

③ 70.2569 = *7 × 10 + 0 + 2/10 + 5/100 + 6/1,000 + 9/10,000*

④ 861.2816 = *8 × 100 + 6 × 10 + 1 + 2/10 + 8/100 + 1/1,000 + 6/10,000*

⑤ 9,030.741 = *9 × 1,000 + 0 × 100 + 3 × 10 + 0 + 7/10 + 4/100 + 1/1,000*

⑥ 10,429.658 = *1 × 10,000 + 0 × 1,000 + 4 × 100 + 2 × 10 + 9 + 6/10 + 5/100 + 8/1,000*

⑦ 21,841.5623 = *2 × 10,000 + 1 × 1,000 + 8 × 100 + 4 × 10 + 1 + 5/10 + 6/100 + 2/1,000 + 3/10,000*

⑧ 4,606.613 = *4 × 1,000 + 6 × 100 + 0 × 10 + 6 + 6/10 + 1/100 + 3/1,000*

⑨ 16.91006 = *1 × 10 + 6 + 9/10 + 1/100 + 0/1,000 + 0/10,000 + 6/100,000*

⑩ 723.4139 = *7 × 100 + 2 × 10 + 3 + 4/10 + 1/100 + 3/1,000 + 9/10,000*

⑪ 987.65432 = *9 × 100 + 8 × 10 + 7 + 6/10 + 5/100 + 4/1,000 + 3/10,000 + 2/100,000*

Place value is the property of our number system which tells us by the *position* of a *digit* what its *value* in the number is.

Back Page Exercises Move the decimal point right two places in each problem above and rework them.

Decimal Number Place Value 55

The Idea

Place value is the property of our number system which tells us by the position of a digit what its value in the number is. As we move to the left from the decimal point, the value of each place is higher. As we move to the right from the decimal point, the value of each place is smaller. To the right of the decimal point, we are talking about fractional parts of the number 1.

How to Use the Idea

The number on the chart is read as 23 and 456 thousandths. We can also write it as 2 × 10 + 3 × 1 + 4/10 + 5/100 + 6/1,000. If we change the fractions to a common denominator of 1,000, we have 400/1,000 + 50/1,000 + 6/1,000 = 456/1,000, which is how we read the number.

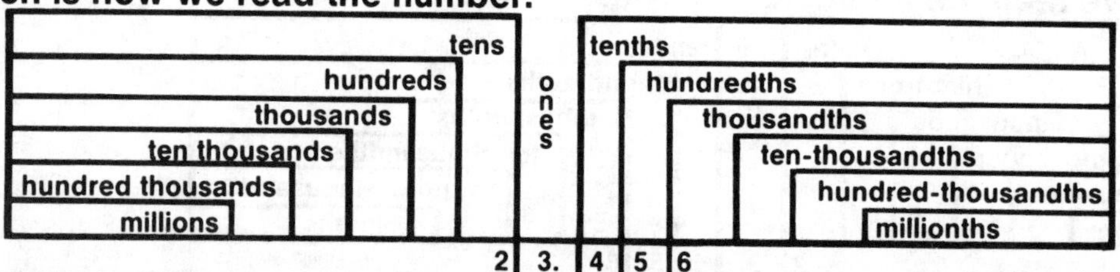

Write each member to show the place values.

① 871.2386 = *8 × 100 + 7 × 10 + 1 + 2/10 + 3/100 + 8/1,000 + 6/10,000*

② 1,289.3014 =

③ 70.2569 =

④ 861.2816 =

⑤ 9,030.741 =

⑥ 10,429.658 =

⑦ 21,841.5623 =

⑧ 4,606.613 =

⑨ 16.91006 =

⑩ 723.4139 =

⑪ 987.65432 =

________________ is the property of our number system which tells us by the ________________ of a ________________ what its ________________ in the number is.

Back Page Exercises — **Move the decimal point right two places in each problem above and rework them.**

Adding Decimals

The Idea

Place value means that each place in a number, on either side of the decimal, tells the value of the digit in that place.

How to Use the Idea

When we add decimal numbers, it is very important to line up the decimals. When one number has more digits to the right of the decimal than another, we can add or annex zeroes to the same number of places. Two tenths = .2 = .20 = twenty hundredths. Annexing zeroes to the right of a decimal number does not change the value of the number—but we never annex zeroes in the middle of a number. 2.033 = 2.0330   2.033 ≠ 2.0033

A Find the sums. Carry as in whole number addition.

① 6.314 + 4.58*0* = ***10.894***

② 84.604 + 17.34*0* = ***101.944***

③ 108.6*00* + 93.246 = ***201.846***

④ 98.714 + 3.183 = ***101.897***

⑤ 391.26*0* + 118.036 = ***509.296***

⑥ 1,021.608 + 161.11*0* + 29.07*0* = ***1,211.788***

⑦ 7,834.55*0* + 206.004 + 562.1*00* = ***8,602.654***

⑧ 10,664.08*00* + 23.115*0* + 147.0016 = ***10,834.1966***

⑨ 4,389.07 + 246.*00* + 59.1*0* = ***4,694.17***

⑩ 9,000.00 + 481.*00* + 706.1*0* = ***10,187.10***

⑪ 9,164.113*0* + 222.31*00* + 467.006*0* + 1.1403 = ***9,854.5693***

⑫ 306,463.812 + 10,180.06*0* + 4,007.103 + 23,146.024 = ***343,796.999***

⑬ 51,612.06*00* + 47.92*00* + 3.007*0* + 14.0124 = ***51,676.9994***

⑭ 408,106.14*0* + 1,212.23*0* + 41,124.006 + 3,444.123 = ***453,886.499***

⑮ 783.008*0* + 16.121*0* + 5.6201 + 3.2408 = ***807.9899***

B Change each decimal number to the indicated number of places by annexing or dropping zeroes.

① 1.060
hundredths ***1.06***
ten-thousandths ***1.0600***

② 30.41
thousandths ***30.410***
ten-thousandths ***30.4100***

③ 471.800
tenths ***471.8***
hundredths ***471.80***

④ 6
tenths ***6.0***
thousandths ***6.000***

⑤ 70.1
hundredths ***70.10***
ten-thousandths ***70.1000***

⑥ 41.006
hundred-thousandths ***41.00600***
millionths ***41.006000***

Place value means that each ***place*** in a ***number***, on ***either*** side of the decimal, tells the ***value*** of the digit in that ***place***.

Back Page Exercises Create ten problems similar to those in exercise A. Work them.

Adding Decimals

The Idea

Place value means that each place in a number, on either side of the decimal, tells the value of the digit in that place.

How to Use the Idea

When we add decimal numbers, it is very important to line up the decimals. When one number has more digits to the right of the decimal than another, we can add or annex zeroes to the same number of places. Two tenths = .2 = .20 = twenty hundredths. Annexing zeroes to the right of a decimal number does not change the value of the number—but we never annex zeroes in the middle of a number. 2.033 = 2.0330   2.033 ≠ 2.0033

A Find the sums. Carry as in whole number addition.

①	②	③	④	⑤
6.314 + 4.58*0* ***10.894***	84.604 + 17.34	108.6 + 93.246	98.714 + 3.183	391.26 + 118.036

⑥	⑦	⑧	⑨	⑩
1,021.608 161.11 + 29.07	7,834.55 206.004 + 562.1	10,664.08 23.115 + 147.0016	4,389.07 246 + 59.1	9,000.00 481 + 706.1

⑪	⑫	⑬	⑭	⑮
9,164.113 222.31 467.006 + 1.1403	306,463.812 10,180.06 4,007.103 + 23,146.024	51,612.06 47.92 3.007 + 14.0124	408,106.14 1,212.23 41,124.006 + 3,444.123	783.008 16.121 5.6201 + 3.2408

B Change each decimal number to the indicated number of places by annexing or dropping zeroes.

① 1.060
hundredths ***1.06***
ten-thousandths ***1.0600***

② 30.41
thousandths ______
ten-thousandths ______

③ 471.800
tenths ______
hundredths ______

④ 6
tenths ______
thousandths ______

⑤ 70.1
hundredths ______
ten-thousandths ______

⑥ 41.006
hundred-thousandths ______
millionths ______

Place value means that each ______ in a ______, on ______ side of the decimal, tells the ______ of the digit in that ______.

Back Page Exercises Create ten problems similar to those in exercise A. Work them.

Subtracting Decimals

The Idea

Subtraction works the same with decimals as with whole numbers. The decimal places must be lined up so that digits of the same place value are lined up before subtracting. Annex zeroes if needed.

How to Use the Idea

a. (tenths, hundredths, thousandths)

```
  39.586
- 28.475
  ------
  11.111
```

b. (zero annexed)

```
  628.73  =   628.730
- 47.506  =  - 47.506
                -------
              581.224
```

A Find the remainders. Bring decimal points straight down.

① 861.324 − 78.510 = ***782.814***	② 1,506.198 − 619.203 = ***886.995***	③ 35.0614 − 29.1431 = ***5.9183***	④ 516.3184 − 98.5263 = ***417.7921***
⑤ 6,007.417 − 358.229 = ***5,649.188***	⑥ 1.06123 − .94007 = ***.12116***	⑦ 29.8462 − 17.7571 = ***12.0891***	⑧ 140.8670 − 72.7346 = ***68.1324***
⑨ 9,683.830 − 8,684.925 = ***998.905***	⑩ 398.4444 − 299.5432 = ***98.9012***	⑪ 290.0103 − 163.9145 = ***126.0958***	⑫ 783.6741 − 279.5006 = ***504.1735***

B As long as you keep the decimals lined up, you can add (annex) as many zeroes as needed. Find the remainders.

① 2.***0*** − 1.5 = ***.5***	② 8.6***00*** − 2.581 = ***6.019***	③ 10.41***0*** − 6.354 = ***4.056***	④ 116.23***00*** − 98.4613 = ***17.7687***
⑤ 3,006.06***0*** − 1,998.159 = ***1,007.901***	⑥ 806.115***0*** − 707.2355 = ***98.8795***	⑦ 10,003.41***0*** − 8,961.006 = ***1,042.404***	⑧ 860.723***0*** − 458.6007 = ***402.1223***
⑨ 13.46***00*** − 10.5057 = ***2.9543***	⑩ 29.001***0*** − 27.1026 = ***1.8984***	⑪ 504.1183***0*** − 328.00645 = ***176.11185***	⑫ 999.101***0*** − 819.9166 = ***179.1844***

Subtraction works the same with ***decimals*** as with ***whole*** numbers.

Back Page Exercises Move the decimal two places right in each problem above and subtract. You may need to add zeroes to the problem before you begin.

Subtracting Decimals

The Idea

Subtraction works the same with decimals as with whole numbers. The decimal places must be lined up so that digits of the same place value are lined up before subtracting. Annex zeroes if needed.

How to Use the Idea

tenths, hundredths, thousandths

a. $\begin{array}{r} 39.586 \\ -\,28.475 \\ \hline 11.111 \end{array}$

b. $\begin{array}{r} 628.73 \\ -\,47.506 \\ \hline \end{array} = \begin{array}{r} 628.730 \\ -\,47.506 \\ \hline 581.224 \end{array}$ (zero annexed)

A Find the remainders. Bring decimal points straight down.

① $\begin{array}{r} 861.324 \\ -\,78.510 \\ \hline \textit{782.814} \end{array}$
② $\begin{array}{r} 1{,}506.198 \\ -\,619.203 \\ \hline \end{array}$
③ $\begin{array}{r} 35.0614 \\ -\,29.1431 \\ \hline \end{array}$
④ $\begin{array}{r} 516.3184 \\ -\,98.5263 \\ \hline \end{array}$

⑤ $\begin{array}{r} 6{,}007.417 \\ -\,358.229 \\ \hline \end{array}$
⑥ $\begin{array}{r} 1.06123 \\ -\,.94007 \\ \hline \end{array}$
⑦ $\begin{array}{r} 29.8462 \\ -\,17.7571 \\ \hline \end{array}$
⑧ $\begin{array}{r} 140.8670 \\ -\,72.7346 \\ \hline \end{array}$

⑨ $\begin{array}{r} 9{,}683.830 \\ -\,8{,}684.925 \\ \hline \end{array}$
⑩ $\begin{array}{r} 398.4444 \\ -\,299.5432 \\ \hline \end{array}$
⑪ $\begin{array}{r} 290.0103 \\ -\,163.9145 \\ \hline \end{array}$
⑫ $\begin{array}{r} 783.6741 \\ -\,279.5006 \\ \hline \end{array}$

B As long as you keep the decimals lined up, you can add (annex) as many zeroes as needed. Find the remainders.

① $\begin{array}{r} 2.\textit{0} \\ -\,1.5 \\ \hline \textit{.5} \end{array}$
② $\begin{array}{r} 8.6 \\ -\,2.581 \\ \hline \end{array}$
③ $\begin{array}{r} 10.41 \\ -\,6.354 \\ \hline \end{array}$
④ $\begin{array}{r} 116.23 \\ -\,98.4613 \\ \hline \end{array}$

⑤ $\begin{array}{r} 3{,}006.06 \\ -\,1{,}998.159 \\ \hline \end{array}$
⑥ $\begin{array}{r} 806.115 \\ -\,707.2355 \\ \hline \end{array}$
⑦ $\begin{array}{r} 10{,}003.41 \\ -\,8{,}961.006 \\ \hline \end{array}$
⑧ $\begin{array}{r} 860.723 \\ -\,458.6007 \\ \hline \end{array}$

⑨ $\begin{array}{r} 13.46 \\ -\,10.5057 \\ \hline \end{array}$
⑩ $\begin{array}{r} 29.001 \\ -\,27.1026 \\ \hline \end{array}$
⑪ $\begin{array}{r} 504.1183 \\ -\,328.00645 \\ \hline \end{array}$
⑫ $\begin{array}{r} 999.101 \\ -\,819.9166 \\ \hline \end{array}$

✲ ____________ works the same with ____________ as with ____________ numbers.

Back Page Exercises — Move the decimal two places right in each problem above and subtract. You may need to add zeroes to the problem before you begin.

Multiplying Decimals

The Idea

A decimal is a way of writing a fraction that has 10; 100; 1,000; 10,000; or another power of 10 as a denominator.

How to Use the Idea

1/10 = .1 1/100 = .01 1/1,000 = .001

The number of decimal places in the product is the sum of the decimal places in the factors.

.25	5	.6	.08
× .5	× .3	× .2	× .04
.125	1.5	.12	.0032

Multiply.

① .35 × .12 70 35 .0420	② .75 × .15 375 75 .1125	③ 2.68 × .75 1340 1876 2.0100	④ 40.15 × 1.6 24090 4015 64.240
⑤ 17.64 × 1.23 5292 3528 1764 21.6972	⑥ 8.56 × 1.7 5992 856 14.552	⑦ 10.84 × 2.52 2168 5420 2168 27.3168	⑧ 113.21 × 3.42 22642 45284 33963 387.1782
⑨ 3,008.25 × 1.05 1504125 3008250 3,158.6625	⑩ 720.65 × 320 1441300 216195 230,608.00	⑪ 10,620.55 × 30.06 6372330 318616500 319,253.7330	⑫ 8,210.75 × 4.66 4926450 4926450 3284300 38,262.0950
⑬ 10,000.55 × 8.66 6000330 6000330 8000440 86,604.7630	⑭ 4,466.44 × 23.2 893288 1339932 893288 103,621.408	⑮ 5,006.88 × 240 20027520 1001376 1,201,651.20	⑯ 122.45 × 3.64 48980 73470 36735 445.7180

A *decimal* is a way of writing a *fraction* that has 10; 100; 1,000; 10,000; or another power of *10* as a denominator.

Back Page Exercises Multiply each product by 2.49.

Multiplying Decimals

The Idea

A decimal is a way of writing a fraction that has 10; 100; 1,000; 10,000; or another power of 10 as a denominator.

How to Use the Idea

1/10 = .1 1/100 = .01 1/1,000 = .001

The number of decimal places in the product is the sum of the decimal places in the factors.

$$\begin{array}{r} .25 \\ \times .5 \\ \hline .125 \end{array} \qquad \begin{array}{r} 5 \\ \times .3 \\ \hline 1.5 \end{array} \qquad \begin{array}{r} .6 \\ \times .2 \\ \hline .12 \end{array} \qquad \begin{array}{r} .08 \\ \times .04 \\ \hline .0032 \end{array}$$

Multiply.

① $\begin{array}{r} .35 \\ \times .12 \\ \hline 70 \\ 35 \\ \hline .0420 \end{array}$ ② $\begin{array}{r} .75 \\ \times .15 \\ \hline \end{array}$ ③ $\begin{array}{r} 2.68 \\ \times .75 \\ \hline \end{array}$ ④ $\begin{array}{r} 40.15 \\ \times 1.6 \\ \hline \end{array}$

⑤ $\begin{array}{r} 17.64 \\ \times 1.23 \\ \hline \end{array}$ ⑥ $\begin{array}{r} 8.56 \\ \times 1.7 \\ \hline \end{array}$ ⑦ $\begin{array}{r} 10.84 \\ \times 2.52 \\ \hline \end{array}$ ⑧ $\begin{array}{r} 113.21 \\ \times 3.42 \\ \hline \end{array}$

⑨ $\begin{array}{r} 3{,}008.25 \\ \times 1.05 \\ \hline \end{array}$ ⑩ $\begin{array}{r} 720.65 \\ \times 320 \\ \hline \end{array}$ ⑪ $\begin{array}{r} 10{,}620.55 \\ \times 30.06 \\ \hline \end{array}$ ⑫ $\begin{array}{r} 8{,}210.75 \\ \times 4.66 \\ \hline \end{array}$

⑬ $\begin{array}{r} 10{,}000.55 \\ \times 8.66 \\ \hline \end{array}$ ⑭ $\begin{array}{r} 4{,}466.44 \\ \times 23.2 \\ \hline \end{array}$ ⑮ $\begin{array}{r} 5{,}006.88 \\ \times 240 \\ \hline \end{array}$ ⑯ $\begin{array}{r} 122.45 \\ \times 3.64 \\ \hline \end{array}$

A ________________ is a way of writing a ________________ that has 10; 100; 1,000; 10,000; or another power of ________________ as a denominator.

Back Page Exercises **Multiply each product by 2.49.**

Dividing Decimals

The Idea

When we divide with decimals, we use a caret (‸) to mark where the decimal place goes in the quotient.

How to Use the Idea

When dividing decimals, count the places to the right of the decimal in the divisor and move the decimal point in the dividend that many places to the right.

0.25) 1.00‸ = 4. 100	0.75) 30.00‸ = 40. 300	2.8) 56.0‸ = 20. 56	0.15) .36‸0 = 2.4 30 60 60

Find the quotients. Use a caret (‸) to mark the new position of the decimal point in each problem.

① 0.5) 1.5‸ = *3.* *15*	② 0.6) .3‸*0* = *.5* *30*	③ 0.4) 20.*0*‸ = *50.* *20* *0*	④ 0.2) 1.6‸ = *8.* *16*
⑤ 0.25) 5.5*0*‸ = *22.* *50* *50* *50*	⑥ 0.35) 7.7*0*‸ = *22.* *70* *70* *70*	⑦ 0.75) 33.*00*‸ = *44.* *300* *300* *300*	⑧ 1.8) 3.6‸18 = *2.01* *36* *18* *18*
⑨ 9.8) 15.6‸8 = *1.6* *98* *588* *588*	⑩ 0.23) 9.66‸ = *42.* *92* *46* *46*	⑪ 0.56) 1.06‸4 = *1.9* *56* *504* *504*	⑫ 7.1) 1.8‸46 = *0.26* *142* *426* *426*
⑬ 0.82) 254.2*0*‸ = *310.* *246* *82* *82* *0*	⑭ 5.7) 193.8‸ = *34.* *171* *228* *228*	⑮ 3.9) 0.8‸19 = *0.21* *78* *39* *39*	⑯ 8.3) 14.1‸1 = *1.7* *83* *581* *581*

When we divide with *decimals*, we use a *caret* (‸) to mark where the decimal place goes in the *quotient*.

Back Page Exercises Create ten decimal division problems. Work them.

Dividing Decimals

The Idea

When we divide with decimals, we use a caret (‸) to mark where the decimal place goes in the quotient.

How to Use the Idea

When dividing decimals, count the places to the right of the decimal in the divisor and move the decimal point in the dividend that many places to the right.

$0.25\overline{)1.00_\wedge}$ = 4. ; 100

$0.75\overline{)30.00_\wedge}$ = 40. ; 300

$2.8\overline{)56.0_\wedge}$ = 20. ; 56

$0.15\overline{).36_\wedge0}$ = 2.4 ; 30 ; 60 ; 60

Find the quotients. Use a caret (‸) to mark the new position of the decimal point in each problem.

(1) $0.5\overline{)1.5_\wedge}$ = *3.* ; *15*

(2) $0.6\overline{).3}$

(3) $0.4\overline{)20.}$

(4) $0.2\overline{)1.6}$

(5) $0.25\overline{)5.5}$

(6) $0.35\overline{)7.7}$

(7) $0.75\overline{)33.}$

(8) $1.8\overline{)3.618}$

(9) $9.8\overline{)15.68}$

(10) $0.23\overline{)9.66}$

(11) $0.56\overline{)1.064}$

(12) $7.1\overline{)1.846}$

(13) $0.82\overline{)254.2}$

(14) $5.7\overline{)193.8}$

(15) $3.9\overline{)0.819}$

(16) $8.3\overline{)14.11}$

When we divide with ________________, we use a ________________ (‸) to mark where the decimal place goes in the ________________.

Back Page Exercises Create ten decimal division problems. Work them.

Converting Decimals to Fractions

The Idea

A decimal is a way of writing a fraction that has 10; 100; 1,000; 10,000; or another power of 10 as a denominator. The word "decimal" comes from the Latin word for "ten".

How to Use the Idea

Each place to the right of the decimal means that digit divided by 10 or 100 or 1,000 . . . whatever place it holds.

$0.4 = \frac{4}{10} = \frac{2}{5}$ $0.25 = \frac{25}{100} = \frac{1}{4}$ $.75 = \frac{75}{100} = \frac{3}{4}$

✱ **Convert each decimal to a fraction. Reduce fractions to lowest terms.**

① $0.625 = \frac{625}{1,000} = \frac{5}{8}$	② $0.875 = \frac{875}{1,000} = \frac{7}{8}$	③ $0.35 = \frac{35}{100} = \frac{7}{20}$	④ $0.252 = \frac{252}{1,000} = \frac{63}{250}$
⑤ $0.32 = \frac{32}{100} = \frac{8}{25}$	⑥ $0.685 = \frac{685}{1,000} = \frac{137}{200}$	⑦ $0.45 = \frac{45}{100} = \frac{9}{20}$	⑧ $0.56 = \frac{56}{100} = \frac{14}{25}$
⑨ $0.1 = \frac{1}{10}$	⑩ $0.15 = \frac{15}{100} = \frac{3}{20}$	⑪ $0.325 = \frac{325}{1,000} = \frac{13}{40}$	⑫ $0.125 = \frac{125}{1,000} = \frac{1}{8}$
⑬ $0.2 = \frac{2}{10} = \frac{1}{5}$	⑭ $0.01 = \frac{1}{100}$	⑮ $0.55 = \frac{55}{100} = \frac{11}{20}$	⑯ $0.375 = \frac{375}{1,000} = \frac{3}{8}$
⑰ $0.5 = \frac{5}{10} = \frac{1}{2}$	⑱ $0.335 = \frac{335}{1,000} = \frac{67}{200}$	⑲ $0.75 = \frac{75}{100} = \frac{3}{4}$	⑳ $0.44 = \frac{44}{100} = \frac{11}{25}$
㉑ $0.8 = \frac{8}{10} = \frac{4}{5}$	㉒ $0.9 = \frac{9}{10}$	㉓ $0.09 = \frac{9}{100}$	㉔ $0.275 = \frac{275}{1,000} = \frac{11}{40}$
㉕ $0.57 = \frac{57}{100}$	㉖ $0.16 = \frac{16}{100} = \frac{4}{25}$	㉗ $0.95 = \frac{95}{100} = \frac{19}{20}$	㉘ $0.02 = \frac{2}{100} = \frac{1}{50}$
㉙ $0.65 = \frac{65}{100} = \frac{13}{20}$	㉚ $0.45 = \frac{45}{100} = \frac{9}{20}$	㉛ $0.555 = \frac{555}{1,000} = \frac{111}{200}$	㉜ $0.6 = \frac{6}{10} = \frac{3}{5}$
㉝ $0.075 = \frac{75}{1,000} = \frac{3}{40}$	㉞ $0.88 = \frac{88}{100} = \frac{22}{25}$	㉟ $0.910 = \frac{910}{1,000} = \frac{91}{100}$	㊱ $0.055 = \frac{55}{1,000} = \frac{11}{200}$

The word *"decimal"* comes from the Latin word for *"ten"*.

Back Page Exercises Write fifteen decimals. Convert each to a fraction and reduce.

Converting Decimals to Fractions

The Idea

A decimal is a way of writing a fraction that has 10; 100; 1,000; 10,000; or another power of 10 as a denominator. The word "decimal" comes from the Latin word for "ten".

How to Use the Idea

Each place to the right of the decimal means that digit divided by 10 or 100 or 1,000 . . . whatever place it holds.

$0.4 = \frac{4}{10} = \frac{2}{5}$ $0.25 = \frac{25}{100} = \frac{1}{4}$ $.75 = \frac{75}{100} = \frac{3}{4}$

Convert each decimal to a fraction. Reduce fractions to lowest terms.

① $0.625 = \frac{625}{1,000} = \frac{5}{8}$	② 0.875 =	③ 0.35 =	④ 0.252 =
⑤ 0.32 =	⑥ 0.685 =	⑦ 0.45 =	⑧ 0.56 =
⑨ 0.1 =	⑩ 0.15 =	⑪ 0.325 =	⑫ 0.125 =
⑬ 0.2 =	⑭ 0.01 =	⑮ 0.55 =	⑯ 0.375 =
⑰ 0.5 =	⑱ 0.335 =	⑲ 0.75 =	⑳ 0.44 =
㉑ 0.8 =	㉒ 0.9 =	㉓ 0.09 =	㉔ 0.275 =
㉕ 0.57 =	㉖ 0.16 =	㉗ 0.95 =	㉘ 0.02 =
㉙ 0.65 =	㉚ 0.45 =	㉛ 0.555 =	㉜ 0.6 =
㉝ 0.075 =	㉞ 0.88 =	㉟ 0.910 =	㊱ 0.055 =

The word ____________________ comes from the Latin word for ____________.

Back Page Exercises **Write fifteen decimals. Convert each to a fraction and reduce.**

Percents

The Idea

Percent means "in a hundred." "Cent" comes from a Latin word meaning "hundred." We get the word "century" from this word, and we call a penny a cent because there are 100 pennies in $1.00.

How to Use the Idea

The symbol for percent is %. When we read the decimal 0.35, we say thirty-five hundredths. This is also thirty-five percent, and we write this as 35%.
Notice that when we change a decimal to percent, the decimal point moves two places to the right.

A Change each decimal to a percent.

① 0.45 = ***45%***	⑦ 0.2 = ***20%***	⑬ 0.3 = ***30%***	⑲ 0.15 = ***15%***
② 0.25 = ***25%***	⑧ 0.75 = ***75%***	⑭ 0.41 = ***41%***	⑳ 3.40 = ***340%***
③ 0.10 = ***10%***	⑨ 0.8 = ***80%***	⑮ 2.50 = ***250%***	㉑ 0.19 = ***19%***
④ 0.50 = ***50%***	⑩ 0.90 = ***90%***	⑯ 0.7 = ***70%***	㉒ 0.24 = ***24%***
⑤ 0.65 = ***65%***	⑪ 0.22 = ***22%***	⑰ 1.25 = ***125%***	㉓ 4.63 = ***463%***
⑥ 0.01 = ***1%***	⑫ 0.86 = ***86%***	⑱ 0.55 = ***55%***	㉔ 0.05 = ***5%***

B To find a percent of some number, change the percent to a decimal (move the decimal point two places to the left) and multiply.

① 10% of 50 = ***.10 × 50 = 5***	⑨ 60% of 40 = ***.60 × 40 = 24***
② 30% of 4 = ***.30 × 4 = 1.2***	⑩ 50% of 12 = ***.50 × 12 = 6***
③ 20% of 5 = ***.20 × 5 = 1***	⑪ 90% of 30 = ***.90 × 30 = 27***
④ 100% of 6 = ***1 × 6 = 6***	⑫ 22% of 20 = ***.22 × 20 = 4.4***
⑤ 80% of 20 = ***.80 × 20 = 16***	⑬ 10% of 10 = ***.10 × 10 = 1***
⑥ 65% of 100 = ***.65 × 100 = 65***	⑭ 75% of 40 = ***.75 × 40 = 30***
⑦ 40% of 10 = ***.40 × 10 = 4***	⑮ 70% of 30 = ***.70 × 30 = 21***
⑧ 25% of 20 = ***.25 × 20 = 5***	⑯ 20% of 35 = ***.20 × 35 = 7***

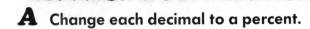

Percent means "in a hundred." ***"Cent"*** comes from a Latin word meaning ***"hundred"***.

Back Page Exercises Find 51 % of each number in exercise B.

Percents

The Idea

Percent means "in a hundred." "Cent" comes from a Latin word meaning "hundred." We get the word "century" from this word, and we call a penny a cent because there are 100 pennies in $1.00.

How to Use the Idea

The symbol for percent is %. When we read the decimal 0.35, we say thirty-five hundredths. This is also thirty-five percent, and we write this as 35%.

Notice that when we change a decimal to percent, the decimal point moves two places to the right.

A Change each decimal to a percent.

① 0.45 = ***45%***
② 0.25 =
③ 0.10 =
④ 0.50 =
⑤ 0.65 =
⑥ 0.01 =
⑦ 0.2 =
⑧ 0.75 =
⑨ 0.8 =
⑩ 0.90 =
⑪ 0.22 =
⑫ 0.86 =
⑬ 0.3 =
⑭ 0.41 =
⑮ 2.50 =
⑯ 0.7 =
⑰ 1.25 =
⑱ 0.55 =
⑲ 0.15 =
⑳ 3.40 =
㉑ 0.19 =
㉒ 0.24 =
㉓ 4.63 =
㉔ 0.05 =

B To find a percent of some number, change the percent to a decimal (move the decimal point two places to the left) and multiply.

① 10% of 50 = ***.10 × 50 = 5***
② 30% of 4 =
③ 20% of 5 =
④ 100% of 6 =
⑤ 80% of 20 =
⑥ 65% of 100 =
⑦ 40% of 10 =
⑧ 25% of 20 =
⑨ 60% of 40 =
⑩ 50% of 12 =
⑪ 90% of 30 =
⑫ 22% of 20 =
⑬ 10% of 10 =
⑭ 75% of 40 =
⑮ 70% of 30 =
⑯ 20% of 35 =

________________ means "in a hundred." ________________ comes from a Latin word meaning ________________.

Back Page Exercises — **Find 51 % of each number in exercise B.**

Proportion

The Idea

A proportion is a sentence stating two ratios are equal.

How to Use the Idea

If three numbers in a proportion are known, we can solve for the fourth number.

$\frac{2}{3} = \frac{4}{?}$; $? \times \frac{2}{3} = \frac{4}{?} \times ?$; $(?)\frac{2}{3} \times 3 = 4(3)$; $2(?) = (12)$; $2(?) \times \frac{1}{2} = (12)\frac{1}{2}$; $? = 6$

Solve the proportions.

① $\frac{3}{8} = \frac{?}{16}$
$(16)(\frac{3}{8}) = (16)(\frac{?}{16})$
$6 = ?$

② $\frac{1}{2} = \frac{5}{?}$
$(?)(2)(\frac{1}{2}) = (?)(2)(\frac{5}{?})$
$? = 10$

③ $\frac{3}{4} = \frac{?}{8}$
$(8)(\frac{3}{4}) = (8)(\frac{?}{8})$
$6 = ?$

④ $\frac{2}{5} = \frac{?}{25}$
$(25)(\frac{2}{5}) = (25)(\frac{?}{25})$
$10 = ?$

⑤ $\frac{5}{6} = \frac{15}{?}$
$(6)(?)(\frac{5}{6}) = (6)(?)(\frac{15}{?})$
$5(?) = 90$
$? = 18$

⑥ $\frac{2}{3} = \frac{8}{?}$
$(?)(3)(\frac{2}{3}) = (?)(3)(\frac{8}{?})$
$2(?) = 24$
$? = 12$

⑦ $\frac{3}{10} = \frac{?}{30}$
$(30)(\frac{3}{10}) = (30)(\frac{?}{30})$
$9 = ?$

⑧ $\frac{1}{4} = \frac{25}{?}$
$(4)(?)(\frac{1}{4}) = (4)(?)(\frac{25}{?})$
$? = 100$

⑨ $\frac{5}{7} = \frac{15}{?}$
$(7)(?)(\frac{5}{7}) = (7)(?)(\frac{15}{?})$
$5(?) = 105$
$? = 21$

⑩ $\frac{5}{3} = \frac{?}{12}$
$(12)(\frac{5}{3}) = (12)(\frac{?}{12})$
$20 = ?$

⑪ $\frac{4}{4} = \frac{?}{8}$
$(8)(\frac{4}{4}) = (8)(\frac{?}{8})$
$8 = ?$

⑫ $\frac{5}{8} = \frac{25}{?}$
$(8)(?)(\frac{5}{8}) = (8)(?)(\frac{25}{?})$
$5(?) = 200$
$? = 40$

⑬ $\frac{1}{?} = \frac{6}{300}$
$(?)(300)(\frac{1}{?}) = (?)(300)(\frac{6}{300})$
$300 = 6(?)$
$50 = ?$

⑭ $\frac{2}{25} = \frac{?}{150}$
$(150)(\frac{2}{25}) = (150)(\frac{?}{150})$
$12 = ?$

⑮ $\frac{4}{15} = \frac{20}{?}$
$(15)(?)(\frac{4}{15}) = (15)(?)(\frac{20}{?})$
$4(?) = 300$
$? = 75$

A ___*proportion*___ is a ___*sentence*___ stating two ratios are ___*equal*___.

Back Page Exercises Create ten problems similar to those above. Work them.

Proportion

The Idea

A proportion is a sentence stating two ratios are equal.

How to Use the Idea

If three numbers in a proportion are known, we can solve for the fourth number.

$\frac{2}{3} = \frac{4}{?}$; $? \times \frac{2}{3} = \frac{4}{?} \times ?$; $(?)\frac{2}{3} \times 3 = 4(3)$; $2(?) = (12)$; $2(?) \times \frac{1}{2} = (12)\frac{1}{2}$; $? = 6$

Solve the proportions.

① $\frac{3}{8} = \frac{?}{16}$

$(16)\left(\frac{3}{8}\right) = (16)\left(\frac{?}{16}\right)$

$6 = ?$

⑥ $\frac{2}{3} = \frac{8}{?}$

⑪ $\frac{4}{4} = \frac{?}{8}$

② $\frac{1}{2} = \frac{5}{?}$

⑦ $\frac{3}{10} = \frac{?}{30}$

⑫ $\frac{5}{8} = \frac{25}{?}$

③ $\frac{3}{4} = \frac{?}{8}$

⑧ $\frac{1}{4} = \frac{25}{?}$

⑬ $\frac{1}{?} = \frac{6}{300}$

④ $\frac{2}{5} = \frac{?}{25}$

⑨ $\frac{5}{7} = \frac{15}{?}$

⑭ $\frac{2}{25} = \frac{?}{150}$

⑤ $\frac{5}{6} = \frac{15}{?}$

⑩ $\frac{5}{3} = \frac{?}{12}$

⑮ $\frac{4}{15} = \frac{20}{?}$

A ____________________ is a ____________________ stating two ratios are ____________________.

Back Page Exercises **Create ten problems similar to those above. Work them.**

Ratio

The Idea

A ratio is a pair of numbers that describes a rate or compares two quantities. Fractions, decimals, and percents are all ways of expressing ratios.

How to Use the Idea

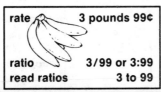

rate — 3 pounds 99¢

ratio — 3/99 or 3:99

read ratios — 3 to 99

comparison

△ △ △ △ △ △

□ □ □ □

ratio △ to □ — 6/4 or 6:4

read ratios — 6 to 4

A Write a ratio to describe each rate. Rewrite the ratio as a fraction.

① Socks are 3 pairs for $2.29.
3:$2.29 — $\frac{3}{\$2.29}$

② Shirts are 2 for $15.00.
2:$15.00 — $\frac{2}{\$15.00}$

③ Corn is priced at 73¢ for 2 cans.
73¢:2 — $\frac{73¢}{2}$

④ Tim goes 160 miles in 3 hours.
160:3 — $\frac{160}{3}$

⑤ Eric types 175 words in 4 minutes.
175:4 — $\frac{175}{4}$

⑥ In one week, Ann reads three books.
1:3 — $\frac{1}{3}$

⑦ One pound of sausage serves 4.
1:4 — $\frac{1}{4}$

⑧ A car gets 28 miles per gallon.
1:28 — $\frac{1}{28}$

B A percent is a ratio whose second term is 100 or a fraction whose denominator is 100. Fill in this chart.

percent	decimal fraction	ratio	fraction	simplified fraction
35%	*0.35*	*35:100*	*35/100*	*7/20*
80%	*0.80*	*80:100*	*80/100*	*4/5*
10%	*0.10*	*10:100*	*10/100*	*1/10*
100%	*1.00*	*100:100*	*100/100*	*1*
5%	*0.05*	*5:100*	*5/100*	*1/20*
65%	*0.65*	*65:100*	*65/100*	*13/20*
25%	*0.25*	*25:100*	*25/100*	*1/4*
75%	*0.75*	*75:100*	*75/100*	*3/4*
2%	*0.02*	*2:100*	*2/100*	*1/50*
15%	*0.15*	*15:100*	*15/100*	*3/20*

A ___*ratio*___ is a pair of numbers that describe a ___*rate*___ or compares two ___*quantities*___.

Back Page Exercises — Create fifteen ratios and something to decribe them.

Ratio

The Idea

A ratio is a pair of numbers that describes a rate or compares two quantities. Fractions, decimals, and percents are all ways of expressing ratios.

How to Use the Idea

rate	3 pounds 99¢
ratio	3/99 or 3:99
read ratios	3 to 99

comparison	△ △ △ △ △ △ □ □ □ □
ratio △ to □	6/4 or 6:4
read ratios	6 to 4

A Write a ratio to describe each rate. Rewrite the ratio as a fraction.

① Socks are 3 pairs for $2.29.
3:$2.29 *3/$2.29*

② Shirts are 2 for $15.00.

③ Corn is priced at 73¢ for 2 cans.

④ Tim goes 160 miles in 3 hours.

⑤ Eric types 175 words in 4 minutes.

⑥ In one week, Ann reads three books.

⑦ One pound of sausage serves 4.

⑧ A car gets 28 miles per gallon.

B A percent is a ratio whose second term is 100 or a fraction whose denominator is 100. Fill in this chart.

percent	decimal fraction	ratio	fraction	simplified fraction
35%	*0.35*	*35:100*	*35/100*	*7/20*
80%				
10%				
100%				
5%				
65%				
25%				
75%				
2%				
15%				

A ______________________ is a pair of numbers that describe a ______________________ or compares two ____________________.

Back Page Exercises Create fifteen ratios and something to decribe them.

Identity Elements

The Idea

The identity element for addition and subtraction is zero because $a + 0 = 0 + a = a$ and $a - 0 = a$. The identity element for multiplication and division is one because $1 \times a = a \times 1 = a$ and $a/1 = a$.

How to Use the Idea

$5 + 0 = 5$	$0 + 5 = 5$	$5 - 0 = 5$
$7 \times 1 = 7$	$1 \times 7 = 7$	$7/1 = 7$

A Solve the problems.

① $5 + 3 - 3 =$ ***5***

② $14 \times (4 - 1) + 8 - 8 =$ ***14 × 3 = 42***

③ $(8 - 7) \times 9 =$ ***1 × 9 = 9***

④ $7 - 7 + 11 =$ ***0 + 11 = 11***

⑤ $23 + 16 - 23 =$ ***16***

⑥ $27 \times (11 - 10) =$ ***27 × 1 = 27***

⑦ $43 + 9 - 9 =$ ***43***

⑧ $112 \times (14 - 13) =$ ***112 × 1 = 112***

⑨ $(22 - 21) \times 56 =$ ***1 × 56 = 56***

⑩ $19 + 18 - 19 =$ ***18***

⑪ $51 \times (36 - 35) =$ ***51 × 1 = 51***

⑫ $322 - 4 + 4 =$ ***322***

⑬ $78 \times (56 - 55) =$ ***78 × 1 = 78***

⑭ $65 - 18 + 18 =$ ***65***

B Read the equations and answer the questions.

① $8 - n = 8$ What number is represented by n? ***0***

② $16 + n = 16$ What number is represented by n? ***0***

③ $7 \times n = 7$ What number is represented by n? ***1***

④ $9 \div n = 9$ What number is represented by n? ***1***

⑤ $n + 23 = 23$ What number is represented by n? ***0***

⑥ $n \times 11 = 11$ What number is represented by n? ***1***

⑦ $a + b = a$ What number is represented by b? ***0***

The identity element for ***addition*** and subtraction is ***zero***. The identity element for multiplication and ***division*** is ***one***.

Back Page Exercises Create fifteen problems similar to those in A. Work them.

Identity Elements

The Idea

The identity element for addition and subtraction is zero because $a + 0 = 0 + a = a$ and $a - 0 = a$. The identity element for multiplication and division is one because $1 \times a = a \times 1 = a$ and $a/1 = a$.

How to Use the Idea

$5 + 0 = 5$	$0 + 5 = 5$	$5 - 0 = 5$
$7 \times 1 = 7$	$1 \times 7 = 7$	$7/1 = 7$

A Solve the problems.

① $5 + 3 - 3 =$ **5**

② $14 \times (4 - 1) + 8 - 8 =$

③ $(8 - 7) \times 9 =$

④ $7 - 7 + 11 =$

⑤ $23 + 16 - 23 =$

⑥ $27 \times (11 - 10) =$

⑦ $43 + 9 - 9 =$

⑧ $112 \times (14 - 13) =$

⑨ $(22 - 21) \times 56 =$

⑩ $19 + 18 - 19 =$

⑪ $51 \times (36 - 35) =$

⑫ $322 - 4 + 4 =$

⑬ $78 \times (56 - 55) =$

⑭ $65 - 18 + 18 =$

B Read the equations and answer the questions.

① $8 - n = 8$ What number is represented by n? ***0***

② $16 + n = 16$ What number is represented by n? ______

③ $7 \times n = 7$ What number is represented by n? ______

④ $9 \div n = 9$ What number is represented by n? ______

⑤ $n + 23 = 23$ What number is represented by n? ______

⑥ $n \times 11 = 11$ What number is represented by n? ______

⑦ $a + b = a$ What number is represented by b? ______

The identity element for ____________ and subtraction is ____________. The identity element for multiplication and ____________ is ____________.

Back Page Exercises Create fifteen problems similar to those in A. Work them.

Equations

The Idea

An equation is a statement that two expressions are equal. When an equation has an unknown, we can solve for the unknown. Whatever we do to one side, we must do to the other side.

How to Use the Idea

a. $n + 3 = 9$
$n + 3 - 3 = 9 - 3 = 6$

b. $n - 7 = 11$
$n - 7 + 7 = 11 + 7 = 18$

Solve the equations.

① $n + 2 = 6$
$n + 2 - 2 = 6 - 2$
$n = 4$

② $6n = 12$
$\frac{6}{6}n = \frac{12}{6}$
$n = 2$

③ $6 + n = 12$
$6 + n - 6 = 12 - 6$
$n = 6$

④ $7n = 14$
$\frac{7}{7}n = \frac{14}{7}$
$n = 2$

⑤ $n + 12 = 17$
$n + 12 - 12 = 17 - 12$
$n = 5$

⑥ $5n = 25$
$\frac{5}{5}n = \frac{25}{5}$
$n = 5$

⑦ $15n = 45$
$\frac{15}{15}n = \frac{45}{15}$
$n = 3$

⑧ $n + 6 = 15$
$n + 6 - 6 = 15 - 6$
$n = 9$

⑨ $12n = 48$
$\frac{12}{12}n = \frac{48}{12}$
$n = 4$

⑩ $n - 20 = 40$
$n - 20 + 20 = 40 + 20$
$n = 60$

⑪ $8n = 40$
$\frac{8}{8}n = \frac{40}{8}$
$n = 5$

⑫ $21 + n = 22$
$21 + n - 21 = 22 - 21$
$n = 1$

⑬ $10n = 120$
$\frac{10}{10}n = \frac{120}{10}$
$n = 12$

⑭ $n - 17 = 3$
$n - 17 + 17 = 3 + 17$
$n = 20$

⑮ $5n = 65$
$\frac{5}{5}n = \frac{65}{5}$
$n = 13$

⑯ $n + 23 = 30$
$n + 23 - 23 = 30 - 23$
$n = 7$

⑰ $11n = 44$
$\frac{11}{11}n = \frac{44}{11}$
$n = 4$

⑱ $32n = 96$
$\frac{32}{32}n = \frac{96}{32}$
$n = 3$

An ___*equation*___ is a statement that two expressions are ___*equal*___.

Back Page Exercises Solve the following: $1x = 26$, $26 \times 3 = n$, $9n = 117$, $n + 43 = 176$, $20 - n = 17$, $19 \div n = 19$, and $47n = 141$.

The Idea

An equation is a statement that two expressions are equal. When an equation has an unknown, we can solve for the unknown. Whatever we do to one side, we must do to the other side.

How to Use the Idea

a. $n + 3 = 9$

$n + 3 - 3 = 9 - 3 = 6$

b. $n - 7 = 11$

$n - 7 + 7 = 11 + 7 = 18$

Solve the equations.

① $n + 2 = 6$

$n + 2 - 2 = 6 - 2$

$n = 4$

② $6n = 12$

③ $6 + n = 12$

④ $7n = 14$

⑤ $n + 12 = 17$

⑥ $5n = 25$

⑦ $15n = 45$

⑧ $n + 6 = 15$

⑨ $12n = 48$

⑩ $n - 20 = 40$

⑪ $8n = 40$

⑫ $21 + n = 22$

⑬ $10n = 120$

⑭ $n - 17 = 3$

⑮ $5n = 65$

⑯ $n + 23 = 30$

⑰ $11n = 44$

⑱ $32n = 96$

An ____________________ is a statement that two expressions are ____________________.

Back Page Exercises Solve the following: $1x = 26$, $26 \times 3 = n$, $9n = 117$, $n + 43 = 176$, $20 - n = 17$, $19 \div n = 19$, and $47n = 141$.

Parentheses and Brackets

The Idea

Parentheses ( ) and brackets [ ] are used to show us in what order to perform the operations in a problem. Perform those within the parentheses first; next perform those within the brackets; then perform any other operations in the problem.

How to Use the Idea

(a) $3[(16 + 2) \div 2] = 3[18 \div 2] = 3[9] = 27$

(b) $(7 + 3)\ [12 \div (7 - 3)] = 10[12 \div 4] = 10[3] = 30$

Solve these problems.

① $(14 \div 7)\ [(16 - 7) \times 2] = 2[9 \times 2] = 2[18] = 36$

② $[(8 - 3) \div 5] + [(10 + 2) \div 3] = [5 \div 5] + [12 \div 3] = 1 + 4 = 5$

③ $(10 - 1)\ [(15 - 11) \times (16 \div 8)] = 9[4 \times 2] = 9[8] = 72$

④ $(17 + 3)\ [16 - (21 \div 7)] = 20\ [16 - 3] = 20[13] = 260$

⑤ $\frac{[5 - (2 \times 1)]}{3}\ [(18 \div 9) + 4] = \frac{5 - 2}{3}\ [2 + 4] = \frac{3}{3}\ [6] = 1[6] = 6$

⑥ $(13 - 3) + [17 - (3 \times 3)] = 10 + [17 - 9] = 10 + 8 = 18$

⑦ $(15 \div 3)\ [12 + (2 \times 4)] = 5[12 + 8] = 5[20] = 100$

⑧ $(6 - 3)\ [15 \div (3 + 2)] = 3[15 \div 5] = 3[3] = 9$

⑨ $[(25 \div 5) + 3(8 \div 4)]\ (8 - 3) = [5 + 3(2)](5) = 11(5) = 55$

⑩ $(36 \div 9)[(13 - 7) \times 3] = 4[6 \times 3] = 4(18) = 72$

⑪ $[(45 \div 15) \times 6] + [(24 \div 12) + 4] = [3 \times 6] + [2 + 4] = 18 + 6 = 24$

⑫ $[7 + (\frac{1}{2} \times 16)]\ [(16 \times \frac{1}{4}) - 3] = [7 + 8]\ [4 - 3] = [15]\ [1] = 15$

⑬ $[5 + (6 \div 3) - 6] + [(8 \div 4) + 6] = [5 + 2 - 6] + [2 + 6] = 1 + 8 = 9$

Parentheses and *brackets* are used to show us what *order* to perform the *operations* in a problem.

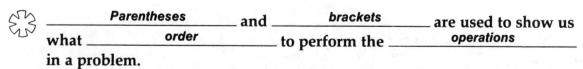

Back Page Exercises Create and work fifteen problems similar to those above.

Parentheses and Brackets

The Idea

Parentheses ( ) and brackets [ ] are used to show us in what order to perform the operations in a problem. Perform those within the parentheses first; next perform those within the brackets; then perform any other operations in the problem.

How to Use the Idea

(a) $3[(16 + 2) \div 2] = 3[18 \div 2] = 3[9] = 27$

(b) $(7 + 3)\ [12 \div (7 - 3)] = 10[12 \div 4] = 10[3] = 30$

Solve these problems.

① $(14 \div 7)\ [(16 - 7) \times 2] = 2[9 \times 2] = 2[18] = 36$

② $[(8 - 3) \div 5] + [(10 + 2) \div 3] =$

③ $(10 - 1)\ [(15 - 11) \times (16 \div 8)] =$

④ $(17 + 3)\ [16 - (21 \div 7)] =$

⑤ $\frac{[5 - (2 \times 1)]}{3}\ [(18 \div 9) + 4] =$

⑥ $(13 - 3) + [17 - (3 \times 3)] =$

⑦ $(15 \div 3)\ [12 + (2 \times 4)] =$

⑧ $(6 - 3)\ [15 \div (3 + 2)] =$

⑨ $[(25 \div 5) + 3(8 \div 4)]\ (8 - 3) =$

⑩ $(36 \div 9)[(13 - 7) \times 3] =$

⑪ $[(45 \div 15) \times 6] + [(24 \div 12) + 4] =$

⑫ $[7 + (\frac{1}{2} \times 16)]\ [(16 \times \frac{1}{4}) - 3] =$

⑬ $[5 + (6 \div 3) - 6] + [(8 \div 4) + 6] =$

________________ and ________________ are used to show us what ________________ to perfom the ________________ in a problem.

Back Page Exercises Create and work fifteen problems similar to those above.

The Idea

We can use x, or any other letter or symbol, to stand for a number which is unknown. We solve for the unknown, or find a solution to the equation.

How to Use the Idea To perform the indicated operations, we find the number which makes each number sentence true.

(a)

$$7x - 3 = 11$$
$$7x - 3 + 3 = 11 + 3$$
$$7x = 14$$
$$\frac{1}{7} \bullet \frac{7}{1}x = 14 \bullet \frac{1}{7}$$
$$x = 2$$

(b)

$$\frac{1}{6}x + 4 = 7$$
$$\frac{1}{6}x + 4 - 4 = 7 - 4$$
$$\frac{1}{6}x = 3$$
$$\frac{6}{1} \bullet \frac{1}{6}x = 3 \bullet \frac{6}{1}$$
$$x = 18$$

Find the value of x and solve each equation.

① $\frac{1}{2}x - 5 = 5$

$$\frac{1}{2}x - 5 + 5 = 5 + 5$$
$$\frac{1}{2}x = 10$$
$$\frac{2}{1} \bullet \frac{1}{2}x = 10 \bullet \frac{2}{1}$$
$$x = 20$$

② $4x - 3 = 1$

$$4x - 3 + 3 = 1 + 3$$
$$4x = 4$$
$$\frac{4x}{4} = \frac{4}{4}$$
$$x = 1$$

③ $2x + 4 = 8$

$$2x + 4 - 4 = 8 - 4$$
$$2x = 4$$
$$\frac{2x}{2} = \frac{4}{2}$$
$$x = 2$$

④ $5x + 3 = 18$

$$5x + 3 - 3 = 18 - 3$$
$$5x = 15$$
$$\frac{5x}{5} = \frac{15}{5}$$
$$x = 3$$

⑤ $x + \frac{1}{2} = 0$

$$x + \frac{1}{2} - \frac{1}{2} = 0 - \frac{1}{2}$$
$$x = -\frac{1}{2}$$

⑥ $6x - 6 = 18$

$$6x - 6 + 6 = 18 + 6$$
$$6x = 24$$
$$\frac{6x}{6} = \frac{24}{6}$$
$$x = 4$$

⑦ $8x - 2 = 4$

$$8x - 2 + 2 = 4 + 2$$
$$8x = 6$$
$$\frac{8x}{8} = \frac{6}{8}$$
$$x = \frac{3}{4}$$

⑧ $3x + 3 = 42$

$$3x + 3 - 3 = 42 - 3$$
$$3x = 39$$
$$\frac{3x}{3} = \frac{39}{3}$$
$$x = 13$$

⑨ $4x - 2 = 58$

$$4x - 2 + 2 = 58 + 2$$
$$4x = 60$$
$$\frac{4x}{4} = \frac{60}{4}$$
$$x = 15$$

We can use ___*x*___, or any other letter or symbol, to stand for a number which is ___*unknown*___.

Back Page Exercises Create and work twelve problems similar to those above.

Finding X

The Idea

We can use x, or any other letter or symbol, to stand for a number which is unknown. We solve for the unknown, or find a solution to the equation.

How to Use the Idea

To perform the indicated operations, we find the number which makes each number sentence true.

(a)
$$7x - 3 = 11$$
$$7x - 3 + 3 = 11 + 3$$
$$7x = 14$$
$$\frac{1}{7} \bullet \frac{7}{1}x = 14 \bullet \frac{1}{7}$$
$$x = 2$$

(b)
$$\frac{1}{6}x + 4 = 7$$
$$\frac{1}{6}x + 4 - 4 = 7 - 4$$
$$\frac{1}{6}x = 3$$
$$\frac{6}{1} \bullet \frac{1}{6}x = 3 \bullet \frac{6}{1}$$
$$x = 18$$

Find the value of x and solve each equation.

① $\frac{1}{2}x - 5 = 5$

$$\frac{1}{2}x - 5 + 5 = 5 + 5$$
$$\frac{1}{2}x = 10$$
$$\frac{2}{1} \bullet \frac{1}{2}x = 10 \bullet \frac{2}{1}$$
$$x = 20$$

② $4x - 3 = 1$

③ $2x + 4 = 8$

④ $5x + 3 = 18$

⑤ $x + \frac{1}{2} = 0$

⑥ $6x - 6 = 18$

⑦ $8x - 2 = 4$

⑧ $3x + 3 = 42$

⑨ $4x - 2 = 58$

We can use ____________________, or any other letter or symbol, to stand for a number which is ____________________.

Back Page Exercises Create and work twelve problems similar to those above.

Finding Two Missing Factors

The Idea

When we are given two equations about two unknowns, we can use both equations to solve for both unknowns.

How to Use the Idea

a. $x + y = 5$

$x - y = 1$ Add the equations.

$2x = 6$

$x = 3$ Replace x with 3 in either equation.

$3 + y = 5$

$y = 5 - 3 = 2$

b. $2x + y = 9$ Multiply both sides by 2.

$x - 2y = 2$

$4x = 18$ Add the equations.

$5x = 20$

$x = 4$ Replace x with 4.

$2(4) + y = 9$

$y = 9 - 8 = 1$

Solve each pair of equations.

① $\frac{1}{2}x + \frac{1}{3}y = 2$

$x - \frac{1}{3}y = 1$

$\frac{3}{2}x = 3$

$\frac{2}{3} \cdot \frac{3}{2}x = 3 \cdot \frac{2}{3}$

$x = 2$

$\frac{1}{2}(2) + \frac{1}{3}y = 2$

$\frac{1}{3}y = 1$

$y = 3$

② $3x + 4y = 1$

$2x + 2y = 2$

$4x + 4y = 4$

$3x + 4y = 1$

$x = 3$

$2(3) + 2y = 2$

$2y = -4$

$y = -2$

③ $4x - y = 10$

$2x + y = 20$

$6x = 30$

$x = 5$

$2(5) + y = 20$

$y = 10$

④ $x - 6y = 2$

$2x + y = 17$

$2x + 12y = 4$

$13y = 13$

$y = 1$

$2x + 1 = 17$

$2x = 16$

$x = 8$

⑤ $11x - y = 18$

$x + y = 6$

$12x = 24$

$x = 2$

$2 + y = 6$

$y = 4$

⑥ $4x + 4y = 8$

$4x - 4y = 24$

$8x = 32$

$x = 4$

$4(4) + 4y = 8$

$4y = -8$

$y = -2$

⑦ $x - 3y = 7$

$2x - 2y = 18$

$2x - 6y = 14$

$4y = 4$

$y = 1$

$x - 3(1) = 7$

$x = 10$

⑧ $x + y = 3$

$2x - y = 6$

$3x = 9$

$x = 3$

$3 + y = 3$

$y = 0$

When we are given ___*two*___ equations about two ___*unknowns*___, we can use both ___*equations*___ to solve for both ___*unknowns*___.

Back Page Exercises Create and work eight problems similar to those above.

Finding Two Missing Factors

The Idea

When we are given two equations about two unknowns, we can use both equations to solve for both unknowns.

How to Use the Idea

a.
$x + y = 5$
$x - y = 1$ Add the equations.
$2x = 6$
$x = 3$ Replace x with 3 in either equation.
$3 + y = 5$
$y = 5 - 3 = 2$

b.
$2x + y = 9$ Multiply both sides by 2.
$x - 2y = 2$
$4x = 18$ Add the equations.
$5x = 20$
$x = 4$ Replace x with 4.
$2(4) + y = 9$
$y = 9 - 8 = 1$

Solve each pair of equations.

① $\frac{1}{2}x + \frac{1}{3}y = 2$
$x - \frac{1}{3}y = 1$

$\frac{3}{2}x = 3$
$\frac{2}{3} \cdot \frac{3}{2}x = 3 \cdot \frac{2}{3}$
$x = 2$

$\frac{1}{2}(2) + \frac{1}{3}y = 2$
$\frac{1}{3}y = 1$
$y = 3$

② $3x + 4y = 1$
$2x + 2y = 2$

③ $4x - y = 10$
$2x + y = 20$

④ $x - 6y = 2$
$2x + y = 17$

⑤ $11x - y = 18$
$x + y = 6$

⑥ $4x + 4y = 8$
$4x - 4y = 24$

⑦ $x - 3y = 7$
$2x - 2y = 18$

⑧ $x + y = 3$
$2x - y = 6$

When we are given ______________ equations about two ______________, we can use both ______________ to solve for both ______________.

Back Page Exercises Create and work eight problems similar to those above.

Solving Equations

The Idea

An equation is a statement of equality between two expressions.

How to Use the Idea

a.

$$13 - 4x = 5$$
$$13 - 4x + 4x - 5 = 5 - 5 + 4x$$
$$8 = 4x$$
$$2 = x$$

b.

$$\frac{2}{x} = 4$$
$$\frac{x}{1} \bullet \frac{2}{x} = 4 \bullet \frac{x}{1}$$
$$2 = 4x$$
$$\frac{2}{4} = x = \frac{1}{2}$$

c.

$$5x - 6 = 19$$
$$5x - 6 + 6 = 19 + 6$$
$$5x = 25$$
$$x = 5$$

d.

$$6 - \frac{9}{x} = 3$$
$$6 - \frac{9}{x} + \frac{9}{x} - 3 = 3 - 3 + \frac{9}{x}$$
$$3 = \frac{9}{x}$$
$$3x = 9$$
$$x = 3$$

Solve each equation for x.

① $12x + 4 = -8$
$$12x + 4 - 4 = -8 - 4$$
$$12x = -12$$
$$x = -1$$

② $13 + 6x = 1$
$$13 + 6x - 13 = 1 - 13$$
$$6x = -12$$
$$x = \frac{-12}{6}$$
$$x = -2$$

③ $12 - 5x = 2$
$$12 - 5x + 5x - 2 = 2 + 5x - 2$$
$$10 = 5x$$
$$2 = x$$

④ $16x - 18 = 30$
$$16x - 18 + 18 = 30 + 18$$
$$16x = 48$$
$$x = 3$$

⑤ $\frac{3}{x} + 2 = 11$
$$\frac{3}{x} + 2 - 2 = 11 - 2$$
$$\frac{3}{x} = 9$$
$$x \bullet \frac{3}{x} = 9 \bullet x$$
$$3 = 9x$$
$$\frac{1}{3} = x$$

⑥ $4 - \frac{1}{x} = 5$
$$4 - \frac{1}{x} + \frac{1}{x} - 5 = 5 + \frac{1}{x} - 5$$
$$-1 = \frac{1}{x}$$
$$x(-1) = \frac{1}{x}(x)$$
$$-x = 1$$
$$x = -1$$

⑦ $7 + 9x = 25$
$$7 + 9x - 7 = 25 - 7$$
$$9x = 18$$
$$x = 2$$

⑧ $8 + \frac{x}{3} = 10$
$$8 + \frac{x}{3} - 8 = 10 - 8$$
$$\frac{x}{3} = 2$$
$$x = 6$$

⑨ $3x + 7 = -2$
$$3x + 7 - 7 = -2 - 7$$
$$3x = -9$$
$$x = \frac{-9}{3} = -3$$

An *equation* is a statement of *equality* between two *expressions*.

Back Page Exercises Solve the following: $\frac{3}{x} = 6$, $5 + \frac{2}{3} = x$, and $9x + 13 = -5$.

The Idea

An equation is a statement of equality between two expressions.

How to Use the Idea

a.

$$13 - 4x = 5$$
$$13 - 4x + 4x - 5 = 5 - 5 + 4x$$
$$8 = 4x$$
$$2 = x$$

b.

$$\frac{2}{x} = 4$$
$$\frac{x}{1} \bullet \frac{2}{x} = 4 \bullet \frac{x}{1}$$
$$2 = 4x$$
$$\frac{2}{4} = x = \frac{1}{2}$$

c.

$$5x - 6 = 19$$
$$5x - 6 + 6 = 19 + 6$$
$$5x = 25$$
$$x = 5$$

d.

$$6 - \frac{9}{x} = 3$$
$$6 - \frac{9}{x} + \frac{9}{x} - 3 = 3 - 3 + \frac{9}{x}$$
$$3 = \frac{9}{x}$$
$$3x = 9$$
$$x = 3$$

Solve each equation for x.

① $12x + 4 = -8$

$12x + 4 - 4 = -8 - 4$

$12x = -12$

$x = -1$

② $13 + 6x = 1$

③ $12 - 5x = 2$

④ $16x - 18 = 30$

⑤ $\frac{3}{x} + 2 = 11$

⑥ $4 - \frac{1}{x} = 5$

⑦ $7 + 9x = 25$

⑧ $8 + \frac{x}{3} = 10$

⑨ $3x + 7 = -2$

An ______________ is a statement of ______________ between two ______________.

Back Page Exercises Solve the following: $\frac{3}{x} = 6$, $5 + \frac{2}{3} = x$, and $9x + 13 = -5$.

Multiple Operations

The Idea

Addition, subtraction, multiplication, and division are separate operations. A problem may require each operation. One operation may be used several times in the same problem.

How to Use the Idea

$$N = [2\,(8-5)\,(\tfrac{13-3}{5})] \div 4 = [2\,(3)\,(\tfrac{10}{5})] \div 4 = 12 \div 4 = 3$$

In this problem subtraction was used twice, multiplication twice, and division twice.

Solve the problems. Then indicate how many times each operation is used.

① $N = 10 - [(\frac{17-3}{7})(\frac{21+3}{6})] = 10 - [(\frac{14}{7})(\frac{24}{6})] =$
$10 - (2)(4) = 10 - 8 = 2$

② $P = [17 - (\frac{23-9}{7})(\frac{19+6}{5})] \times 3 = [17 - (\frac{14}{7})(\frac{25}{5})] \times 3 =$
$[17 - (2)(5)] \times 3 = [17 - 10] \times 3 = 7 \times 3 = 21$

③ $x = [19 + (\frac{36+12}{8})(\frac{45+5}{10})] \div 7 = [19 + (\frac{48}{8})(\frac{50}{10})] \div 7 =$
$[19 + (6)(5)] \div 7 = [19 + 30] \div 7 = 49 \div 7 = 7$

④ $T = [15 + (\frac{8-5}{3})(\frac{6+3}{3})] \div 6 = [15 + (\frac{3}{3})(\frac{9}{3})] \div 6 =$
$[15 + (1)(3)] \div 6 = [15 + 3] \div 6 = 18 \div 6 = 3$

⑤ $W = [\frac{1}{2}(\frac{10-4}{3})(\frac{16-4}{6})] + 3 = [\frac{1}{2}(\frac{6}{3})(\frac{12}{6})] + 3 =$
$[\frac{1}{2}(2)(2)] + 3 = \frac{1}{2}(4) + 3 = 2 + 3 = 5$

⑥ $S = [26 - (\frac{17-5}{2})(\frac{39+15}{27})] \div 7 = [26 - (\frac{12}{2})(\frac{54}{27})] \div 7 =$
$[26 - (6)(2)] \div 7 = [26 - 12] \div 7 = 14 \div 7 = 2$

Problem	$+$	$-$	$\times$	$\div$
①	1	2	1	2
②	1	2	2	2
③	3	0	1	3
④	2	1	1	3
⑤	1	2	2	3
⑥	1	2	1	3

Addition, *subtraction*, *multiplication*, and *division* are separate operations. A *problem* may require each operation. One *operation* may be used several times in the *same* problem.

Back Page Exercises Create ten problems similar to those above.

Multiple Operations

The Idea

Addition, subtraction, multiplication, and division are separate operations. A problem may require each operation. One operation may be used several times in the same problem.

How to Use the Idea

$N = [2\,(8 - 5)\,(\frac{13-3}{5})] \div 4 = [2\,(3)\,(\frac{10}{5})] \div 4 = 12 \div 4 = 3$

In this problem subtraction was used twice, multiplication twice, and division twice.

Solve the problems. Then indicate how many times each operation is used.

	+	−	×	÷
① $N = 10 - [(\frac{17-3}{7})\,(\frac{21+3}{6})] = 10 - [(\frac{14}{7})\,(\frac{24}{6})] = 10 - (2)\,(4) = 10 - 8 = 2$	1	2	1	2
② $P = [17 - (\frac{23-9}{7})\,(\frac{19+6}{5})] \times 3 =$	____	____	____	____
③ $x = [19 + (\frac{36+12}{8})\,(\frac{45+5}{10})] \div 7 =$	____	____	____	____
④ $T = [15 + (\frac{8-5}{3})\,(\frac{6+3}{3})] \div 6 =$	____	____	____	____
⑤ $W = [\frac{1}{2}\,(\frac{10-4}{3})\,(\frac{16-4}{6})] + 3 =$	____	____	____	____
⑥ $S = [26 - (\frac{17-5}{2})\,(\frac{39+15}{27})] \div 7 =$	____	____	____	____

________________, ________________, ________________, and ________________ are separate operations. A ________________ may require each operation. One ________________ may be used several times in the ________________ problem.

Back Page Exercises Create ten problems similar to those above.

Problems with Multiple Operations

The Idea

Each time we add, subtract, multiply, or divide, we perform one mathematical operation. One problem may require several operations to complete it.

How to Use the Idea

a. $X = [(3 + 2)\ (\frac{15 - 3}{4})] \div 3 = [5\ (\frac{12}{4})] \div 3 = [\frac{60}{4}] \div 3 = 15 \div 3 = 5$

b. $N = [\frac{1}{2}\ (7 - 3)\ (\frac{16 + 5}{7})] \div 6 = [\frac{1}{2}(4)\ (\frac{21}{7})] \div 6 = [(2)\ (3)] \div 6 = 6 \div 6 = 1$

Solve the problems.

① $X = [(\frac{13+3}{8})\ (7 - 5)] \div 2 =$ *$[(\frac{16}{8})\ (2)] \div 2 = [(2)\ (2)] \div 2 = 4 \div 2 = 2$*

② $Z = [(\frac{6 \times 9}{27})\ (18 - 3)] \div 15 =$ *$[(\frac{54}{27})\ (15)] \div 15 = [(2)\ (15)] \div 15 = 30 \div 15 = 2$*

③ $N = [(\frac{17+8}{5})\ (10 + 2)] \div 4 =$ *$[(\frac{25}{5})\ (12)] \div 4 = [(5)\ (12)] \div 4 = 60 \div 4 = 15$*

④ $W = 35 \div [(\frac{7-2}{4+1})\ (\frac{32+18}{8+2})] =$ *$35 \div [(\frac{5}{5})\ (\frac{50}{10})] = 35 \div 5 = 7$*

⑤ $Y = [(23 - 8)\ (\frac{3}{9-4})] \div 9 =$ *$[(15)\ (\frac{3}{5})] \div 9 = 9 \div 9 = 1$*

⑥ $T = [(\frac{2 \times 32}{16})\ (31 - 6)] \div 10 =$ *$[(\frac{64}{16})\ (25)] \div 10 = [(4)\ (25)] \div 10 = 100 \div 10 = 10$*

⑦ $S = [(13 + 7)\ (\frac{19 - 11}{10})] \times \frac{1}{8} =$ *$[(20)\ (\frac{8}{10})] \times \frac{1}{8} = 16 \times \frac{1}{8} = 2$*

⑧ $Q = [(\frac{6 \times 7}{14})\ (19 - 4)] \div 5 =$ *$[(\frac{42}{14})\ (15)] \div 5 = [(3)\ (15)] \div 5 = 45 \div 5 = 9$*

⑨ $V = [(16 + 4)\ (\frac{9+7}{4})] \div 40 =$ *$[(20)\ (\frac{16}{4})] \div 40 = 80 \div 40 = 2$*

⑩ $R = 120 \div [(\frac{6 \times 15}{2})\ (\frac{9-7}{1})] =$ *$120 \div [(\frac{90}{2})\ (\frac{2}{1})] = 120 \div 90 = \frac{12}{9} = \frac{4}{3} = 1\frac{1}{3}$*

⑪ $T = [(\frac{4 \times 9}{6})\ (\frac{12+3}{5})] \times \frac{1}{6} =$ *$[(\frac{36}{6})\ (\frac{15}{5})] \times \frac{1}{6} = [(6)\ (3)] \times \frac{1}{6} = 3$*

⑫ $Y = [(\frac{6 \times 12}{4 \times 9})\ (\frac{75 - 15}{4})] \div 6 =$ *$[(\frac{72}{36})\ (\frac{60}{4})] \div 6 = [(2)\ (15)] \div 6 = 30 \div 6 = 5$*

Each time we ___*add*___, ___*subtract*___, ___*multiply*___, or ___*divide*___, we perform one mathematical operation. One ___*problem*___ may require several ___*operations*___ to complete it.

Back Page Exercises Create ten problems similar to those above.

Problems with Multiple Operations

The Idea

Each time we add, subtract, multiply, or divide, we perform one mathematical operation. One problem may require several operations to complete it.

How to Use the Idea

a. $X = [(3 + 2)\,(\frac{15-3}{4})] \div 3 = [5\,(\frac{12}{4})] \div 3 = [\frac{60}{4}] \div 3 = 15 \div 3 = 5$

b. $N = [\frac{1}{2}\,(7 - 3)\,(\frac{16+5}{7})] \div 6 = [\frac{1}{2}(4)\,(\frac{21}{7})] \div 6 = [(2)\,(3)] \div 6 = 6 \div 6 = 1$

Solve the problems.

① $X = [(\frac{13+3}{8})\,(7 - 5)] \div 2 =$ ***$[(\frac{16}{8})\,(2)] \div 2 = [(2)\,(2)] \div 2 = 4 \div 2 = 2$***

② $Z = [(\frac{6 \times 9}{27})\,(18 - 3)] \div 15 =$

③ $N = [(\frac{17+8}{5})\,(10 + 2)] \div 4 =$

④ $W = 35 \div [(\frac{7-2}{4+1})\,(\frac{32+18}{8+2})] =$

⑤ $Y = [(23 - 8)\,(\frac{3}{9-4})] \div 9 =$

⑥ $T = [(\frac{2 \times 32}{16})\,(31 - 6)] \div 10 =$

⑦ $S = [(13 + 7)\,(\frac{19-11}{10})] \times \frac{1}{8} =$

⑧ $Q = [(\frac{6 \times 7}{14})\,(19 - 4)] \div 5 =$

⑨ $V = [(16 + 4)\,(\frac{9+7}{4})] \div 40 =$

⑩ $R = 120 \div [(\frac{6 \times 15}{2})\,(\frac{9-7}{1})] =$

⑪ $T = [(\frac{4 \times 9}{6})\,(\frac{12+3}{5})] \times \frac{1}{6} =$

⑫ $Y = [(\frac{6 \times 12}{4 \times 9})\,(\frac{75-15}{4})] \div 6 =$

Each time we ________________, ________________, ________________, or ________________, we perform one mathematical operation. One ________________ may require several ________________ to complete it.

Back Page Exercises Create ten problems similar to those above.

Time-Related Problems

The Idea

The natural division of time is between night (darkness) and day (light). Because the lengths change with the seasons, we use a standard division of time called "days" of 24 hours of 60 minutes each. Each "day" goes from midnight to midnight. We may call midnight to noon "a.m." and noon to midnight "p.m.," or we may count from midnight to 24:00, midnight, as pilots and the military do.

Find how many hours and minutes are in each of these blocks of time.

① 7:00 a.m. to 9:15 a.m.

9:15 − 7:00 = 2 hours, 15 minutes

② 9:15 a.m. to 7:00 p.m.

12:00 − 9:15 = 2 hours, 45 minutes
+ 7 hours
9 hours, 45 minutes

③ 1:03 p.m. to 9:21 p.m.

9:21 − 1:03 = 8 hours, 18 minutes

④ 6:32 p.m. to 2:20 a.m.

12:00 − 6:32 = 5 hours, 28 minutes
+ 2 hours, 20 minutes
7 hours, 48 minutes

⑤ 11:35 a.m. to 12:45 p.m.

12:00 − 11:35 = 25 minutes
+ 45 minutes
1 hour, 10 minutes

⑥ 1:47 a.m. to 7:21 p.m.

12:00 − 1:47 = 10 hours, 13 minutes
+ 7 hours, 21 minutes
17 hours, 34 minutes

⑦ 7:21 p.m. to 1:47 a.m.

12:00 − 7:21 = 4 hours, 39 minutes
+ 1 hour, 47 minutes
5 hours, 86 minutes
= 6 hours, 26 minutes

⑧ 8:00 a.m. to 8:00 a.m.

= 24 hours

⑨ 11:00 to 18:45

18:45 − 11:00 = 7 hours, 45 minutes

⑩ 17:00 to 8:00

24:00 − 17:00 = 7 hours
+ 8 hours
15 hours

⑪ 23:00 to 5:17

24:00 − 23:00 = 1 hour
+ 5 hours 17 minutes
6 hours, 17 minutes

⑫ 6:13 a.m. to 9:20 p.m.

12:00 − 6:13 = 5 hours, 47 minutes
+ 9 hours, 20 minutes
14 hours, 67 minutes
= 15 hours, 7 minutes

The natural division of time is between *night* and *day*.

Back Page Exercises Write the time you wake, leave for school, arrive at school, eat lunch, arrive at home, and go to sleep. Figure the time between each.

Time-Related Problems

The Idea

The natural division of time is between night (darkness) and day (light). Because the lengths change with the seasons, we use a standard division of time called "days" of 24 hours of 60 minutes each. Each "day" goes from midnight to midnight. We may call midnight to noon "a.m." and noon to midnight "p.m.," or we may count from midnight to 24:00, midnight, as pilots and the military do.

Find how many hours and minutes are in each of these blocks of time.

① 7:00 a.m. to 9:15 a.m.
9:15 − 7:00 = 2 hours, 15 minutes

② 9:15 a.m. to 7:00 p.m.

③ 1:03 p.m. to 9:21 p.m.

④ 6:32 p.m. to 2:20 a.m.

⑤ 11:35 a.m. to 12:45 p.m.

⑥ 1:47 a.m. to 7:21 p.m.

⑦ 7:21 p.m. to 1:47 a.m.

⑧ 8:00 a.m. to 8:00 a.m.

⑨ 11:00 to 18:45

⑩ 17:00 to 8:00

⑪ 23:00 to 5:17

⑫ 6:13 a.m. to 9:20 p.m.

The natural division of time is between ________________ and ________________.

Back Page Exercises Write the time you wake, leave for school, arrive at school, eat lunch, arrive at home, and go to sleep. Figure the time between each.

Adding Money

The Idea

Addition of money is similar to addition of decimal numbers. The decimal points must be lined up and the dollar sign must always be shown in the sum.

How to Use the Idea

a.	b.	c.	d.
$8.33 + 7.15 = $15.48	$4.67 + 2.49 = $7.16	$6.48 + 3.19 = $9.67	$12.86 + 9.53 = $22.39

Find the sums.

① $7.05 + 3.25 = ***$10.30***	② $16.27 + 6.43 = ***$22.70***	③ $23.02 + 19.26 = ***$42.28***	④ $27.31 + 12.17 = ***$39.48***
⑤ $31.67 + 14.23 = ***$45.90***	⑥ $38.72 + 14.19 = ***$52.91***	⑦ $41.18 + 23.23 = ***$64.41***	⑧ $46.98 + 25.25 = ***$72.23***
⑨ $26.02, 17.91, + 15.87 = ***$59.80***	⑩ $37.23, 28.35, + 21.16 = ***$86.74***	⑪ $48.45, 19.98, + 16.43 = ***$84.86***	⑫ $53.09, 47.23, + 11.84 = ***$112.16***
⑬ $57.13, 23.87, 19.01, + 18.99 = ***$119.00***	⑭ $61.14, 47.23, 38.46, + 17.43 = ***$164.26***	⑮ $84.07, 61.26, 43.38, + 17.15 = ***$205.86***	⑯ $91.26, 43.98, 38.59, + 13.97 = ***$187.80***
⑰ $106.19, 101.54, 98.63, + 90.54 = ***$396.90***	⑱ $221.19, 186.53, 95.47, + 63.04 = ***$566.23***	⑲ $358.26, 269.59, 193.75, + 88.14 = ***$909.74***	⑳ $491.38, 327.43, 369.71, + 283.26 = ***$1,471.78***

Addition of ___*money*___ is similar to addition of ___*decimal*___ numbers.

Back Page Exercises Create ten money addition problems.

Adding Money

The Idea

Addition of money is similar to addition of decimal numbers. The decimal points must be lined up and the dollar sign must always be shown in the sum.

How to Use the Idea

a.	b.	c.	d.
$8.33 + 7.15 = $15.48	$4.67 + 2.49 = $7.16	$6.48 + 3.19 = $9.67	$12.86 + 9.53 = $22.39

Find the sums.

1. $7.05 + 3.25 = *$10.30*
2. $16.27 + 6.43
3. $23.02 + 19.26
4. $27.31 + 12.17
5. $31.67 + 14.23
6. $38.72 + 14.19
7. $41.18 + 23.23
8. $46.98 + 25.25
9. $26.02, 17.91, + 15.87
10. $37.23, 28.35, + 21.16
11. $48.45, 19.98, + 16.43
12. $53.09, 47.23, + 11.84
13. $57.13, 23.87, 19.01, + 18.99
14. $61.14, 47.23, 38.46, + 17.43
15. $84.07, 61.26, 43.38, + 17.15
16. $91.26, 43.98, 38.59, + 13.97
17. $106.19, 101.54, 98.63, + 90.54
18. $221.19, 186.53, 95.47, + 63.04
19. $358.26, 269.59, 193.75, + 88.14
20. $491.38, 327.43, 369.71, + 283.26

Addition of ____________ is similar to addition of ____________ numbers.

Back Page Exercises Create ten money addition problems.

Subtracting Money

The Idea

We are dealing with whole dollars and decimal parts of dollars when we subtract money. Subtracting money is just like subtracting decimals. Keep the decimal points lined up.

How to Use the Idea

a.	b.	c.	d.
$7.89	$20.00	$106.43	$229.98
− 6.78	− 15.88	− 55.38	− 171.22
$1.11	$4.12	$51.05	$58.76

Find the remainders.

① $8.62 − 5.55 = ***$3.07***	② $9.12 − 7.24 = ***$1.88***	③ $11.73 − 4.69 = ***$7.04***	④ $10.00 − 9.99 = ***$.01***
⑤ $15.85 − 13.89 = ***$1.96***	⑥ $20.00 − 19.98 = ***$.02***	⑦ $25.16 − 18.45 = ***$6.71***	⑧ $31.61 − 27.58 = ***$4.03***
⑨ $312.46 − 280.50 = ***$31.96***	⑩ $150.00 − 99.99 = ***$50.01***	⑪ $741.41 − 359.60 = ***$381.81***	⑫ $886.53 − 649.77 = ***$236.76***
⑬ $453.00 − 69.16 = ***$383.84***	⑭ $942.42 − 189.43 = ***$752.99***	⑮ $912.86 − 414.93 = ***$497.93***	⑯ $784.19 − 555.22 = ***$228.97***
⑰ $1,276.36 − 943.99 = ***$332.37***	⑱ $1,891.06 − 1,448.29 = ***$442.77***	⑲ $2,904.13 − 2,315.28 = ***$588.85***	⑳ $2,190.60 − 1,819.78 = ***$370.82***
㉑ $3,411.81 − 2,724.93 = ***$686.88***	㉒ $8,410.28 − 6,829.83 = ***$1,580.45***	㉓ $10,014.61 − 2,173.58 = ***$7,841.03***	㉔ $12,961.48 − 6,009.50 = ***$6,951.98***

We are dealing with ***whole*** dollars and ***decimal*** parts of dollars when we subtract money.

Back Page Exercises Create ten problems subtracting money.

Subtracting Money

The Idea

We are dealing with whole dollars and decimal parts of dollars when we subtract money. Subtracting money is just like subtracting decimals. Keep the decimal points lined up.

How to Use the Idea

	a.	b.	c.	d.
	$7.89	$20.00	$106.43	$229.98
	− 6.78	− 15.88	− 55.38	− 171.22
	$1.11	$4.12	$51.05	$58.76

Find the remainders.

① $8.62 − 5.55 = *$3.07*	② $9.12 − 7.24	③ $11.73 − 4.69	④ $10.00 − 9.99
⑤ $15.85 − 13.89	⑥ $20.00 − 19.98	⑦ $25.16 − 18.45	⑧ $31.61 − 27.58
⑨ $312.46 − 280.50	⑩ $150.00 − 99.99	⑪ $741.41 − 359.60	⑫ $886.53 − 649.77
⑬ $453.00 − 69.16	⑭ $942.42 − 189.43	⑮ $912.86 − 414.93	⑯ $784.19 − 555.22
⑰ $1,276.36 − 943.99	⑱ $1,891.06 − 1,448.29	⑲ $2,904.13 − 2,315.28	⑳ $2,190.60 − 1,819.78
㉑ $3,411.81 − 2,724.93	㉒ $8,410.28 − 6,829.83	㉓ $10,014.61 − 2,173.58	㉔ $12,961.48 − 6,009.50

We are dealing with ____________ dollars and ____________ parts of dollars when we subtract money.

Back Page Exercises Create ten problems subtracting money.

Multiplying Money

The Idea

Multiplying money is the same as multiplying decimal numbers.

How to Use the Idea

a.
```
  $16.50
  × 4
  ------
  $66.00
```

b.
```
  $12.10
  × 12
  -------
    2420
   1210
  -------
  $145.20
```

c.
```
  $25.15
  × 30
  -------
  $754.50
```

d.
```
  $230.45
  × 200
  ----------
  $46,090.00
```

Find the products.

① $261.20 × 9 = *$2,350.80*

② $8,756.37 × 8 = *$70,050.96*

③ $3,007.41 × 7 = *$21,051.87*

④ $4,872.12 × 5 = *$24,360.60*

⑤ $109.50 × 25
54750
21900
$2,737.50

⑥ $223.10 × 31
22310
66930
$6,916.10

⑦ $489.15 × 43
146745
195660
$21,033.45

⑧ $502.30 × 51
50230
251150
$25,617.30

⑨ $1,123.40 × 75
561700
786380
$84,255.00

⑩ $2,367.21 × 45
1183605
946884
$106,524.45

⑪ $3,168.12 × 62
633624
1900872
$196,423.44

⑫ $4,382.23 × 99
3944007
3944007
$433,840.77

⑬ $313.25 × 111
31325
31325
31325
$34,770.75

⑭ $227.18 × 213
68154
22718
45436
$48,389.34

⑮ $341.91 × 324
136764
68382
102573
$110,778.84

⑯ $500.20 × 415
250100
50020
200080
$207,583.00

Multiplying *money* is the same as multiplying *decimal numbers*.

Back Page Exercises Multiply 784 by the multiplicand in each problem above.

Multiplying Money

The Idea

Multiplying money is the same as multiplying decimal numbers.

How to Use the Idea

a. $16.50 × 4 = $66.00

b. $12.10 × 12
2420
1210
$145.20

c. $25.15 × 30 = $754.50

d. $230.45 × 200 = $46,090.00

Find the products.

① $261.20 × 9 = *$2,350.80*

② $8,756.37 × 8

③ $3,007.41 × 7

④ $4,872.12 × 5

⑤ $109.50 × 25

⑥ $223.10 × 31

⑦ $489.15 × 43

⑧ $502.30 × 51

⑨ $1,123.40 × 75

⑩ $2,367.21 × 45

⑪ $3,168.12 × 62

⑫ $4,382.23 × 99

⑬ $313.25 × 111

⑭ $227.18 × 213

⑮ $341.91 × 324

⑯ $500.20 × 415

Multiplying ____________ is the same as multiplying ____________.

Back Page Exercises Multiply 784 by the multiplicand in each problem above.

Dividing Money

The Idea

Dividing money is the same as dividing decimal numbers.

How to Use the Idea

a.
```
      $.50
  4 ) $2.00
       20
```

b.
```
      $2.60
  6 ) $15.60
       12
        36
        36
```

c.
```
       $5.25
  20 ) $105.00
        100
          50
          40
          100
          100
```

d.
```
       $23.02
  35 ) $805.70
        70
        105
        105
           70
           70
```

Find the quotients.

①
```
       *$5.40*
  25 ) $135.00
        125
         100
         100
```

②
```
       *$1.20*
  15 ) $18.00
        15
         30
         30
```

③
```
        *$7.50*
  100 ) $750.00
         700
         500
         500
```

④
```
       *$5.06*
  16 ) $80.96
        80
          96
          96
```

⑤
```
       *$21.30*
  30 ) $639.00
        60
         39
         30
          90
          90
```

⑥
```
       *$22.02*
  45 ) $990.90
        90
         90
         90
           90
           90
```

⑦
```
       *$21.00*
  43 ) $903.00
        86
         43
         43
```

⑧
```
       *$4.60*
  10 ) $46.00
        40
         60
         60
```

⑨
```
       *$4.00*
  68 ) $272.00
        272
```

⑩
```
       *$3.00*
  72 ) $216.00
        216
```

⑪
```
       *$50.00*
  18 ) $900.00
        90
```

⑫
```
        *$4.00*
  500 ) $2,000.00
         2000
```

⑬
```
       *$3.02*
  55 ) $166.10
        165
          110
          110
```

⑭
```
       *$3.02*
  75 ) $226.50
        225
          150
          150
```

⑮
```
       *$3.03*
  80 ) $242.40
        240
          240
          240
```

⑯
```
       *$3.20*
  27 ) $86.40
        81
         54
         54
```

Dividing *money* is the same as dividing *decimal numbers*.

Back Page Exercises Create ten money division problems.

Dividing Money

The Idea

Dividing money is the same as dividing decimal numbers.

How to Use the Idea

a. $4 \overline{)\$2.00}$ = $.50
   20

b. $6 \overline{)\$15.60}$ = $2.60
   12
   36
   36

c. $20 \overline{)\$105.00}$ = $5.25
   100
   50
   40
   100
   100

d. $35 \overline{)\$805.70}$ = $23.02
   70
   105
   105
   70
   70

Find the quotients.

① 25) $135.00 — *$5.40*
125
100
100

② 15) $18.00

③ 100) $750.00 — *$7.50*

④ 16) $80.96

⑤ 30) $639.00

⑥ 45) $990.90

⑦ 43) $903.00

⑧ 10) $46.00

⑨ 68) $272.00

⑩ 72) $216.00

⑪ 18) $900.00

⑫ 500) $2,000.00

⑬ 55) $166.10

⑭ 75) $226.50

⑮ 80) $242.40

⑯ 27) $86.40

Dividing ______________ is the same as dividing ______________.

Back Page Exercises Create ten money division problems.

Writing Checks

The Idea

A check is a draft written to a place or person substituting for bills and coins.

How to Use the Idea

When we write a check, we must fill in this information.

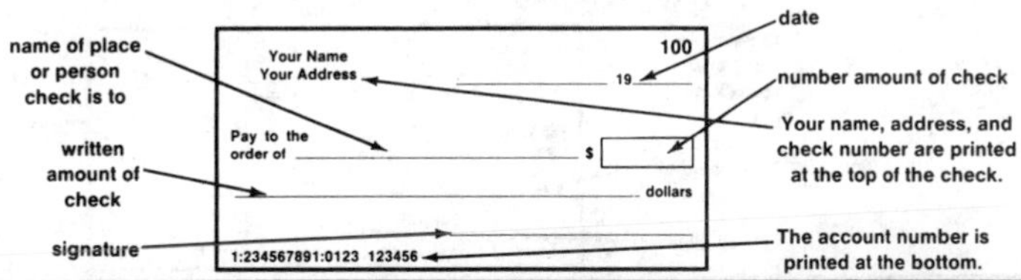

Fill out the checks.

① $5.98 to Bill Smith on July 8, 1987

> 100
> *July 8* 19 *87*
> Pay to the order of *Bill Smith* $ *5.98*
> *five and 98/100* — — — — — — — — — — dollars
> *Student's Signature*
> 1:234567891:0123 123456

② $17.43 to City Natural Gas on September 21, 1987

> 101
> *September 21* 19 *87*
> Pay to the order of *City Natural Gas* $ *17.43*
> *seventeen and 43/100* — — — — — — — dollars
> *Student's Signature*
> 1:234567891:0123 123456

③ $26.17 to Freeman's Market on October 1, 1987

> 102
> *October 1* 19 *87*
> Pay to the order of *Freeman's Market* $ *26.17*
> *twenty-six and 17/100* — — — — — — — dollars
> *Student's Signature*
> 1:234567891:0123 123456

④ $109.01 to City Electric Company on August 25, 1987

> 103
> *August 25* 19 *87*
> Pay to the order of *City Electric Company* $ *109.01*
> *one hundred nine and 01/100* — — — — dollars
> *Student's Signature*
> 1:234567891:0123 123456

⑤ $210.00 to Joe Landlord on December 1, 1987

> 104
> *December 1* 19 *87*
> Pay to the order of *Joe Landlord* $ *210.00*
> *two hundred ten and no/100* — — — — — dollars
> *Student's Signature*
> 1:234567891:0123 123456

⑥ $59.50 to Gray's Department Store on December 23, 1987

> 105
> *December 23* 19 *87*
> Pay to the order of *Gray's Department Store* $ *59.50*
> *fifty-nine and 50/100* — — — — — — — — dollars
> *Student's Signature*
> 1:234567891:0123 123456

A ___*check*___ is a draft written to a place or person ___*substituting*___ for ___*bills*___ and ___*coins*___.

Back Page Exercises Draw four checks. Write them to pay bills.

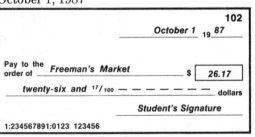

Writing Checks

The Idea

A check is a draft written to a place or person substituting for bills and coins.

How to Use the Idea

When we write a check, we must fill in this information.

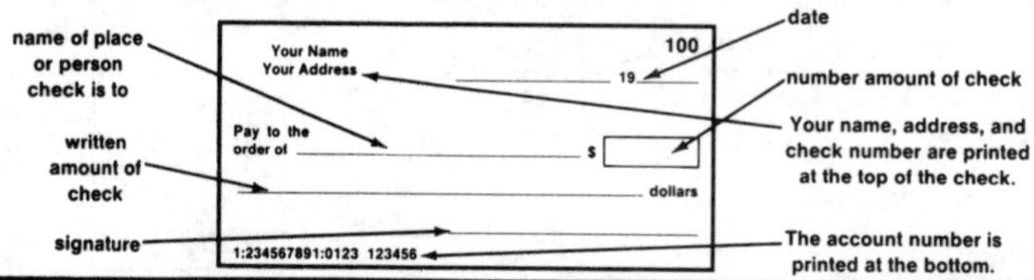

Fill out the checks.

① $5.98 to Bill Smith on July 8, 1987

100
July 8 19 *87*
Pay to the order of *Bill Smith* $ *5.98*
five and 98/100 — — — — — — — — — — dollars
Student's Signature
1:234567891:0123 123456

② $17.43 to City Natural Gas on September 21, 1987

101
______ 19____
Pay to the order of ______________ $ [   ]
______________ dollars
____
1:234567891:0123 123456

③ $26.17 to Freeman's Market on October 1, 1987

102
______ 19____
Pay to the order of ______________ $ [   ]
______________ dollars
____
1:234567891:0123 123456

④ $109.01 to City Electric Company on August 25, 1987

103
______ 19____
Pay to the order of ______________ $ [   ]
______________ dollars
____
1:234567891:0123 123456

⑤ $210.00 to Joe Landlord on December 1, 1987

104
______ 19____
Pay to the order of ______________ $ [   ]
______________ dollars
____
1:234567891:0123 123456

⑥ $59.50 to Gray's Department Store on December 23, 1987

105
______ 19____
Pay to the order of ______________ $ [   ]
______________ dollars
____
1:234567891:0123 123456

A ______________ is a draft written to a place or person ______________ for ______________ and ______________.

Back Page Exercises Draw four checks. Write them to pay bills.

Keeping a Checkbook

The Idea

A checkbook is a record of checks written against a checking account.

How to Use the Idea

When we keep a checkbook, we enter all deposits to the account and add them to the balance. We enter all checks written and subtract them from the balance.

check #	date	check issued to	amount of check	deposit	balance
					200.00
701	8/3	Big Harry's	56.00		144.00
702	8/4	Dr. Thomas	34.00		110.00
	8/4			106.00	216.00

Fill in the checkbook.

Jason Hatcher had a balance of $311.67 on December 3. On that same day he wrote four checks, beginning with number 267, to three different businesses. The first was to Sue's Bakery for $15.20, the second to 66 Gas for $10, the third to P.J.'s for $36.50, and the fourth check was to Sue's Bakery for $26.76. On December 5, Jason deposited $500. On December 6, he made a house payment to Home Federal for $475. On December 8, Jason wrote a check to the Carosel for $120 and deposited $300 into his account. On December 10, Jason deposited $500; then he went Christmas shopping and wrote the following checks: one to Supertots for $26.87, one to Halliday's for $65.78, one to Ima's for $25.08, and one to Toyland for $88.99. On December 12, Jason went shopping for the food to cook his family's Christmas dinner. He spent $56.75 at Big Save and $73.48 at Harold's. On December 15, Jason paid all his monthly bills. He paid City Water $10, City Electric $65, City Phone $36, and City Gas $17.65. On December 17, Jason deposited $200 in his account.

check #	date	check issued to	amount of check	deposit	balance
					311.67
267	*12/3*	*Sue's Bakery*	*15.20*		*296.47*
268	*12/3*	*66 Gas*	*10.00*		*286.47*
269	*12/3*	*P.J.'s*	*36.50*		*249.97*
270	*12/3*	*Sue's Bakery*	*26.76*		*223.21*
	12/5			*500.00*	*723.21*
271	*12/6*	*Home Federal*	*475.00*		*248.21*
272	*12/8*	*Carosel*	*120.00*		*128.21*
	12/8			*300.00*	*428.21*
	12/10			*500.00*	*928.21*
273	*12/10*	*Supertots*	*26.87*		*901.34*
274	*12/10*	*Halliday's*	*65.78*		*835.56*
275	*12/10*	*Ima's*	*25.08*		*810.48*
276	*12/10*	*Toyland*	*88.99*		*721.49*
277	*12/12*	*Big Save*	*56.75*		*664.74*
278	*12/12*	*Harold's*	*73.48*		*591.26*
279	*12/15*	*City Water*	*10.00*		*581.26*
280	*12/15*	*City Electric*	*65.00*		*516.26*
281	*12/15*	*City Phone*	*36.00*		*480.26*
282	*12/15*	*City Gas*	*17.65*		*462.61*
	12/17			*200.00*	*662.61*

A ___*checkbook*___ is a ___*record*___ of checks written against a checking account.

Back Page Exercises — **Delete the $500 deposit on 12-10 and refigure the checkbook. Does Jason have enough money to cover his checks?**

Keeping a Checkbook

The Idea

A checkbook is a record of checks written against a checking account.

How to Use the Idea

When we keep a checkbook, we enter all deposits to the account and add them to the balance. We enter all checks written and subtract them from the balance.

check #	date	check issued to	amount of check	deposit	balance
					200.00
701	8/3	Big Harry's	56.00		144.00
702	8/4	Dr. Thomas	34.00		110.00
	8/4			106.00	216.00

Fill in the checkbook.

Jason Hatcher had a balance of $311.67 on December 3. On that same day he wrote four checks, beginning with number 267, to three different businesses. The first was to Sue's Bakery for $15.20, the second to 66 Gas for $10, the third to P.J.'s for $36.50, and the fourth check was to Sue's Bakery for $26.76. On December 5, Jason deposited $500. On December 6, he made a house payment to Home Federal for $475. On December 8, Jason wrote a check to the Carosel for $120 and deposited $300 into his account. On December 10, Jason deposited $500; then he went Christmas shopping and wrote the following checks: one to Supertots for $26.87, one to Halliday's for $65.78, one to Ima's for $25.08, and one to Toyland for $88.99. On December 12, Jason went shopping for the food to cook his family's Christmas dinner. He spent $56.75 at Big Save and $73.48 at Harold's. On December 15, Jason paid all his monthly bills. He paid City Water $10, City Electric $65, City Phone $36, and City Gas $17.65. On December 17, Jason deposited $200 in his account.

check #	date	check issued to	amount of check	deposit	balance
					311.67
267	*12/3*	*Sue's Bakery*	*15.20*		*296.47*

A ______________________ is a ______________________ of checks written against a checking account.

Back Page Exercises Delete the $500 deposit on 12-10 and refigure the checkbook. Does Jason have enough money to cover his checks?

Exponents

The Idea

An exponent is a number placed above and to the right of a number or symbol called the base. It tells us to raise the base number to that power, to use the base number as a factor the number of times shown by the exponent.

How to Use the Idea

(a) $2^4 = 2 \times 2 \times 2 \times 2 = 16$ (b) $3^3 = 3 \times 3 \times 3 = 27$ (c) $x^5 = x \cdot x \cdot x \cdot x \cdot x$

Write out what each expression means.

① $2^3 = 2 \times 2 \times 2 = 8$

② $3^2 = 3 \times 3 = 9$

③ $5^2 = 5 \times 5 = 25$

④ $1^2 = 1 \times 1 = 1$

⑤ $2^5 = 2 \times 2 \times 2 \times 2 \times 2 = 32$

⑥ $4^2 = 4 \times 4 = 16$

⑦ $5^3 = 5 \times 5 \times 5 = 125$

⑧ $1^3 = 1 \times 1 \times 1 = 1$

⑨ $6^2 = 6 \times 6 = 36$

⑩ $2^6 = 2 \times 2 \times 2 \times 2 \times 2 \times 2 = 64$

⑪ $4^3 = 4 \times 4 \times 4 = 64$

⑫ $7^2 = 7 \times 7 = 49$

⑬ $1^4 = 1 \times 1 \times 1 \times 1 = 1$

⑭ $3^4 = 3 \times 3 \times 3 \times 3 = 81$

⑮ $2^7 = 2 \times 2 \times 2 \times 2 \times 2 \times 2 \times 2 = 128$

⑯ $8^2 = 8 \times 8 = 64$

⑰ $(\frac{1}{2})^2 = \frac{1}{2} \times \frac{1}{2} = \frac{1}{4}$

⑱ $(\frac{1}{3})^2 = \frac{1}{3} \times \frac{1}{3} = \frac{1}{9}$

⑲ $1^5 = 1 \times 1 \times 1 \times 1 \times 1 = 1$

⑳ $(\frac{1}{4})^2 = \frac{1}{4} \times \frac{1}{4} = \frac{1}{16}$

㉑ $(\frac{1}{2})^3 = \frac{1}{2} \times \frac{1}{2} \times \frac{1}{2} = \frac{1}{8}$

㉒ $x^6 = x \cdot x \cdot x \cdot x \cdot x \cdot x$

㉓ $a^2 = a \cdot a$

㉔ $9^2 = 9 \times 9 = 81$

An ___*exponent*___ is a number placed ___*above*___ and to the ___*right*___ of a number or symbol called the ___*base*___. It tells us to ___*raise*___ the base number to that ___*power*___, to use the ___*base*___ number as a ___*factor*___ the number of ___*times*___ shown by the exponent.

Back Page Exercises Raise each problem above to the ninth power.

Exponents

The Idea

An exponent is a number placed above and to the right of a number or symbol called the base. It tells us to raise the base number to that power, to use the base number as a factor the number of times shown by the exponent.

How to Use the Idea

(a) $2^4 = 2 \times 2 \times 2 \times 2 = 16$ **(b)** $3^3 = 3 \times 3 \times 3 = 27$ **(c)** $x^5 = x \bullet x \bullet x \bullet x \bullet x$

Write out what each expression means.

① $2^3 = 2 \times 2 \times 2 = 8$

② $3^2 =$

③ $5^2 =$

④ $1^2 =$

⑤ $2^5 =$

⑥ $4^2 =$

⑦ $5^3 =$

⑧ $1^3 =$

⑨ $6^2 =$

⑩ $2^6 =$

⑪ $4^3 =$

⑫ $7^2 =$

⑬ $1^4 =$

⑭ $3^4 =$

⑮ $2^7 =$

⑯ $8^2 =$

⑰ $(\frac{1}{2})^2 =$

⑱ $(\frac{1}{3})^2 =$

⑲ $1^5 =$

⑳ $(\frac{1}{4})^2 =$

㉑ $(\frac{1}{2})^3 =$

㉒ $x^6 =$

㉓ $a^2 =$

㉔ $9^2 =$

An ________________ is a number placed ________________ and to the ________________ of a number or symbol called the ________________. It tells us to ________________ the base number to that ________________, to use the ________________ number as a ________________ the number of ________________ shown by the exponent.

Back Page Exercises **Raise each problem above to the ninth power.**

Square Measure 80

The Idea

We measure the area of surfaces in square units. Whatever unit we are using, a square measuring one unit per side is one square unit.

How to Use the Idea

We find the area of a rectangle by multiplying the length times the width.

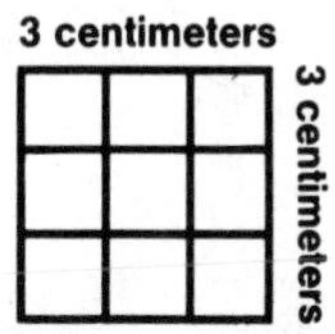

A = LW
A = 3 × 3
A = 9 sq. cm

Find the areas.

① length = 2 meters
width = 5 meters
A = LW
A = 2 × 5
A = 10 sq. m

② length = 3 inches
width = 4 inches
A = LW
A = 3 × 4
A = 12 sq. in.

③ length = 4 feet
width = 4 feet
A = LW
A = 4 × 4
A = 16 sq. ft.

④ length = 5 yards
width = 5 yards
A = LW
A = 5 × 5
A = 25 sq. yds.

⑤ length = 3 yards
width = 5 yards
A = LW
A = 3 × 5
A = 15 sq. yds.

⑥ length = 1 mile
width = 1 mile
A = LW
A = 1 × 1
A = 1 sq. mi.

⑦ length = 2 miles
width = 2 miles
A = LW
A = 2 × 2
A = 4 sq. mi.

⑧ length = 4 inches
width = 1 inch
A = LW
A = 4 × 1
A = 4 sq. in.

⑨ length = 7 centimeters
width = 3 centimeters
A = LW
A = 7 × 3
A = 21 sq. cm

⑩ length = 6 meters
width = 6 meters
A = LW
A = 6 × 6
A = 36 sq. m

⑪ length = 4 kilometers
width = 7 kilometers
A = LW
A = 4 × 7
A = 28 sq. km

⑫ length = 9 meters
width = 12 meters
A = LW
A = 9 × 12
A = 108 sq. m

⑬ length = 10 yards
width = 14 yards
A = LW
A = 10 × 14
A = 140 sq. yds.

⑭ length = 22 inches
width = 4 inches
A = LW
A = 22 × 4
A = 88 sq. in.

⑮ length = 10 miles
width = 7 miles
A = LW
A = 10 × 7
A = 70 sq. mi.

We measure the ___*area*___ of surfaces in ___*square*___ units.

Back Page Exercises Find the areas of the following rectangles: 10 × 18, 23 × 6, 99 × 38, 54 × 13, 12 × 12, 13 × 146, and 48 × 57.

Square Measure

The Idea

We measure the area of surfaces in square units. Whatever unit we are using, a square measuring one unit per side is one square unit.

How to Use the Idea

We find the area of a rectangle by multiplying the length times the width.

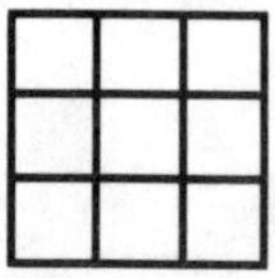

A = LW
A = 3 × 3
A = 9 sq. cm

Find the areas.

① length = 2 meters
width = 5 meters
A = LW
A = 2 × 5
A = 10 sq. m

② length = 3 inches
width = 4 inches

③ length = 4 feet
width = 4 feet

④ length = 5 yards
width = 5 yards

⑤ length = 3 yards
width = 5 yards

⑥ length = 1 mile
width = 1 mile

⑦ length = 2 miles
width = 2 miles

⑧ length = 4 inches
width = 1 inch

⑨ length = 7 centimeters
width = 3 centimeters

⑩ length = 6 meters
width = 6 meters

⑪ length = 4 kilometers
width = 7 kilometers

⑫ length = 9 meters
width = 12 meters

⑬ length = 10 yards
width = 14 yards

⑭ length = 22 inches
width = 4 inches

⑮ length = 10 miles
width = 7 miles

We measure the ______________ of surfaces in ______________ units.

Back Page Exercises **Find the areas of the following rectangles: 10 × 18, 23 × 6, 99 × 38, 54 × 13, 12 × 12, 13 × 146, and 48 × 57.**

Cubic Measure

The Idea

When we measure length and depth and height of a solid or a container, we can use cubic measure to tell the volume.

How to Use the Idea

A cube which measures one inch on each edge has a volume of 1 inch × 1 inch × 1 inch = 1 cubic inch. When we determine the volume of a larger cube or rectangular prism, we are finding out how many of those one inch cubes it takes to build the larger cube or prism.

Find the volumes of figures with these dimensions.

① length = 4 centimeters
width = 2 centimeters
height = 2 centimeters
V = LWH
V = 4 × 2 × 2
V = 16 cu. cm

② length = 2 inches
width = 1 inch
height = 6 inches
V = LWH
V = 2 × 1 × 6
V = 12 cu. in.

③ length = 4 feet
width = 4 feet
height = 2 feet
V = LWH
V = 4 × 4 × 2
V = 32 cu. ft.

④ length = 1 centimeter
width = 1 centimeter
height = 2 centimeters
V = LWH
V = 1 × 1 × 2
V = 2 cu. cm

⑤ length = 5 centimeters
width = 1 centimeter
height = 5 centimeters
V = LWH
V = 5 × 1 × 5
V = 25 cu. cm

⑥ length = 4 feet
width = 2 feet
height = 3 feet
V = LWH
V = 4 × 2 × 3
V = 24 cu. ft.

⑦ length = 6 inches
width = 2 inches
height = 6 inches
V = LWH
V = 6 × 2 × 6
V = 72 cu. in.

⑧ length = 3 centimeters
width = 3 centimeters
height = 3 centimeters
V = LWH
V = 3 × 3 × 3
V = 27 cu. cm

⑨ length = 10 inches
width = 4 inches
height = 5 inches
V = LWH
V = 10 × 4 × 5
V = 200 cu. in.

⑩ length = 17 inches
width = 6 inches
height = 9 inches
V = LWH
V = 17 × 6 × 9
V = 918 cu. in.

⑪ length = 5 feet
width = 2 feet
height = 4 feet
V = LWH
V = 5 × 2 × 4
V = 40 cu. ft.

⑫ length = 11 inches
width = 7 inches
height = 8 inches
V = LWH
V = 11 × 7 × 8
V = 616 cu. in.

When we *measure* length and depth and height of a *solid* or a *container*, we can use *cubic* measure to tell the *volume*.

Back Page Exercises Find the volumes of the following: 10 × 18 × 23, 6 × 99 × 38, 54 × 13 × 12, 12 × 13 × 146, and 48 × 75 × 1.

Cubic Measure

The Idea

When we measure length and depth and height of a solid or a container, we can use cubic measure to tell the volume.

How to Use the Idea

A cube which measures one inch on each edge has a volume of 1 inch × 1 inch × 1 inch = 1 cubic inch. When we determine the volume of a larger cube or rectangular prism, we are finding out how many of those one inch cubes it takes to build the larger cube or prism.

Find the volumes of figures with these dimensions.

① length = 4 centimeters
width = 2 centimeters
height = 2 centimeters

V = LWH
V = 4 × 2 × 2
V = 16 cu. cm

② length = 2 inches
width = 1 inch
height = 6 inches

③ length = 4 feet
width = 4 feet
height = 2 feet

④ length = 1 centimeter
width = 1 centimeter
height = 2 centimeters

⑤ length = 5 centimeters
width = 1 centimeter
height = 5 centimeters

⑥ length = 4 feet
width = 2 feet
height = 3 feet

⑦ length = 6 inches
width = 2 inches
height = 6 inches

⑧ length = 3 centimeters
width = 3 centimeters
height = 3 centimeters

⑨ length = 10 inches
width = 4 inches
height = 5 inches

⑩ length = 17 inches
width = 6 inches
height = 9 inches

⑪ length = 5 feet
width = 2 feet
height = 4 feet

⑫ length = 11 inches
width = 7 inches
height = 8 inches

When we ________ length and depth and height of a ________ or a ________, we can use ________ measure to tell the ________.

Back Page Exercises Find the volumes of the following: 10 × 18 × 23, 6 × 99 × 38, 54 × 13 × 12, 12 × 13 × 146, and 48 × 75 × 1.

English Units of Length

The Idea

Inches, feet, yeards, and miles are English units of length.

How to Use the Idea

1 inch = 1/12 foot	3 feet = 1 yard	5,280 feet = 1 mile
12 inches = 1 foot	1 inch = 1/36 yard	1,760 yards = 1 mile
1 foot = 1/3 yard	36 inches = 1 yard	

A Match the equivalent measures.

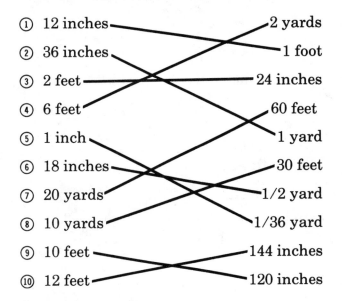

① 12 inches	2 yards	⑪ 5,280 feet	2 miles
② 36 inches	1 foot	⑫ 3,520 yards	1 mile
③ 2 feet	24 inches	⑬ 360 inches	10 yards
④ 6 feet	60 feet	⑭ 5 miles	270 feet
⑤ 1 inch	1 yard	⑮ 100 feet	1/2 mile
⑥ 18 inches	30 feet	⑯ 90 yards	1,200 inches
⑦ 20 yards	1/2 yard	⑰ 2,640 feet	26,400 feet
⑧ 10 yards	1/36 yard	⑱ 440 yards	63,360 inches
⑨ 10 feet	144 inches	⑲ 1 mile	12,320 yards
⑩ 12 feet	120 inches	⑳ 7 miles	1/4 mile

B Fill in the blanks.

① An *inch* is a unit of length equaling 1/12 foot.

② A *foot* is a unit of length equaling 12 inches.

③ A *yard* is a unit of length equaling 36 inches.

④ A *mile* is a unit of length equaling 5,280 feet.

⑤ In this lesson, the shortest unit of length is the *inch*.

⑥ In this lesson, the longest unit of length is the *mile*.

⑦ Compared to inches, a foot is *longer*.

⑧ A yard is *shorter* than a mile.

⑨ A mile is *longer* than a foot.

⑩ Two yards *equal* six feet.

Inches, feet, yards, and miles are *English* units of length.

Back Page Exercises Name ten instances where you would use English units of length.

English Units of Length

The Idea

Inches, feet, yeards, and miles are English units of length.

How to Use the Idea

1 inch = 1/12 foot	3 feet = 1 yard	5,280 feet = 1 mile
12 inches = 1 foot	1 inch = 1/36 yard	1,760 yards = 1 mile
1 foot = 1/3 yard	36 inches = 1 yard	

A Match the equivalent measures.

① 12 inches	2 yards	⑪ 5,280 feet	2 miles
② 36 inches	1 foot	⑫ 3,520 yards	1 mile
③ 2 feet	24 inches	⑬ 360 inches	10 yards
④ 6 feet	60 feet	⑭ 5 miles	270 feet
⑤ 1 inch	1 yard	⑮ 100 feet	1/2 mile
⑥ 18 inches	30 feet	⑯ 90 yards	1,200 inches
⑦ 20 yards	1/2 yard	⑰ 2,640 feet	26,400 feet
⑧ 10 yards	1/36 yard	⑱ 440 yards	63,360 inches
⑨ 10 feet	144 inches	⑲ 1 mile	12,320 yards
⑩ 12 feet	120 inches	⑳ 7 miles	1/4 mile

B Fill in the blanks.

① An ___inch___ is a unit of length equaling 1/12 foot.

② A __________ is a unit of length equaling 12 inches.

③ A __________ is a unit of length equaling 36 inches.

④ A __________ is a unit of length equaling 5,280 feet.

⑤ In this lesson, the shortest unit of length is the __________ .

⑥ In this lesson, the longest unit of length is the __________ .

⑦ Compared to inches, a foot is __________ .

⑧ A yard is __________ than a mile.

⑨ A mile is __________ than a foot.

⑩ Two yards __________ six feet.

Inches, feet, yards, and miles are __________ units of length.

Back Page Exercises Name ten instances where you would use English units of length.

Metric Units of Length

The Idea

Millimeters, centimeters, meters, and kilometers are metric units of length.

How to Use the Idea

1 centimeter = 10 millimeters
100 centimeters = 1 meter
1,000 millimeters = 1 meter
1,000 meters = 1 kilometer
100,000 centimeters = 1 kilometer

A Match the equivalent measures.

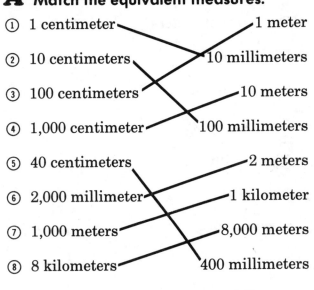

① 1 centimeter	1 meter
② 10 centimeters	10 millimeters
③ 100 centimeters	10 meters
④ 1,000 centimeter	100 millimeters
⑤ 40 centimeters	2 meters
⑥ 2,000 millimeter	1 kilometer
⑦ 1,000 meters	8,000 meters
⑧ 8 kilometers	400 millimeters
⑨ 90 millimeters	4 kilometers
⑩ 400,000 centimeters	9 centimeters

⑪ 700,000 centimeters	10 meters
⑫ 500 centimeters	7 kilometers
⑬ 1,000 millimeters	1 meter
⑭ 1 centimeter	1/100 meter
⑮ 10,000 millimeters	5 meters
⑯ 1 millimeter	1/1,000 meter
⑰ 11,000 meters	9 kilometers
⑱ 900,000 centimeters	13,000 meters
⑲ 13 kilometers	11 kilometers
⑳ 1 meter	1/1,000 kilometer

B Fill in the blanks.

① A ___*centimeter*___ is a metric unit of length equaling 10 millimeters.

② A ___*meter*___ is a metric unit of length equaling 100 centimeters.

③ A ___*kilometer*___ is a metric unit of length equaling 1,000 meters.

④ In this lesson, the ___*millimeter*___ is the shortest unit of length.

⑤ In this lesson, the ___*kilometer*___ is the longest unit of length.

___*Millimeters*___, ___*centimeters*___, ___*meters*___, and ___*kilometers*___ are metric units of length.

Back Page Exercises Name ten instances where you would use metric units of length.

Metric Units of Length 83

The Idea

Millimeters, centimeters, meters, and kilometers are metric units of length.

How to Use the Idea

1 centimeter = 10 millimeters
100 centimeters = 1 meter
1,000 millimeters = 1 meter
1,000 meters = 1 kilometer
100,000 centimeters = 1 kilometer

A Match the equivalent measures.

① 1 centimeter	1 meter	⑪ 700,000 centimeters	10 meters
② 10 centimeters	10 millimeters	⑫ 500 centimeters	7 kilometers
③ 100 centimeters	10 meters	⑬ 1,000 millimeters	1 meter
④ 1,000 centimeter	100 millimeters	⑭ 1 centimeter	1/100 meter
⑤ 40 centimeters	2 meters	⑮ 10,000 millimeters	5 meters
⑥ 2,000 millimeter	1 kilometer	⑯ 1 millimeter	1/1,000 meter
⑦ 1,000 meters	8,000 meters	⑰ 11,000 meters	9 kilometers
⑧ 8 kilometers	400 millimeters	⑱ 900,000 centimeters	13,000 meters
⑨ 90 millimeters	4 kilometers	⑲ 13 kilometers	11 kilometers
⑩ 400,000 centimeters	9 centimeters	⑳ 1 meter	1/1,000 kilometer

B Fill in the blanks.

① A ______________ is a metric unit of length equaling 10 millimeters.

② A ______________ is a metric unit of length equaling 100 centimeters.

③ A ______________ is a metric unit of length equaling 1,000 meters.

④ In this lesson, the ______________ is the shortest unit of length.

⑤ In this lesson, the ______________ is the longest unit of length.

______________, ______________, ______________, and ______________ are metric units of length.

Back Page Exercises Name ten instances where you would use metric units of length.

Conversion — Length

The Idea

Conversion is the process of changing units of measure from one system to another.

How to Use the Idea

From English to Metric

inches × 25 → millimeters
inches × 250 → centimeters
feet × 30 → centimeters
yards × .9 → meters

Measures are approximate.

A Convert inches to millimeters.

① 10 inches × __25__ = __250__ millimeters
② 126 inches × __25__ = __3,150__ millimeters
③ 1 inch × __25__ = __25__ millimeters
④ 72 inches × __25__ = __1,800__ millimeters
⑤ 37 inches × __25__ = __925__ millimeters
⑥ 108 inches × __25__ = __2,700__ millimeters

B Convert inches to centimeters.

① 5 inches × __250__ = __1,250__ centimeters
② 1 inch × __250__ = __250__ centimeters
③ 28 inches × __250__ = __7,000__ centimeters
④ 9 inches × __250__ = __2,250__ centimeters
⑤ 17 inches × __250__ = __4,250__ centimeters
⑥ 60 inches × __250__ = __15,000__ centimeters

C Convert feet to centimeters.

① 3 feet × __30__ = __90__ centimeters
② 12 feet × __30__ = __360__ centimeters
③ 10 feet × __30__ = __300__ centimeters
④ 1/2 foot × __30__ = __15__ centimeters
⑤ 1 foot × __30__ = __30__ centimeters
⑥ 5 feet × __30__ = __150__ centimeters

D Convert yards to meters.

① 7 yards × __.9__ = __6.3__ meters
② 6 yards × __.9__ = __5.4__ meters
③ 1 yard × __.9__ = __.9__ meters
④ 26 yards × __.9__ = __23.4__ meters
⑤ 10 yards × __.9__ = __9__ meters
⑥ 1,000 yards × __.9__ = __900__ meters

__Conversion__ is the process of __changing__ units of measure from one system to another.

Back Page Exercises Which system of measuring lengths is easier — the English or the metric system? Explain your answer.

Conversion — Length

The Idea

Conversion is the process of changing units of measure from one system to another.

From English to Metric

How to Use the Idea

inches × 25 → millimeters
inches × 250 → centimeters
feet × 30 → centimeters
yards × .9 → meters

Measures are approximate.

A Convert inches to millimeters.

① 10 inches × __25__ = __250__ millimeters
② 126 inches × ______ = ______ millimeters
③ 1 inch × ______ = ______ millimeters
④ 72 inches × ______ = ______ millimeters
⑤ 37 inches × ______ = ______ millimeters
⑥ 108 inches × ______ = ______ millimeters

B Convert inches to centimeters.

① 5 inches × __250__ = __1,250__ centimeters
② 1 inch × ______ = ______ centimeters
③ 28 inches × ______ = ______ centimeters
④ 9 inches × ______ = ______ centimeters
⑤ 17 inches × ______ = ______ centimeters
⑥ 60 inches × ______ = ______ centimeters

C Convert feet to centimeters.

① 3 feet × __30__ = __90__ centimeters
② 12 feet × ______ = ______ centimeters
③ 10 feet × ______ = ______ centimeters
④ 1/2 foot × ______ = ______ centimeters
⑤ 1 foot × ______ = ______ centimeters
⑥ 5 feet × ______ = ______ centimeters

D Convert yards to meters.

① 7 yards × __.9__ = __6.3__ meters
② 6 yards × ______ = ______ meters
③ 1 yard × ______ = ______ meters
④ 26 yards × ______ = ______ meters
⑤ 10 yards × ______ = ______ meters
⑥ 1,000 yards × ______ = ______ meters

______________ is the process of ______________ units of measure from one system to another.

Back Page Exercises Which system of measuring lengths is easier — the English or the metric system? Explain your answer.

English Units of Weight

The Idea

Ounces and pounds are English units of weight.

How to Use the Idea

1 oz. = 1/16 lb.	12 oz. = 3/4 lb.	1 lb. = 16 oz.
4 oz. = 1/4 lb.	16 oz. = 1 lb.	1 lb. = 1/2,000 T.
8 oz. = 1/2 lb.	32 oz. = 2 lbs.	2,000 lbs. = 1 T.

A Match the equivalent measures.

① 16 ounces	1 pound	⑪ 1,000 pounds	1 ton
② 8 ounces	1/4 pound	⑫ 500 pounds	1/2 ton
③ 4 ounces	10 pounds	⑬ 1,500 pounds	1/4 ton
④ 64 ounces	128 ounces	⑭ 2,000 pounds	3/4 ton
⑤ 160 ounces	1/2 pound	⑮ 4,000 pounds	60,000 pounds
⑥ 112 ounces	400 pounds	⑯ 10,000 pounds	2 tons
⑦ 8 pounds	4 pounds	⑰ 1 pound	1/2,000 ton
⑧ 6,400 ounces	640 ounces	⑱ 30 tons	5 tons
⑨ 25 pounds	7 pounds	⑲ 96,000 ounces	3 tons
⑩ 40 pounds	400 ounces	⑳ 50 tons	100,000 pounds

B Fill in the blanks.

① An ___ounce___ is an English unit of weight equaling 1/16 pound.

② A ___pound___ is an English unit of weight equaling 16 ounces.

③ Ounces are ___lighter___ than pounds.

④ Pounds are ___heavier___ than ounces.

⑤ Ounces and pounds are ___English___ units of weight.

___Ounces___ and ___pounds___ are English units of weight.

Back Page Exercises Name ten instances where you would use English units of weight.

English Units of Weight

The Idea

Ounces and pounds are English units of weight.

How to Use the Idea

1 oz. = 1/16 lb.	12 oz. = 3/4 lb.	1 lb. = 16 oz.
4 oz. = 1/4 lb.	16 oz. = 1 lb.	1 lb. = 1/2,000 T.
8 oz. = 1/2 lb.	32 oz. = 2 lbs.	2,000 lbs. = 1 T.

A Match the equivalent measures.

(1)	16 ounces	1 pound	(11)	1,000 pounds	1 ton
(2)	8 ounces	1/4 pound	(12)	500 pounds	1/2 ton
(3)	4 ounces	10 pounds	(13)	1,500 pounds	1/4 ton
(4)	64 ounces	128 ounces	(14)	2,000 pounds	3/4 ton
(5)	160 ounces	1/2 pound	(15)	4,000 pounds	60,000 pounds
(6)	112 ounces	400 pounds	(16)	10,000 pounds	2 tons
(7)	8 pounds	4 pounds	(17)	1 pound	1/2,000 ton
(8)	6,400 ounces	640 ounces	(18)	30 tons	5 tons
(9)	25 pounds	7 pounds	(19)	96,000 ounces	3 tons
(10)	40 pounds	400 ounces	(20)	50 tons	100,000 pounds

B Fill in the blanks.

(1) An ________ is an English unit of weight equaling 1/16 pound.

(2) A ________ is an English unit of weight equaling 16 ounces.

(3) Ounces are ________ than pounds.

(4) Pounds are ________ than ounces.

(5) Ounces and pounds are ________ units of weight.

________________ and ________________ are English units of weight.

Back Page Exercises Name ten instances where you would use English units of weight.

Metric Units of Weight

The Idea

Grams and kilograms are metric units of weight.

How to Use the Idea

1 g = .001 kg	50 g = .05 kg	1 kg = 1,000 g
2 g = .002 kg	500 g = .5 kg	1 kg = .001 t
5 g = .005 kg	1,000 g = 1 kg	1,000 kg = 1 t

A Match the equivalent measures.

① .01 kilogram	.1 kilogram	⑪ 1,000 kilograms	.007 metric ton
② 100 grams	10 grams	⑫ 1,000 grams	1 kilogram
③ 4,000 grams	4 kilograms	⑬ 7 kilograms	90 grams
④ 400 grams	.04 kilogram	⑭ 8,000 grams	1 metric ton
⑤ 40 grams	4 metric tons	⑮ .009 metric ton	9 kilograms
⑥ 4 grams	.4 kilogram	⑯ .09 kilograms	19 kilograms
⑦ 4 kilograms	.004 metric ton	⑰ .9 kilograms	8 kilograms
⑧ 4,000 kilograms	400 metric tons	⑱ 19,000 grams	9 metric tons
⑨ 40,000 grams	.004 kilograms	⑲ 9,000 kilograms	.001 kilogram
⑩ 400,000 kilograms	40 kilograms	⑳ 1 gram	900 grams

B Fill in the blanks.

① A *gram* is a metric unit of weight equaling .001 kilogram.

② A *kilogram* is a metric unit of weight equaling 1,000 grams.

③ A gram is *lighter* than a kilogram.

④ A kilogram is *heavier* than a gram.

⑤ Grams and kilograms are *metric* units of weight.

✲ *Grams* and *kilograms* are metric units of weight.

Back Page Exercises **Name ten instances where you would use metric units of weight.**

Metric Units of Weight

The Idea

Grams and kilograms are metric units of weight.

How to Use the Idea

1 g = .001 kg	50 g = .05 kg	1 kg = 1,000 g
2 g = .002 kg	500 g = .5 kg	1 kg = .001 t
5 g = .005 kg	1,000 g = 1 kg	1,000 kg = 1 t

A Match the equivalent measures.

① .01 kilogram	.1 kilogram	⑪ 1,000 kilograms	.007 metric ton
② 100 grams	10 grams	⑫ 1,000 grams	1 kilogram
③ 4,000 grams	4 kilograms	⑬ 7 kilograms	90 grams
④ 400 grams	.04 kilogram	⑭ 8,000 grams	1 metric ton
⑤ 40 grams	4 metric tons	⑮ .009 metric ton	9 kilograms
⑥ 4 grams	.4 kilogram	⑯ .09 kilograms	19 kilograms
⑦ 4 kilograms	.004 metric ton	⑰ .9 kilograms	8 kilograms
⑧ 4,000 kilograms	400 metric tons	⑱ 19,000 grams	9 metric tons
⑨ 40,000 grams	.004 kilograms	⑲ 9,000 kilograms	.001 kilogram
⑩ 400,000 kilograms	40 kilograms	⑳ 1 gram	900 grams

B Fill in the blanks.

① A ______________ is a metric unit of weight equaling .001 kilogram.

② A ______________ is a metric unit of weight equaling 1,000 grams.

③ A gram is ______________ than a kilogram.

④ A kilogram is ______________ than a gram.

⑤ Grams and kilograms are ______________ units of weight.

______________ and ______________ are metric units of weight.

Back Page Exercises **Name ten instances where you would use metric units of weight.**

Conversion — Weight

The Idea

Conversion is the process of changing units of measure from one system to another.

How to Use the Idea

From English to Metric

Measures are approximate.

pounds × .45→kilograms **ounces × 28→grams** **tons × .9→metric tons**

A Convert ounces to grams.

① 1 ounce × *28* = *28* grams

② 15 ounces × *28* = *420* grams

③ 5 ounces × *28* = *140* grams

④ 16 ounces × *28* = *448* grams

⑤ 10 ounces × *28* = *280* grams

⑥ 25 ounces × *28* = *700* grams

⑦ 12 ounces × *28* = *336* grams

⑧ 50 ounces × *28* = *1,400* grams

B Convert pounds to kilograms.

① 3 pounds × *.45* = *1.35* kilograms

② 1 pound × *.45* = *.45* kilogram

③ 10 pounds × *.45* = *4.5* kilograms

④ 50 pounds × *.45* = *22.5* kilograms

⑤ 65 pounds × *.45* = *29.25* kilograms

⑥ 100 pounds × *.45* = *45* kilograms

⑦ 150 pounds × *.45* = *67.5* kilograms

⑧ 175 pounds × *.45* = *78.75* kilograms

C Convert tons to metric tons.

① 1 ton × *.9* = *.9* metric ton

② 5 tons × *.9* = *4.5* metric tons

③ 12 tons × *.9* = *10.8* metric tons

④ 10 tons × *.9* = *9* metric tons

⑤ 20 tons × *.9* = *18* metric tons

⑥ 6 tons × *.9* = *5.4* metric tons

⑦ 100 tons × *.9* = *90* metric tons

⑧ 2 tons × *.9* = *1.8* metric tons

Conversion is the process of changing *units of measure* from one system to another.

Back Page Exercises **Create five conversion problems for each section above. Work them.**

Conversion — Weight

The Idea

Conversion is the process of changing units of measure from one system to another.

How to Use the Idea

From English to Metric

Measures are approximate.

pounds × .45 → kilograms **ounces × 28 → grams** **tons × .9 → metric tons**

A Convert ounces to grams.

① 1 ounce × __28__ = __28__ grams

② 15 ounces × ______ = ______ grams

③ 5 ounces × ______ = ______ grams

④ 16 ounces × ______ = ______ grams

⑤ 10 ounces × ______ = ______ grams

⑥ 25 ounces × ______ = ______ grams

⑦ 12 ounces × ______ = ______ grams

⑧ 50 ounces × ______ = ______ grams

B Convert pounds to kilograms.

① 3 pounds × __.45__ = __1.35__ kilograms

② 1 pound × ______ = ______ kilogram

③ 10 pounds × ______ = ______ kilograms

④ 50 pounds × ______ = ______ kilograms

⑤ 65 pounds × ______ = ______ kilograms

⑥ 100 pounds × ______ = ______ kilograms

⑦ 150 pounds × ______ = ______ kilograms

⑧ 175 pounds × ______ = ______ kilograms

C Convert tons to metric tons.

① 1 ton × __.9__ = __.9__ metric ton

② 5 tons × ______ = ______ metric tons

③ 12 tons × ______ = ______ metric tons

④ 10 tons × ______ = ______ metric tons

⑤ 20 tons × ______ = ______ metric tons

⑥ 6 tons × ______ = ______ metric tons

⑦ 100 tons × ______ = ______ metric tons

⑧ 2 tons × ______ = ______ metric tons

Conversion is the process of changing ____________________ from one system to another.

Back Page Exercises Create five conversion problems for each section above. Work them.

English Units of Volume

The Idea

Ounces, cups, pints, quarts, and gallons are English units of volume.

How to Use the Idea

1/2 cup = 4 ounces	2 pints = 4 cups	1 gallon = 4 quarts
1 cup = 8 ounces	1 quart = 2 pints	1 gallon = 8 pints
2 cups = 16 ounces	1 quart = 4 cups	1 gallon = 16 cups
1 pint = 2 cups	1 quart = 32 ounces	1 gallon = 128 ounces

A Match the equivalent measures.

① 1 cup	2 cups
② 1 pint	4 quarts
③ 1 quart	8 ounces
④ 1 gallon	256 ounces
⑤ 2 gallons	2 pints
⑥ 6 quarts	1 1/2 gallons
⑦ 1 ounce	20 cups
⑧ 10 pints	32 ounces
⑨ 5 gallons	1/8 cup
⑩ 1 quart	20 quarts

⑪ 64 ounces	1/4 cup
⑫ 2 ounces	1/2 gallon
⑬ 1/2 quart	2 cups
⑭ 18 pints	1 cup
⑮ 180 cups	32 ounces
⑯ 1/2 pint	45 quarts
⑰ 1 quart	9 quarts
⑱ 10 cups	20 pints
⑲ 10 quarts	5 pints
⑳ 1 1/4 quarts	5 cups

B Fill in the blanks.

① One ounce equals *1/8* cup.

② One cup equals *eight* ounces.

③ Two cups equal *one* pint.

④ One pint equals *sixteen* ounces.

⑤ One pint equals *1/2* quart.

⑥ One quart equals *two* pints.

⑦ One quart equals *four* cups.

⑧ One quart equals *thirty-two* ounces.

⑨ One gallon equals *four* quarts.

⑩ One gallon equals *eight* pints.

✻ *Ounces*, *cups*, *pints*, *quarts*, and *gallons* are English units of volume.

Back Page Exercises Triple the first measurement in each problem in exercise B and rework the exercise.

English Units of Volume

The Idea

Ounces, cups, pints, quarts, and gallons are English units of volume.

How to Use the Idea

1/2 cup = 4 ounces	2 pints = 4 cups	1 gallon = 4 quarts
1 cup = 8 ounces	1 quart = 2 pints	1 gallon = 8 pints
2 cups = 16 ounces	1 quart = 4 cups	1 gallon = 16 cups
1 pint = 2 cups	1 quart = 32 ounces	1 gallon = 128 ounces

A Match the equivalent measures.

① 1 cup	2 cups	⑪ 64 ounces	1/4 cup
② 1 pint	4 quarts	⑫ 2 ounces	1/2 gallon
③ 1 quart	8 ounces	⑬ 1/2 quart	2 cups
④ 1 gallon	256 ounces	⑭ 18 pints	1 cup
⑤ 2 gallons	2 pints	⑮ 180 cups	32 ounces
⑥ 6 quarts	1 1/2 gallons	⑯ 1/2 pint	45 quarts
⑦ 1 ounce	20 cups	⑰ 1 quart	9 quarts
⑧ 10 pints	32 ounces	⑱ 10 cups	20 pints
⑨ 5 gallons	1/8 cup	⑲ 10 quarts	5 pints
⑩ 1 quart	20 quarts	⑳ 1 1/4 quarts	5 cups

B Fill in the blanks.

① One ounce equals __1/8__ cup.

② One cup equals ________ ounces.

③ Two cups equal ________ pint.

④ One pint equals ________ ounces.

⑤ One pint equals ________ quart.

⑥ One quart equals ________ pints.

⑦ One quart equals ________ cups.

⑧ One quart equals ________ ounces.

⑨ One gallon equals ________ quarts.

⑩ One gallon equals ________ pints.

* ________, ________, ________, ________, and ________ are English units of volume.

Back Page Exercises Triple the first measurement in each problem in exercise B and rework the exercise.

Metric Units of Volume

The Idea

Milliliters, centiliters, and liters are metric units of volume.

How to Use the Idea

1,000 milliliters = 1 liter   100 centiliters = 1 liter   1 centiliter = 10 milliliters

A Match the equivalent measures.

① 1 liter	1,000 milliliters
② 2 liters	10 milliliters
③ 1 centiliter	1,100 milliliters
④ 110 centiliters	200 centiliters
⑤ 5,000 centiliters	3 liters
⑥ 400 centiliters	4 liters
⑦ 3,000 milliliters	50 liters
⑧ 500 centiliters	5 liters

⑨ 5 liters	4,000 milliliters
⑩ 50 liters	50,000 milliliters
⑪ 4 liters	500 centiliters
⑫ 400 liters	40,000 centiliters
⑬ 50 milliliters	5 centiliters
⑭ 50 centiliters	2 liters
⑮ 200 centiliters	20 liters
⑯ 20,000 milliliters	1/2 liter

B Underline the larger volumes.

① 1 centiliter
1 milliliter

② 300 centiliters
300 milliliters

③ 4 liters
4,500 milliliters

④ 2,000 centiliters
21 liters

⑤ 1 liter
1,000 centiliters

⑥ 10 liters
5,000 milliliters

⑦ 10 centiliters
50 milliliters

⑧ 1 centiliter
1 liter

⑨ 100 liters
110,000 milliliters

⑩ 500 centiliters
50 liters

⑪ 50 centiliters
3/4 liter

⑫ 1,000 milliliters
150 centiliters

Milliliters, *centiliters*, and *liters* are metric units of volume.

Back Page Exercises Multiply the top volume measure in each problem in exercise B by four and rework the exercise.

Metric Units of Volume

The Idea

Milliliters, centiliters, and liters are metric units of volume.

How to Use the Idea

1,000 milliliters = 1 liter **100 centiliters = 1 liter** **1 centiliter = 10 milliliters**

A Match the equivalent measures.

① 1 liter	1,000 milliliters	⑨ 5 liters	4,000 milliliters
② 2 liters	10 milliliters	⑩ 50 liters	50,000 milliliters
③ 1 centiliter	1,100 milliliters	⑪ 4 liters	500 centiliters
④ 110 centiliters	200 centiliters	⑫ 400 liters	40,000 centiliters
⑤ 5,000 centiliters	3 liters	⑬ 50 milliliters	5 centiliters
⑥ 400 centiliters	4 liters	⑭ 50 centiliters	2 liters
⑦ 3,000 milliliters	50 liters	⑮ 200 centiliters	20 liters
⑧ 500 centiliters	5 liters	⑯ 20,000 milliliters	1/2 liter

B Underline the larger volumes.

① 1 centiliter 1 milliliter	② 300 centiliters 300 milliliters	③ 4 liters 4,500 milliliters	④ 2,000 centiliters 21 liters
⑤ 1 liter 1,000 centiliters	⑥ 10 liters 5,000 milliliters	⑦ 10 centiliters 50 milliliters	⑧ 1 centiliter 1 liter
⑨ 100 liters 110,000 milliliters	⑩ 500 centiliters 50 liters	⑪ 50 centiliters 3/4 liter	⑫ 1,000 milliliters 150 centiliters

________________, ________________, and ________________ are metric units of volume.

Back Page Exercises — **Multiply the top volume measure in each problem in exercise B by four and rework the exercise.**

Conversion — Volume

The Idea

Conversion is the process of changing units of measure from one system to another.

How to Use the Idea

From English to Metric

Measures are approximate.

ounces × 30 → milliliters   pints × .47 → liters   quarts × .95 → liters   gallons × 1.14 → liters

A Convert ounces to milliliters.

① 10 ounces × 30 = 300 milliliters

② 6 ounces × 30 = 180 milliliters

③ 25 ounces × 30 = 750 milliliters

④ 50 ounces × 30 = 1,500 milliliters

⑤ 5 ounces × 30 = 150 milliliters

⑥ 1 ounce × 30 = 30 milliliters

B Convert pints to liters.

① 5 pints × .47 = 2.35 liters

② 12 pints × .47 = 5.64 liters

③ 8 pints × .47 = 3.76 liters

④ 60 pints × .47 = 28.2 liters

⑤ 21 pints × .47 = 9.87 liters

⑥ 1 pint × .47 = .47 liters

C Convert quarts to liters.

① 2 quarts × .95 = 1.9 liters

② 30 quarts × .95 = 28.5 liters

③ 18 quarts × .95 = 17.1 liters

④ 1 quart × .95 = .95 liter

⑤ 7 quarts × .95 = 6.65 liters

⑥ 10 quarts × .95 = 9.5 liters

D Convert gallons to liters.

① 4 gallons × 1.14 = 4.56 liters

② 1 gallon × 1.14 = 1.14 liters

③ 100 gallons × 1.14 = 114 liters

④ 42 gallons × 1.14 = 47.88 liters

⑤ 12 gallons × 1.14 = 13.68 liters

⑥ 10 gallons × 1.14 = 11.4 liters

Conversion is the process of changing units of measure from one system to another.

Back Page Exercises Create five problems for each section above. Work them.

Conversion — Volume

stop.

The Idea

Conversion is the process of changing units of measure from one system to another.

How to Use the Idea

From English to Metric

Measures are approximate.

ounces × 30 ⟶ milliliters   pints × .47 ⟶ liters   quarts × .95 ⟶ liters   gallons × 1.14 ⟶ liters

A Convert ounces to milliliters.

① 10 ounces × *30* = *300* milliliters

② 6 ounces × ______ = ______ milliliters

③ 25 ounces × ______ = ______ milliliters

④ 50 ounces × ______ = ______ milliliters

⑤ 5 ounces × ______ = ______ milliliters

⑥ 1 ounce × ______ = ______ milliliters

B Convert pints to liters.

① 5 pints × *.47* = *2.35* liters

② 12 pints × ______ = ______ liters

③ 8 pints × ______ = ______ liters

④ 60 pints × ______ = ______ liters

⑤ 21 pints × ______ = ______ liters

⑥ 1 pint × ______ = ______ liters

C Convert quarts to liters.

① 2 quarts × *.95* = *1.9* liters

② 30 quarts × ______ = ______ liters

③ 18 quarts × ______ = ______ liters

④ 1 quart × ______ = ______ liter

⑤ 7 quarts × ______ = ______ liters

⑥ 10 quarts × ______ = ______ liters

D Convert gallons to liters.

① 4 gallons × *1.14* = *4.56* liters

② 1 gallon × ______ = ______ liters

③ 100 gallons × ______ = ______ liters

④ 42 gallons × ______ = ______ liters

⑤ 12 gallons × ______ = ______ liters

⑥ 10 gallons × ______ = ______ liters

______________ is the process of changing units of measure from one ______________ to another.

Back Page Exercises Create five problems for each section above. Work them.

Triangles

The Idea

A triangle is a geometric figure with three sides and three angles.

How to Use the Idea

There are different kinds of triangles. A right triangle has one angle of 90°. The area of a triangle is 1/2 the product of the base and the height. The height of a triangle, other than a right triangle, is determined by the length of a perpendicular line going from the base to the opposite vertex or point where two sides of an angle intersect. The perimeter of a triangle is the sum of the lengths of the three sides.

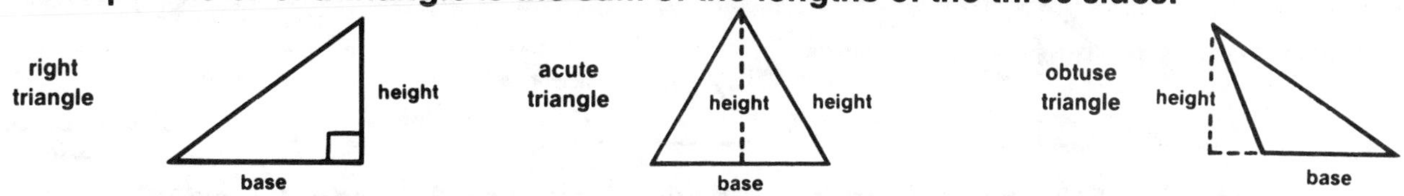

area = 1/2(base × height) **perimeter = side 1 + side 2 + side 3**

Find the areas of the following triangles.

① base = 4 inches
height = 3 inches
A = 1/2(b × h)
A = 1/2(4 × 3)
A = 1/2(12)
A = 6 sq. in.

② base = 6 inches
height = 4 inches
A = 1/2(b × h)
A = 1/2(6 × 4)
A = 1/2(24)
A = 12 sq. in.

③ base = 8 feet
height = 6 feet
A = 1/2(b × h)
A = 1/2(8 × 6)
A = 1/2(48)
A = 24 sq. ft.

④ base = 7 inches
height = 6 inches
A = 1/2(b × h)
A = 1/2(7 × 6)
A = 1/2(42)
A = 21 sq. in.

⑤ base = 10 yards
height = 7 yards
A = 1/2(b × h)
A = 1/2(10 × 7)
A = 1/2(70)
A = 35 sq. yds.

⑥ base = 6 inches
height = 5 inches
A = 1/2(b × h)
A = 1/2(6 × 5)
A = 1/2(30)
A = 15 sq. in.

⑦ base = 9 centimeters
height = 6 centimeters
A = 1/2(b × h)
A = 1/2(9 × 6)
A = 1/2(54)
A = 27 sq. cm

⑧ base = 9 feet
height = 4 feet
A = 1/2(b × h)
A = 1/2(9 × 4)
A = 1/2(36)
A = 18 sq. ft.

⑨ base = 12 meters
height = 9 meters
A = 1/2(b × h)
A = 1/2(12 × 9)
A = 1/2(108)
A = 54 sq. m

A triangle is a geometric figure with *three* sides and *three* angles.

Back Page Exercises **Find the area of the following triangles: 13 × 15, 26 × 9, 31 × 40, and 18 × 54.**

Triangles

The Idea

A triangle is a geometric figure with three sides and three angles.

How to Use the Idea

There are different kinds of triangles. A right triangle has one angle of 90°. The area of a triangle is 1/2 the product of the base and the height. The height of a triangle, other than a right triangle, is determined by the length of a perpendicular line going from the base to the opposite vertex or point where two sides of an angle intersect. The perimeter of a triangle is the sum of the lengths of the three sides.

right triangle

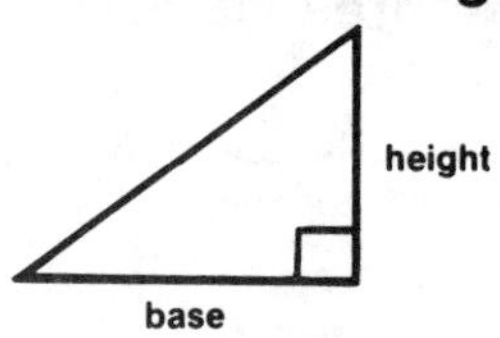

acute triangle

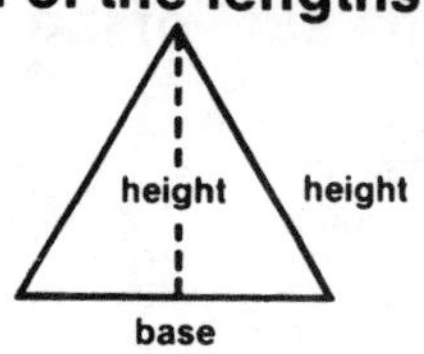

obtuse triangle

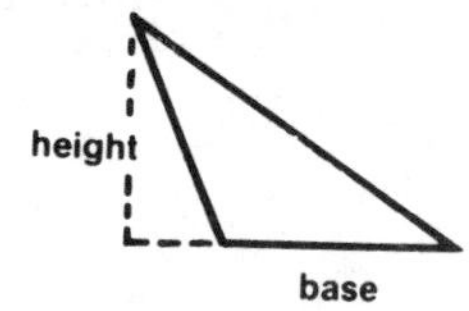

area = 1/2(base × height) **perimeter = side 1 + side 2 + side 3**

Find the areas of the following triangles.

① base = 4 inches
height = 3 inches
A = 1/2(b × h)
A = 1/2(4 × 3)
A = 1/2(12)
A = 6 sq. in.

② base = 6 inches
height = 4 inches

③ base = 8 feet
height = 6 feet

④ base = 7 inches
height = 6 inches

⑤ base = 10 yards
height = 7 yards

⑥ base = 6 inches
height = 5 inches

⑦ base = 9 centimeters
height = 6 centimeters

⑧ base = 9 feet
height = 4 feet

⑨ base = 12 meters
height = 9 meters

A triangle is a geometric figure with ________ sides and ________ angles.

Back Page Exercises — **Find the area of the following triangles: 13 × 15, 26 × 9, 31 × 40, and 18 × 54.**

Squares

The Idea

A square is a special kind of rectangle. It consists of four straight line segments of equal length.

How to Use the Idea

To measure the area of a square, use the formula $A = L^2$. To measure the perimeter of a square, use the formula $P = 4L$.

A Place a check (✓) beside each figure which is a square.

✓ ① 

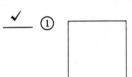

__ ② 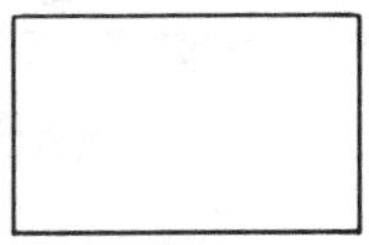

__ ③ 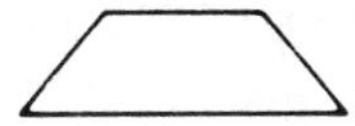

✓ ④ 

__ ⑤ 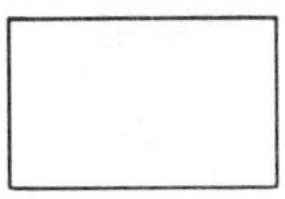

__ ⑥ 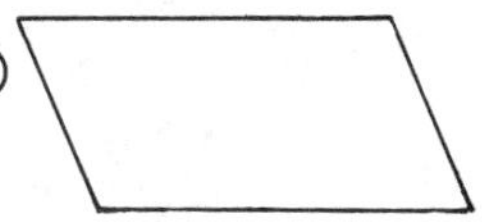

__ ⑦ 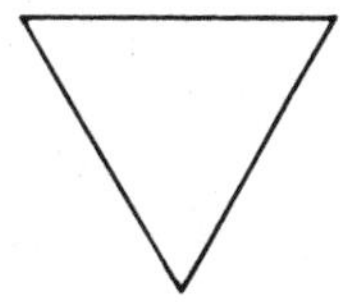

✓ ⑧ 

B Find the perimeter and the area (in square units) of each square.

① 3 inches

$P = 4L$

$P = 4 \times 3$

$P = 12$ in.

$A = L^2$

$A = 3 \times 3$

$A = 9$ sq. in.

② 5 miles

$P = 4L$

$P = 4 \times 5$

$P = 20$ mi.

$A = L^2$

$A = 5 \times 5$

$A = 25$ sq. mi.

③ 4 yards

$P = 4L$

$P = 4 \times 4$

$P = 16$ yds.

$A = L^2$

$A = 4 \times 4$

$A = 16$ sq. yds.

④ 6 centimeters

$P = 4L$

$P = 4 \times 6$

$P = 24$ cm

$A = L^2$

$A = 6 \times 6$

$A = 36$ sq. cm

⑤ 10 yards

$P = 4L$

$P = 4 \times 10$

$P = 40$ yds.

$A = L^2$

$A = 10 \times 10$

$A = 100$ sq. yds.

⑥ 20 feet

$P = 4L$

$P = 4 \times 20$

$P = 80$ ft.

$A = L^2$

$A = 20 \times 20$

$A = 400$ sq. ft.

⑦ 9 inches

$P = 4L$

$P = 4 \times 9$

$P = 36$ in.

$A = L^2$

$A = 9 \times 9$

$A = 81$ sq. in.

⑧ 12 meters

$P = 4L$

$P = 4 \times 12$

$P = 48$ m

$A = L^2$

$A = 12 \times 12$

$A = 144$ sq. m

A ___square___ is a special kind of rectangle. It consists of ___four___ straight line segments of ___equal___ length.

Back Page Exercises Find the perimeter and area of the following squares: 16 feet, 24 inches, 13 yards, 49 centimeters, and 2 miles.

Squares

The Idea

A square is a special kind of rectangle. It consists of four straight line segments of equal length.

How to Use the Idea

To measure the area of a square, use the formula $A = L^2$. To measure the perimeter of a square, use the formula $P = 4L$.

A Place a check (✓) beside each figure which is a square.

✓ ① 

___ ② 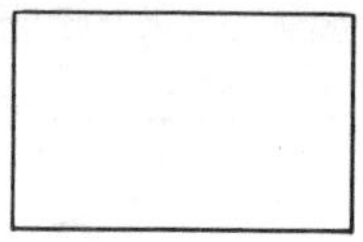

___ ③ 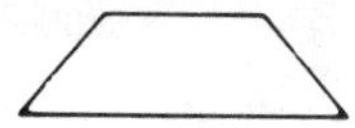

___ ④ 

___ ⑤ 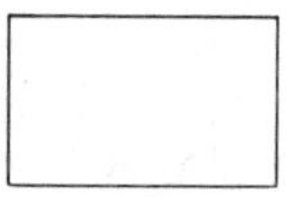

___ ⑥ 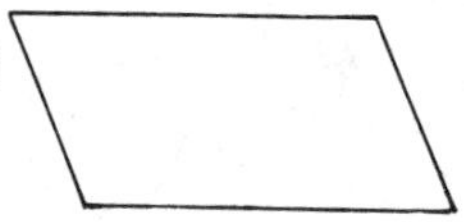

___ ⑦ 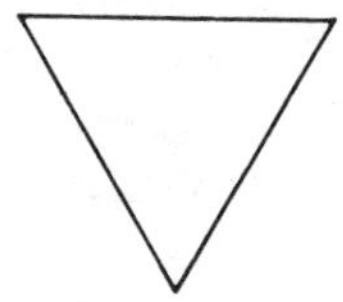

___ ⑧  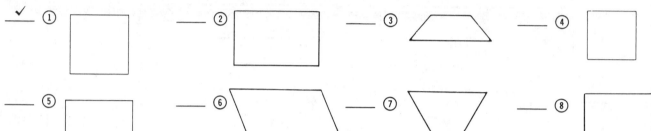

B Find the perimeter and the area (in square units) of each square.

① 3 inches

P = 4L

P = 4 × 3

P = 12 in.

A = L²

A = 3 × 3

A = 9 sq. in.

② 5 miles

③ 4 yards

④ 6 centimeters

⑤ 10 yards

⑥ 20 feet

⑦ 9 inches

⑧ 12 meters

A ______________ is a special kind of rectangle. It consists of ______________ straight line segments of ______________ length.

Back Page Exercises **Find the perimeter and area of the following squares: 16 feet, 24 inches, 13 yards, 49 centimeters, and 2 miles.**

Rectangles

The Idea

A rectangle is a special kind of quadrilateral. Each side is parallel to the opposite side, and each angle is a right angle.

How to Use the Idea

Since the angles in a rectangle are right angles, the area of a rectangle is equal to the product of the length and the width. A = L × W

Since opposite sides of a rectangle are the same length, the perimeter of a rectangle is the sum of twice the length and twice the width. P = 2(L + W)

A Place a check (✓) beside each figure which is a rectangle.

✓ ① 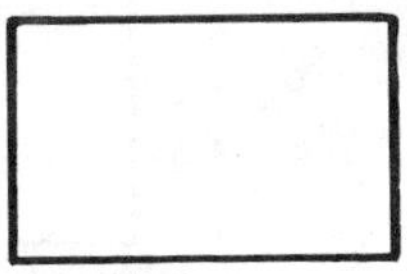

___ ② 

___ ③ 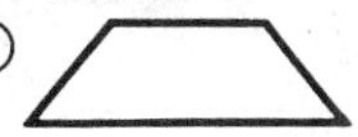

✓ ④ 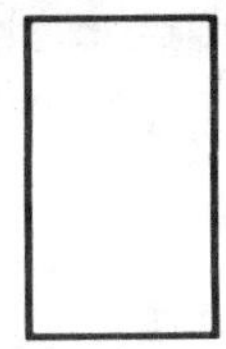

✓ ⑤ 

___ ⑥ 

___ ⑦ 

✓ ⑧ 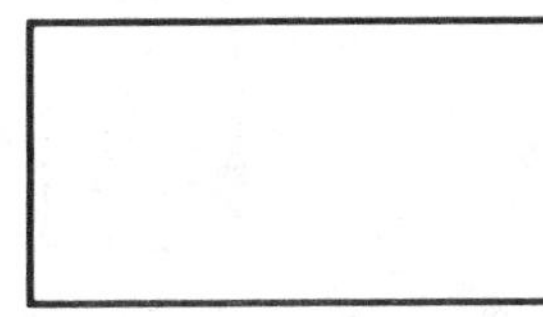

B Find the perimeter and the area (in square units) of each rectangle.

① length = 2 in.
width = 8 in.
P = 2(L + W)
P = 2(2 + 8)
P = 20 in.
A = LW
A = 2 × 8
A = 16 sq. in.

② length = 4 in.
width = 4 in.
P = 2(L + W)
P = 2(4 + 4)
P = 16 in.
A = LW
A = 4 × 4
A = 16 sq. in.

③ length = 3 ft.
width = 6 ft.
P = 2(L + W)
P = 2(3 + 6)
P = 18 ft.
A = LW
A = 3 × 6
A = 18 sq. ft.

④ length = 1 in.
width = 7 in.
P = 2(L + W)
P = 2(1 + 7)
P = 16 in.
A = LW
A = 1 × 7
A = 7 sq. in.

⑤ length = 8 m
width = 3 m
P = 2(L + W)
P = 2(8 + 3)
P = 22 m
A = LW
A = 8 × 3
A = 24 sq. m

⑥ length = 4 yds.
width = 8 yds.
P = 2(L + W)
P = 2(4 + 8)
P = 24 yds.
A = LW
A = 4 × 8
A = 32 sq. yds.

⑦ length = 7 mi.
width = 6 mi.
P = 2(L + W)
P = 2(7 + 6)
P = 26 mi.
A = LW
A = 7 × 6
A = 42 sq. mi.

⑧ length = 2 m
width = 4 m
P = 2(L + W)
P = 2(2 + 4)
P = 12 m
A = LW
A = 2 × 4
A = 8 sq. m

A *rectangle* is a special kind of quadrilateral. Each side is *parallel* to the opposite side, and each angle is a *right* angle.

Back Page Exercises Create ten problems similar to those in exercise B and work them.

Rectangles

The Idea

A rectangle is a special kind of quadrilateral. Each side is parallel to the opposite side, and each angle is a right angle.

How to Use the Idea

Since the angles in a rectangle are right angles, the area of a rectangle is equal to the product of the length and the width. A = L × W

Since opposite sides of a rectangle are the same length, the perimeter of a rectangle is the sum of twice the length and twice the width. P = 2(L + W)

A Place a check (✓) beside each figure which is a rectangle.

✓ ① 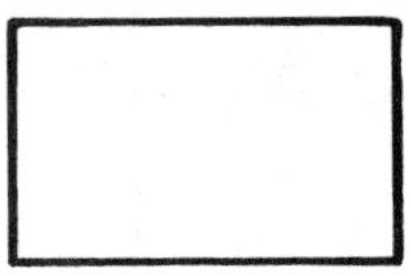

___ ② 

___ ③ 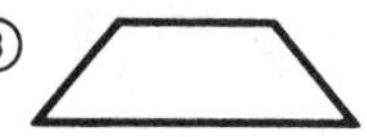

___ ④ 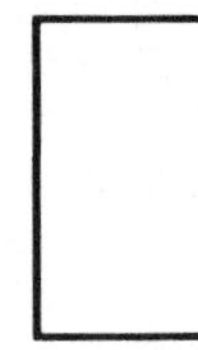

___ ⑤ 

___ ⑥ 

___ ⑦  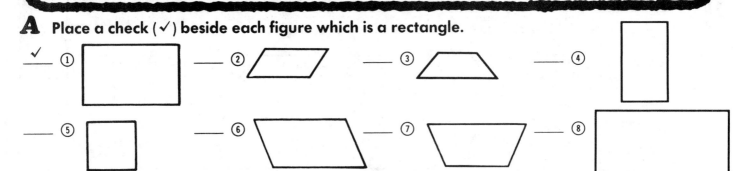

___ ⑧ 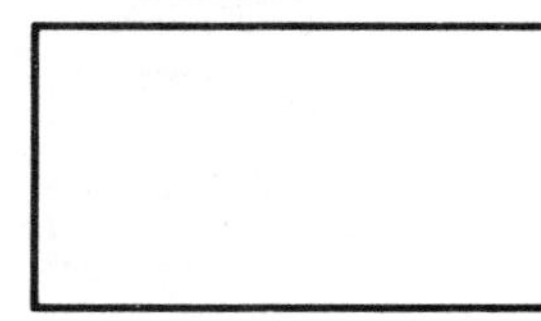

B Find the perimeter and the area (in square units) of each rectangle.

① length = 2 in.
width = 8 in.

P = 2(L + W)
P = 2(2 + 8)
P = 20 in.
A = LW
A = 2 × 8
A = 16 sq. in.

② length = 4 in.
width = 4 in.

③ length = 3 ft.
width = 6 ft.

④ length = 1 in.
width = 7 in.

⑤ length = 8 m
width = 3 m

⑥ length = 4 yds.
width = 8 yds.

⑦ length = 7 mi.
width = 6 mi.

⑧ length = 2 m
width = 4 m

A ________________ is a special kind of quadrilateral. Each side is ________________ to the opposite side, and each angle is a ________________ angle.

Back Page Exercises Create ten problems similar to those in exercise B and work them.

Circles

The Idea

A circle is a closed curved line. All points on the line are the same distance from the center of the circle.

How to Use the Idea

The radius of a circle is a straight line which runs from the center of the circle to the curved line which forms the circle. The diameter of a circle is a straight line which runs through the center of the circle. The circumference is the measure of the curved line which forms the circle. When the circumference is divided by the diameter, the answer is a number very close to 3.14, which is called pi (π). To find the circumference of a circle, use the formula $c = \pi d$. Since any diameter is twice the length of the radius, $c = 2\pi r$. The area of a circle is the product of π and the square of the radius, $A = \pi r^2$.

A Find the circumference of each circle. (Use 3.14 for pi.)

① radius = 3 inches
$c = 2\pi r$
$c = 2(3.14 \times 3)$
$c = 18.84$ in.

② radius = 4 feet
$c = 2\pi r$
$c = 2(3.14 \times 4)$
$c = 25.12$ ft.

③ radius = 2 yards
$c = 2\pi r$
$c = 2(3.14 \times 2)$
$c = 12.56$ yds.

④ radius = 6 miles
$c = 2\pi r$
$c = 2(3.14 \times 6)$
$c = 37.68$ mi.

⑤ radius = 8 inches
$c = 2\pi r$
$c = 2(3.14 \times 8)$
$c = 50.24$ in.

⑥ radius = 5 meters
$c = 2\pi r$
$c = 2(3.14 \times 5)$
$c = 31.40$ m

B Find the area of each circle. (Use 3.14 for pi.)

① radius = 10 inches
$A = \pi r^2$
$A = 3.14(10)^2$
$A = 3.14 \times 100$
$A = 314$ sq. in.

② radius = 9 yards
$A = \pi r^2$
$A = 3.14(9)^2$
$A = 3.14 \times 81$
$A = 254.34$ sq. yds.

③ radius = 1 foot
$A = \pi r^2$
$A = 3.14(1)^2$
$A = 3.14 \times 1$
$A = 3.14$ sq. ft.

④ radius = 7 meters
$A = \pi r^2$
$A = 3.14(7)^2$
$A = 3.14 \times 49$
$A = 153.86$ sq. m

⑤ radius = 12 yards
$A = \pi r^2$
$A = 3.14(12)^2$
$A = 3.14 \times 144$
$A = 452.16$ sq. yds.

⑥ radius = 20 feet
$A = \pi r^2$
$A = 3.14(20)^2$
$A = 3.14 \times 400$
$A = 1{,}256$ sq. ft.

A ___*circle*___ is a closed curved line.

Back Page Exercises Create five similar problems for each section above and work them.

Circles

The Idea

A circle is a closed curved line. All points on the line are the same distance from the center of the circle.

How to Use the Idea

The radius of a circle is a straight line which runs from the center of the circle to the curved line which forms the circle. The diameter of a circle is a straight line which runs through the center of the circle. The circumference is the measure of the curved line which forms the circle. When the circumference is divided by the diameter, the answer is a number very close to 3.14, which is called pi (π). To find the circumference of a circle, use the formula $c = \pi d$. Since any diameter is twice the length of the radius, $c = 2\pi r$. The area of a circle is the product of π and the square of the radius, $A = \pi r^2$.

A Find the circumference of each circle. (Use 3.14 for pi.)

1. radius = 3 inches
   $c = 2\pi r$
   $c = 2(3.14 \times 3)$
   $c = 18.84$ in.
2. radius = 4 feet
   ____
   ____
   ____
3. radius = 2 yards
   ____
   ____
   ____
4. radius = 6 miles
   ____
   ____
   ____
5. radius = 8 inches
   ____
   ____
   ____
6. radius = 5 meters
   ____
   ____
   ____

B Find the area of each circle. (Use 3.14 for pi.)

1. radius = 10 inches
   $A = \pi r^2$
   $A = 3.14(10)^2$
   $A = 3.14 \times 100$
   $A = 314$ sq. in.
2. radius = 9 yards
   ____
   ____
   ____
   ____
3. radius = 1 foot
   ____
   ____
   ____
   ____
4. radius = 7 meters
   ____
   ____
   ____
   ____
5. radius = 12 yards
   ____
   ____
   ____
   ____
6. radius = 20 feet
   ____
   ____
   ____
   ____

A ________________ is a closed curved line.

Back Page Exercises Create five similar problems for each section above and work them.

Time Zones

The Idea

A time zone is an area where the same standard time is used. There are 24 different time zones throughout the world. These zones begin and end with the International Date Line.

How to Use the Idea

The continental United States is divided into four time zones.

A Answer these questions using the above map.

① What country does this map show? *the United States*

② What four time zones divide the continental United States? *Pacific Time, Mountain Time, Central Time, and Eastern Time*

③ Can a state be in more than one time zone? *yes* Give two examples. *Oregon has both Pacific and Mountain time zones; Kentucky has both Central and Eastern time zones.*

④ Do times get earlier or later when traveling east to west? *earlier*
When traveling west to east? *later*

⑤ Could it be both Monday and Tuesday in the United States? *yes*
Give an example. *It if were 12:30 a.m. Tuesday in Georgia, it would be 11:30 p.m. Monday in Arkansas.*

B Complete these time charts.

Pacific Time	Mountain Time	Central Time	Eastern Time
3:00 a.m.	4:00 a.m.	5:00 a.m.	6:00 a.m.
6:15 p.m.	7:15 p.m.	8:15 p.m.	9:15 p.m.
9:30 a.m.	10:30 a.m.	11:30 a.m.	12:30 p.m.
12:05 a.m.	1:05 a.m.	2:05 a.m.	3:05 a.m.
10:45 a.m.	11:45 a.m.	12:45 p.m.	1:45 p.m.
8:00 p.m.	9:00 p.m.	10:00 p.m.	11:00 p.m.
3:00 p.m.	4:00 p.m.	5:00 p.m.	6:00 p.m.

Pacific Time	Mountain Time	Central Time	Eastern Time
2:11 p.m.	3:11 p.m.	4:11 p.m.	5:11 p.m.
9:25 p.m.	10:25 p.m.	11:25 p.m.	12:25 a.m.
1:00 a.m.	2:00 a.m.	3:00 a.m.	4:00 a.m.
11:50 p.m.	12:50 a.m.	1:50 a.m.	2:50 a.m.
6:40 a.m.	7:40 a.m.	8:40 a.m.	9:40 a.m.
1:00 a.m.	2:00 a.m.	3:00 a.m.	4:00 a.m.
5:00 a.m.	6:00 a.m.	7:00 a.m.	8:00 a.m.

A *time zone* is an area where the same standard time is used. There are *24* different time zones throughout the world.

Back Page Exercises Add five lines to each time chart and fill them in.

Time Zones

The Idea

A time zone is an area where the same standard time is used. There are 24 different time zones throughout the world. These zones begin and end with the International Date Line.

How to Use the Idea

The continental United States is divided into four time zones.

A Answer these questions using the above map.

① What country does this map show? ______________________

② What four time zones divide the continental United States? ______________________

____

③ Can a state be in more than one time zone? ______________ Give two examples.

____

____

④ Do times get earlier or later when traveling east to west? ______________________

When traveling west to east? ______________________

⑤ Could it be both Monday and Tuesday in the United States? ______________________

Give an example. ______________________

____

B Complete these time charts.

Pacific Time	Mountain Time	Central Time	Eastern Time
3:00 a.m.	4:00 a.m.	5:00 a.m.	6:00 a.m.
	7:15 p.m.		
			12:30 p.m.
		2:05 a.m.	
	11:45 a.m.		
8:00 p.m.			
		5:00 p.m.	

Pacific Time	Mountain Time	Central Time	Eastern Time
2:11 p.m.			
	10:25 p.m.		
		3:00 a.m.	
			2:50 a.m.
			9:40 a.m.
1:00 a.m.			
		7:00 a.m.	

A ______________ is an area where the same standard time is used. There are ______________ different time zones throughout the world.

Back Page Exercises Add five lines to each time chart and fill them in.

Math Symbols

The Idea

A symbol is a sign that stands for something else.

How to Use the Idea

Common Symbols

+	=	≧	{ }	∠	π	∅	∪
−	>	≦	( )	△	°	∈	∩
÷	<	≯	[ ]	⊥	∴	∉	≡
+	≠	≮		∥	∵	⊆	⊈

Answer these questions.

= ① Which symbol indicates one number is equal to another?
< ② Which symbol indicates a number is less than another?
{ } ③ Which symbol indicates that the enclosed members are a set?
× ④ Which symbol indicates the operation of multiplication?
∠ ⑤ Which symbol indicates an angle?
∴ ⑥ Which symbol stands for the word "therefore"?
∅ ⑦ Which symbol stands for the empty set?
+ ⑧ Which symbol indicates the operation of addition?
> ⑨ Which symbol indicates a number is greater than another?
≧ ⑩ Which symbol indicates a number is greater than or equal to another?
π ⑪ Which symbol stands for the Greek letter "pi"?
⊆ ⑫ Which symbol indicates one set is a subset of another set?
≯ ⑬ Which symbol indicates a number is not greater than another?
△ ⑭ Which symbol stands for "triangle"?
− ⑮ Which symbol indicates the operation of subtraction?
( ) ⑯ Which symbol indicates the operation within it is to be done first?
∪ ⑰ Which symbol indicates a set is the union of two other sets?
∥ ⑱ Which symbol indicates a line is parallel to another line?
÷ ⑲ Which symbol indicates the operation of division?
° ⑳ Which symbol stands for the word "degrees"?
≠ ㉑ Which symbol indicates a number is not equal to another?
∵ ㉒ Which symbol stands for the word "since"?
≮ ㉓ Which symbol indicates a number is not less than another?
∈ ㉔ Which symbol indicates a member is an element of a larger set?
∩ ㉕ Which symbol indicates a set is the intersection of two other sets?
⊥ ㉖ Which symbol indicates two lines are perpendicular?

A *symbol* is a sign that stands for something else.

Back Page Exercises **Create a math problem using each of the 26 symbols. Work the problems.**

Math Symbols

The Idea

A symbol is a sign that stands for something else.

How to Use the Idea

Common Symbols

+	=	≧	{ }	∠	π	∅	∪
−	>	≦	( )	Δ	°	∈	∩
÷	<	≯	[ ]	⊥	∴	∉	≡
+	≠	≮		∥	∵	⊆	⊄

Answer these questions.

_______ ① Which symbol indicates one number is equal to another?
_______ ② Which symbol indicates a number is less than another?
_______ ③ Which symbol indicates that the enclosed members are a set?
_______ ④ Which symbol indicates the operation of multiplication?
_______ ⑤ Which symbol indicates an angle?
_______ ⑥ Which symbol stands for the word "therefore"?
_______ ⑦ Which symbol stands for the empty set?
_______ ⑧ Which symbol indicates the operation of addition?
_______ ⑨ Which symbol indicates a number is greater than another?
_______ ⑩ Which symbol indicates a number is greater than or equal to another?
_______ ⑪ Which symbol stands for the Greek letter "pi"?
_______ ⑫ Which symbol indicates one set is a subset of another set?
_______ ⑬ Which symbol indicates a number is not greater than another?
_______ ⑭ Which symbol stands for "triangle"?
_______ ⑮ Which symbol indicates the operation of subtraction?
_______ ⑯ Which symbol indicates the operation within it is to be done first?
_______ ⑰ Which symbol indicates a set is the union of two other sets?
_______ ⑱ Which symbol indicates a line is parallel to another line?
_______ ⑲ Which symbol indicates the operation of division?
_______ ⑳ Which symbol stands for the word "degrees"?
_______ ㉑ Which symbol indicates a number is not equal to another?
_______ ㉒ Which symbol stands for the word "since"?
_______ ㉓ Which symbol indicates a number is not less than another?
_______ ㉔ Which symbol indicates a member is an element of a larger set?
_______ ㉕ Which symbol indicates a set is the intersection of two other sets?
_______ ㉖ Which symbol indicates two lines are perpendicular?

A _______________ is a sign that stands for something else.

Back Page Exercises — **Create a math problem using each of the 26 symbols. Work the problems.**